CW00858133

Nazi Spies and Collaborators in Britain, 1939–1945

For James Hayward, dear friend,
fellow historian and chaser of the shadows.

Nazi Spies and Collaborators in Britain, 1939–1945

Neil R. Storey

Pen & Sword
MILITARY

First published in Great Britain in 2023 by
Pen & Sword Military
An imprint of Pen & Sword Books Limited
Yorkshire – Philadelphia

Copyright © Neil R. Storey 2023

ISBN 978 1 39908 432 1

The right of Neil R Storey to be identified as
Author of this Work has been asserted by him in accordance
with the Copyright, Designs and Patents Act 1988.

A CIP catalogue record for this book is
available from the British Library

All rights reserved. No part of this book may be reproduced or
transmitted in any form or by any means, electronic or mechanical
including photocopying, recording or by any information storage and
retrieval system, without permission from the Publisher in writing.

Typeset by Mac Style
Printed in the UK by CPI Group (UK) Ltd, Croydon, CR0 4YY.

Pen & Sword Books Limited incorporates the imprints of After
the Battle, Atlas, Archaeology, Aviation, Discovery, Family History,
Fiction, History, Maritime, Military, Military Classics, Politics,
Select, Transport, True Crime, Air World, Frontline Publishing, Leo
Cooper, Remember When, Seaforth Publishing, The Praetorian Press,
Wharncliffe Local History, Wharncliffe Transport, Wharncliffe True
Crime and White Owl.

For a complete list of Pen & Sword titles please contact

PEN & SWORD BOOKS LIMITED
47 Church Street, Barnsley, South Yorkshire, S70 2AS, England
E-mail: enquiries@pen-and-sword.co.uk
Website: www.pen-and-sword.co.uk
or
PEN AND SWORD BOOKS
1950 Lawrence Rd, Havertown, PA 19083, USA
E-mail: Uspen-and-sword@casematepublishers.com
Website: www.penandswordbooks.com

Contents

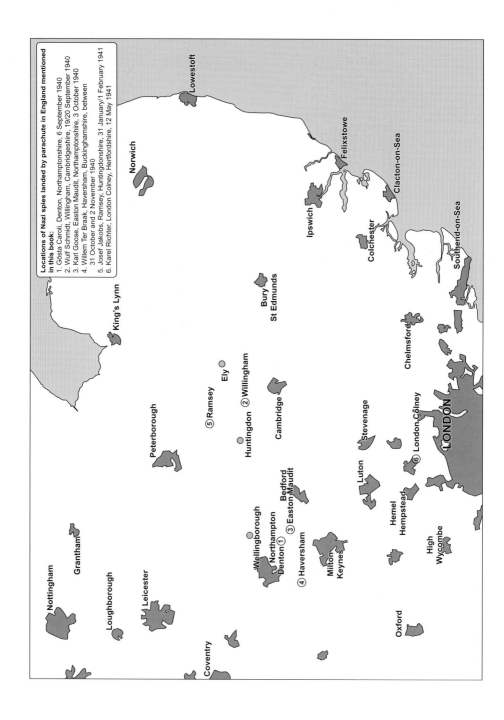

Locations of Nazi spies landed by parachute in England mentioned in this book:
1. Gösta Caroli, Denton, Northamptonshire, 6 September 1940
2. Wulf Schmidt, Willingham, Cambridgeshire, 19/20 September 1940
3. Karl Goose, Easton Maudit, Northamptonshire, 3 October 1940
4. Willem Ter Braak, Haversham, Buckinghamshire, between 31 October and 2 November 1940
5. Josef Jakobs, Ramsey, Huntingdonshire, 31 January/1 February 1941
6. Karel Richter, London Colney, Hertfordshire, 12 May 1941

Nottingham

Grantham

Loughborough

Leicester

Coventry

Peterborough

Oxford

High Wycombe

Hemel Hempstead

Luton

Stevenage

London Colney ⑥

LONDON

Milton Keynes

Wellingborough

Northampton
Denton ①

Bedford
Easton Maudit ③

④ Haversham

② Willingham

Huntingdon

Cambridge

⑤ Ramsey

Ely

Bury
St Edmunds

King's Lynn

Norwich

Lowestoft

Felixstowe

Ipswich

Colchester

Clacton-on-Sea

Chelmsford

Southend-on-Sea

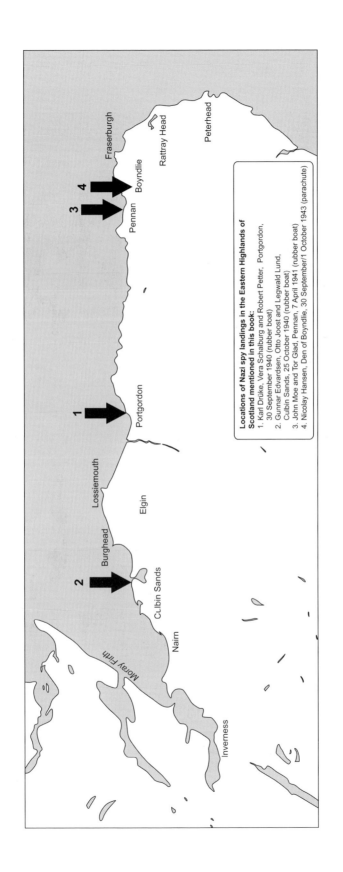

Locations of Nazi spy landings in the Eastern Highlands of Scotland mentioned in this book:

1. Karl Drüke, Vera Schalburg and Robert Petter, Portgordon, 30 September 1940 (rubber boat)
2. Gunnar Edvardsen, Otto Joost and Legwald Lund, Culbin Sands, 25 October 1940 (rubber boat)
3. John Moe and Tor Glad, Pennan, 7 April 1941 (rubber boat)
4. Nicolay Hansen, Den of Boyndlie, 30 September/1 October 1943 (parachute)

A Home Guard checks the identity card of a policeman c1940. Fears of Nazi 'Fifth Columnist' infiltrators in disguise meant that nobody's identity was taken for granted and a challenge to produce your identity card by any civil or military official could not be refused.

Introduction

Ensanguining the skies
How heavily it dies
Into the west away;
Past touch and sight and sound
Not further to be found,
How hopeless under ground
Falls the remorseful day.

A.E. Housman

In *Beating the Nazi Invader,* my first book to focus on Nazi spies and collaborators in Britain, I explored the years leading up to 1939 as the insidious tentacles of the Nazi party and its related security services spread to Britain. During the early war years when our country was under the cloud of invasion, Britain was first penetrated by Nazi spies who landed on our shores by rubber dinghy, fishing boats or were dropped onto fields inland by parachute.

In this book I revisit those stories and complete the accounts of the known agents and sabotage parties who arrived by those means up to the later war years. I also relate some of the cases of those who evaded detection and were only revealed after their escape or their death while in this country. Bearing in mind the space offered by a single volume I draw, in the main, on the cases listed in the 'Most Secret' notes and appendices on the descent and landing of enemy agents compiled by MI5 during the war years now held in The National Archives (KV3/76).

The main content of this book, however, focuses on the previously unpublished case histories of those named on the so-called 'Black List'. This list comprised both 'enemy aliens' and British citizens from all strata of society who, at a time when there were genuine fears of a shadowy 'Fifth Column' of spies and collaborators existing in Britain, raised such concern to civil, military and security services that it was believed their loyalty could not be relied upon and they should not remain at large in the event of an invasion.

Spies and those acting 'as agents of a foreign power' (usually Germany) sent on sabotage missions and other nefarious acts had been a regular and highly popular feature of fact, pseudo-fact and fiction books, magazine features and newspaper stories over the decade of strained Anglo-German political and military relations before the outbreak of the First World War. Books such as *Riddle of the Sands* (1903) where Erskine Childers weaves a tale of two young

Parliament Square, London c1940 when coils of barbed wire and sentries had become common features near significant places for governance and the defence of Britain in wartime.

amateur sailors who uncover a sinister plot that looms over the international community. Other titles such as *The Invasion of 1910* (1906) and *Spies of the Kaiser* (1909) both by William le Queux ably demonstrate the tenor of such literature which reached its zenith in the early years of the war with John Buchan's classic Richard Hannay adventure *The Thirty-Nine Steps* (1915).

Armed with such a canon of literature the dutiful citizens of Great Britain after the declaration of war in 1914 were wanting to 'do their bit'. Fuelled with patriotism and no small measure of xenophobia, rumours and the sort of fear that can emerge in any population under the shadow of war, individuals and groups whose behaviour appeared suspicious were reported in their hundreds to police and military authorities. Particular concern was shown over those of German origin living in Britain; there was talk of Germans having deliberately integrated themselves into British society and were already spying or were waiting to rise up and commit acts of sabotage for the Kaiser.

Germans and Austrians still in Britain were rapidly labelled 'Enemy Aliens' and were sought out by military and police, arrested and interned, but not without rumours almost instantly emerging that those being taken

Thames House, on the corner of Horseferry Road adjacent to Lambeth Bridge and Millbank, Westminster, London c1935. Predominantly offices for Imperial Chemical Industries, between 1934 and August 1939 the top floor of the South Block provided offices for the staff of MI5.

St James's Street from Piccadilly, London c1939. After the MI5 offices at Wormwoods Scrubs were bombed the majority of staff removed to Blenheim Palace, but a London Office was maintained for the Director General and Guy Liddell, some of his counter-espionage officers and a small secretarial staff at 57–58 St. James's Street.

As the declaration of war between Britain and Germany became imminent during late August 1939 tourists and those who needed to flee Britain packed the boat trains for the continent that were leaving from all the major London stations.

away were in 'fact' German spies. Even after the internments the climate of fear was, at times, fanned by rumour and half truth until it bordered on spy hysteria or 'spy mania' and thousands of man hours of the police and military authorities' time were expended on investigating the reports.

During the 1930s the theme of enemy spies, both overtly and thinly veiled operatives of the Nazis, was brought vividly to life on stage and on screen in both A and B movie thrillers. Among the biggest draws were Hitchcock's *The Man Who Knew Too Much* (1934), *The Thirty Nine Steps* (1935) and *The Lady Vanishes* (1938) not to mention Kurt Neumann's *Espionage* (1937) based on Walter. C Hackett's West End play of the same name. There was also Hollywood's first explicitly anti-Nazi film *Confessions of a Nazi Spy* starring Edward G. Robinson, released in May 1939. The theme would continue throughout the Second World War in films such as *Spare A Copper* (1940) starring George Formby, one of the most popular comedy entertainers of the day, Ealing Studios' *The Foreman Went to France* (1942) and *Went the Day Well* (1942).

The difference was, although there were concerns over Nazi agents operating alone or in small cells in Britain the real fear in this new war was over a far wider spread, shadowy organisation which featured in the wartime films and was much bandied around in the popular press, fact and fictional stories in magazines and was the subject of conversations on the street or over the dining table. All members of this organisation were believed to have blind loyalty to the Nazi cause, they could be a neighbour, work colleague, local civic official, captain of industry or a stranger spotted lurking in the shadows. They could be utterly ruthless and use deadly force if required, determined to spy, commit acts of sabotage and ready to rise up and fight the British people from within in the event of an invasion. This group also had a name – The Fifth Column.

Neil R. Storey
Norwich
2023

Chapter 1

The Fifth Column

The term the 'Fifth Column' was not new in 1939, it originated during the Spanish Civil War (1936–39) when Nationalist General Emilio Mola spoke of his four columns of forces advancing on Madrid and a 'Fifth Column' of his militant supporters already within the walls who would rise up in support of the attack. The term remained in generally understood parlance and was easily transferred to the integrated spies and collaborators who appeared out of the woodwork to assist the Nazi forces when they invaded European countries in 1939 and 1940.

The headlines carried by the newspaper vendors on the streets of London say it all on 3 September 1939.

The problem was the people on Britain's home front were confronted with mixed messages. On the one hand eye catching posters in offices, transport hubs, public buildings and meeting places, in fact just about anywhere people gathered, warned 'Careless Talk Costs Lives', 'Walls Have Ears – You Never Know Who's Listening' and 'Keep Mum She's Not So Dumb'. On the other hand British civil authorities, while implying through the poster campaign there must be spies and collaborators anywhere and everywhere, were keen to play down the existence of a Fifth Column to the public to help avoid panics and keep up morale. Those in authority, be they part of the military or civil powers however, were only too aware of the possibility of the existence of a

FIFTH COLUMN

By JOHN LANGDON-DAVIES

Cover of Fifth Column *by John Langdon Davies (1940) one of the dozens of the informative booklets that primed the British people for the new types of warfare that could confront them.*

large body of Nazi infiltrators and collaborators that were already spying and committing acts of sabotage in various forms in preparation for the imminent Nazi invasion.

Churchill was absolutely clear on the matter in a lesser known paragraph of his 'Fight on the Beaches' speech to the House of Commons on 4 June 1940:

Parliament has given us the powers to put down Fifth Column activities with a strong hand, and we shall use those powers subject to the supervision and correction of the House, without the slightest hesitation until we are satisfied, and more than satisfied, that this malignancy in our midst has been effectively stamped out.

By 1940 there was a growing a body of literature by both British and international authors that spoke of the reality of the Fifth Column and warned of its methods. Among them was John Baker White's *Dover-Nürnberg, Return* (1937) and *The Fifth Column* (1940) by John Langdon

Davies. In fact, Davies was the author of numerous booklets that helped to prepare for the dangers of modern warfare and defined the Fifth Columnist succinctly:

> *When does a well meaning man become a traitor? …We certainly cannot distinguish between lawful opposition to a national policy and Fifth Columnist treachery simply by assuming that the latter is paid for by the enemy. It is not on the mercenary weakness, but on the ideals of an individual that the success of Fifth Column tactics depend.*

An insight into how the Fifth Column was perceived by British intelligence agencies working at the sharp end of counter espionage at the height of invasion scares in 1940 can be gained from the circulated notes from the lecture Fifth Column Activities on Other Countries presented by MI5 officer Major Kenneth Younger:

> *The term 'Fifth Column' originated in the Spanish Civil War and has also been used to describe the minorities in Poland. Denmark, Norway, Holland and Belgium who assisted the German invasion. The term implies more than individual spies and traitors in the population who are willing to assist the enemy.*
>
> *As all these countries were invaded without declaration of war, the main work of the Fifth Column was performed by German embassies, consulates, Travel Bureaus and the German Colony generally, against whom no preventive action had been taken before hostilities broke out. In Poland, Holland and Belgium considerable racial and political minorities existed which were openly unpatriotic. In Denmark and Norway the Fifth Column consisted of a smaller number of highly placed people. There is no evidence that Communists assisted the invader in any of these countries.*
>
> *In Poland and Holland the large scale military action was taken mainly by the German Colony and the Dutch NSB. Preparations made by these bodies had not been kept in any way secret before the invasion. Action taken included seizure of key points and aerodromes, sniping and street fighting, issuing false orders and telephone calls. The Fifth Column in Norway had been kept entirely secret. The German Colony seized certain key points, and false orders issued by a few highly placed traitors disorganised the Norwegian defence.*

Racial Minorities of Doubtful Loyalty
1. *Irish: This is the only section likely to take extensive action to assist the Germans.*
2. *Scottish and Welsh Nationalist Movements: Some evidence of German penetration, especially among the Welsh.*

3. *Germans: None still at large except some women of German nationality or extraction. Might give aid on a small scale to parachutists.*
4. *Other Refugees: 10,000 Czechs, 20,000 Dutch and Belgians. Some German agents must be expected, but the vast majority of these refugees may be considered anti-Nazi. British refugees 6,000 to 7,000 returned from the Low Countries, many unable even to speak English.*
5. *Italians: Most of the members of the Italian Fascist Party have either left the country or have been arrested.*

Political Minorities of Doubtful Loyalty in Great Britain

1. *British Union: Membership in March 1940 about 8,000. 600 or 700 interned. Half the membership in London. Policy: authoritarian, anti-Semitic, anti-communist, anti-war. Not organised as a military Fifth Column but focus for people of Nazi sympathies. Subversive action so far discovered the work of individual extremists rather than the organisation. Some half dozen cases since the war show that members deliberately collect secret information. No evidence that they have means of transmitting it to the enemy but much of the information would be useless for any other purpose. Suggested method wireless transmission or crews to Lisbon.*

BUF leader Sir Oswald Mosley inspects his 'Blackshirts' on Royal Mint Street, East London shortly before the clash on Cable Street, 4 October 1936.

Blackshirt sentries at the door of the BUF 'Black House' Headquarters on King's Road near Sloane Square, Chelsea 1934.

2. *Other Pro-Nazi Bodies e,g. Nordic League, Imperial Fascist League etc., small in numbers, now believed inactive.*
3. *Communist Party GB Membership 20,000. Provided no breach of the peace is involved any attempt to stifle such agitation by police action would only arouse additional sympathy for the party*

Conclusion
Subversive action by individuals more likely than mass action, except possibly by the IRA. Most likely methods: signalling to aircraft, bogus telephone calls, rumours, aid to parachutists, isolated acts of sabotage.[1]

BRITISH UNION POLICY.
TEN POINTS.
By OSWALD MOSLEY.

1. PATRIOTISM & REVOLUTION.

BRITISH Union is loyal to King, Country and Empire. Our watchword is "Britain First" and we are determined to build a Nation and an Empire worthy of Patriots. Therefore we stand for revolutionary changes in Government, in economics and in life itself.

2. ACTION.

BRITISH UNION stands for Action in Government which Parliamentary obstruction prevents. British Union will give Government power to act and thus to carry out the will of the people. Government will depend on the vote of the people and will be responsible to the whole Nation.

3. BRITISH UNION MOVEMENT.

OUR Blackshirts united in a voluntary discipline to serve their country because only a creed which puts country before self can save our Nation and our people, Because British Union is a Movement of National revival we have no foreign models as we believe that "Britain Awake" can surpass them all. Our creed of Fascism and National Socialism is the new and universal creed of the 20th century, but in each country it has a policy, method, and character suited to that country and no other because it is a national and not an international creed.

Continued overleaf.

WHAT THE FLASH AND CIRCLE MEAN

The flash of action in the circle of union is the symbol of the British Union. National action can only come from National union that ends the strife of Parties. Let Britons unite with the motto "Britain for the British."

Pre-war leaflet advertising Action *the BUF newspaper*

Despite its parallels and links to the Nazis in Germany and its vile anti-Semitic stance The British Union of Fascists with Sir Oswald Mosley at its helm attracted an ever-growing membership of thousands over the years of its existence between its creation in 1932 up to 1939. Using the skills he

The cover of the Sunday Pictorial *makes the arrest of the Blackshirt activists at the Wortham 'Tithe War' headline news Sunday 18 February 1934*

acquired as a mainstream Labour politician Mosley knew there were large and influential swathes of society whose interests were not being addressed to their satisfaction by Parliament. Mosley had particular success attracting membership and support from land owners and farmers by offering agricultural policies that would appeal to them, especially the abolition of tithes that creamed off a considerable amount of the annual income of those farming lands subject to them.

One particularly infamous intervention became known as 'The Wortham Tithe War'. Author Doreen Wallace and her husband Rowland Rash had decided to make a stand and refused to pay their tithes for Manor Farm at Wortham in Suffolk. In September 1934 the county bailiffs were due to descend on the property to take away livestock to the value of what was owed. Some fifty members of the British Union of Fascists arrived to act as defenders of the farm under the command of their National Political Officer, Richard Plathen. After fortifying the perimeter with barbed wire and obstacles they hoisted their black flag beside the union flag and mounted vigilante patrols to thwart any attempt to remove the livestock. After sixteen days the police had had enough, they shipped in two bus loads of constables, broke the siege and the bailiffs seized the animals, but these events made headline news for the Blackshirts and gained them a lot more supporters from agricultural areas.

To give some idea of the scale of the BUF on the eve of the Second World War it staged a 'Peace Rally' at Earls Court in July 1939. With a tall

Women members of the BUF salute Sir Oswald Mosley, the man many of them simply referred to as 'The Leader', Westminster, 7 May 1939

UP BRITAIN

STOP WAR !

REMEMBER 1914

The call to arms — Millions murdered in cold blood — Thousands maimed and blind — Millions left fatherless — The war wrecks today walk the gutters of Britain — Many without Pensions.   .   .   .   .

MILLIONS MADE THE SUPREME SACRIFICE TO SAVE "POOR LITTLE BELGUIM."   .   .   .   .

THE MILLIONS OF WARRIOR DEAD ARE FORGOTTEN IN 1939

YOU ARE PLEDGED TO DIE FOR POLAND, RUMANIA AND OTHER LITTLE EUROPEAN STATES WHERE JEWISH FINANCIERS HAVE INVESTED THEIR MONEY.   .   .   .   .

WHO MASSED PROFITS IN THE LAST WAR — WHO WILL GAIN BY ANOTHER?

STOP THE MAD DRIVE TO WAR
MIND BRITAINS BUSINESS

UNITE with MOSLEY for

BRITAIN, PEACE AND PEOPLE

Join British Union at 16, Great Smith St, S.W.1. or nearest District H.Q.

Published by J. L. Shepherd, 16, Gt. Smith St, S.W.1. Printed by A. Baker & Co. (Printers) Ltd. T.U. 3R100T8/39

BUF propaganda flyer produced shortly before the outbreak of war in 1939.

rostrum reminiscent of Nazi Party gatherings decked with Union Flags, the militaristic show of processing bands and banners would not have looked out of place at Nuremberg. The sole speaker to address the 30,000 people gathered there was Sir Oswald Mosley.

Members of the BUF could also be found both as members of and holding office within other organisations such as the newly formed British Legion and the Peace Pledge Union. This latter pacifist organisation may seem an odd choice but then consider the aim of the PPU was to stop wars, sometimes by direct action that would hinder the British war effort. BUF members also maintained friends and collaborator contacts among just about every walk of life and occupation, especially those who could be of use to them in Government offices, the Post Office, the Armed Forces and the police. There are many instances of police raiding and searching the homes and properties of BUF members when the organisation was banned after the outbreak of war. The inhabitants, clearly expecting their arrival, had dressed in full BUF uniform and greeted the officers at the door with a Fascist salute.

The BUF maintained strong links with the Nazi Party in Germany right up to the outbreak of war. The main conduit between the two was Rolf Hoffmann of the *Reichspressedienst* (Nazi Press Bureau) in Hamburg. He was in regular correspondence with leading British Fascist Admiral Barry Domvile and time and again his name is mentioned in the case notes of interned and suspect list members of the BUF who would mention how they wrote to him to obtain Nazi books, photographs of Hitler and leading figures of the Nazi Party. Hoffmann also supplied copies of *News from Germany* and offered advice on how to circulate copies when it appeared some of the copies he was sending were being intercepted. He also helped arrange British pro-Hitler supporters attend the Nazi Party rallies at Nuremberg and provided the first point of contact for many of those wishing to become naturalised Germans and attain their goal of becoming fully fledged members of the Nazi Party.[2] Hoffmann openly came to Britain on several occasions through the 1930s visiting principal towns and cities to meet party faithful and recruit a few more to the cause; on a number of occasions he even gave interviews to the press.

However, all may not be quite what it seemed. Mosley was undoubtedly a passionate, and to many a charismatic, orator. He was respected and even idolised as Leader of the British Union but his wife Lady Diana Mosley was far from a woman in the shadow of her husband. Diana and her unmarried sister Unity Mitford had been regular and popular visitors to Nazi Germany in the 1930s. Diana was a personal friend of Hitler and had acted as the main conduit for communication between her husband and the Führer before the outbreak of war. An MI5 report from 1940 recognised that of the husband and wife it was Lady Diana Mosley who was the greater threat, and concluded:

> *Diana Mosley, wife of Sir Oswald Mosley, is reported on the best authority, that of her family and intimate circle, to be a public danger at the present time. Is said to be far cleverer and more dangerous than her husband and will stick at nothing to achieve her ambitions. She is wildly ambitious.*[3]

But as we shall see later in this book, both the Mosleys could have been shunted to the sidelines if the Nazi invasion had taken place and the Major General John Fuller or Leigh Vaughan Henry plots had been successful.

The Mosleys and BUF were far from the only people enamoured with Hitler and Nazi ideals and for a while in the mid 1930s public figures who spoke out against the dangers presented by the Nazis faced derision. Among the most vocal was Lord Robert Vansittart who warned of the Nazi aspirations for European domination. His opposition to appeasement saw him derided for having 'an inflexible mind' and 'Vansittartism' became a byword for a Germanophobia.

The Nazi regime was keen to win international support and embarked on a charm offensive organising exchange visits between British and German students, military veterans and businessmen. Various Anglo-German groups were established and holidaymakers were encouraged to come and see Germany for themselves. Keen to show their prowess and commitment to sport and healthy activities German competitors were supported by Nazi Party officials whenever they competed at major sporting events in Britain and Europe.

A case in point is The Women's League of Health and Beauty which had been founded in 1930 by Mrs Mary 'Mollie' Bagot-Stack on the simple premise that regular exercise will make the people of Britain

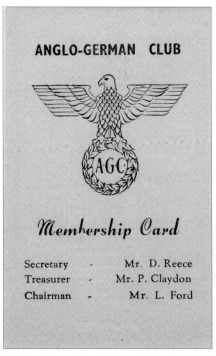

ANGLO-GERMAN CLUB

Membership Card

Secretary	-	Mr. D. Reece
Treasurer	-	Mr. P. Claydon
Chairman	-	Mr. L. Ford

Membership card for the Ipswich Anglo-German Club.

Guests of honour at the Anglo-German Fellowship dinner, 1937. Foreground, left to right, Lord Halifax, Fellowship President Prince Karl Eduard, Duke of Saxe-Coburg and German Ambassador Ribbentrop.

Lapel badge worn by members of the Anglo-German Link founded by Admiral Sir Barry Domvile in 1937.

PUNCH OR THE LONDON CHARIVARI—FEBRUARY 24 1937

SALUT AUX DAMES

["I hope that you will appreciate this gesture of the German Government."—*HERR VON RIBBENTROP*, as reported in a speech last week accepting the plan for banning volunteers to Spain.]

Nazi Ambassador Ribbentrop (the 'von' was an affectation he assumed and was not entitled to) was described in some newspapers as 'one of the most popular men in London' shortly after his appointment. The aggressive behaviour of the Nazis and Ribbentrop's sycophantic loyalty to the Party line soon showed his true colours and he became a frequent target for Punch *magazine.*

healthier and fitter. After Mollie's death in 1935 her daughter Prunella carried on what her mother had begun, but the tone of the group changed. Prunella had visited Germany and had been much impressed by the Nazi public fitness programme, especially the *Bund Deutscher Mädel* (BDM) or League of German Girls, the female wing of the Nazi youth movement. Influenced by what she had seen the public demonstrations of exercise, dance and movement performed my members of the League of Health and Beauty in Britain got bigger, more elaborate and would include thousands of women in uniform outfits all taking part in huge choreographed public performances of graceful but regimented exercise. After film of the Nazi Party rallies and the outdoor gymnastic activities of the girls of the Nazi BDM had been part of the reportage of newsreels shown in British cinemas, it did not take much for both public and press to draw comparisons between the two.

Priscilla also changed the name of the official journal of the League from *Mother & Daughter* to *Health and Beauty* but in doing so she also revised the core aims of the group to a five point plan which was printed on the inside cover of the journal. Four points spoke of encouraging expression of beauty, fostering success, safer and easier motherhood and the final point in the boldest type '*...to promote the cause of national health, which must lead to RACIAL HEALTH AND PEACE.*'[4] At a time when the Nazi vision and aim for racial purity, and the Aryan man was extolled by Nazi theorist Alfred Rosenberg and appearing in magazines and newspapers across Europe, many would wonder if The Women's League of Health and Beauty was indeed a 'fellow traveller' of the Nazis.

German travel brochure c1937. In the late 1930s the Nazi German charm offensive was on and the people of Britain were urged to come and see for themselves rather than judge Germany by what they heard.

Reichsfrauenführerin *Gertrud Scholtz-Klink described by Hitler as the 'perfect Nazi woman'.*

Girls of the Bund Deutscher Mädel *(BDM) or League of German Girls, the female wing of the Nazi youth movement. Note the similarities between their gym kit and that worn by members of The Women's League of Health and Beauty.*

By 1938 the aggressive acts of Nazi Germany on the world stage saw Europe drawn to the brink of war. Toleration and appeasement may have been evinced at Munich but earlier in the year the British public were already uncomfortable about the anti-Semitism and militaristic aggression being shown by the Nazis. Coverage of an arena display by the Women's Health and Beauty in the *Daily Express* described the dancers as 'Stormtroops' and Prunella Stack as 'a radiant, strapping, 23-year-old Nordic, with excellent teeth'. They captioned a photograph of her as 'Führer Stack' adding that she studied new methods of physical training last year in Berlin and 'she's frightfully keen on anything German.'[5] If anyone was left in any doubt *Reichsfrauenführerin* Frau Gertrud Scholtz-Klink, the head of the (NS-Frauenschaft) National Socialist Women's Union, the most senior woman in the Nazi Party in 1939 made a high profile visit to England. She was not only photographed being heartily welcomed at a display arranged by Stack and members of the League of Health and Beauty, but she attended an Anglo-German Fellowship dinner in her honour at Claridges where both Klink and Stack were keynote speakers. After the outbreak of war the League was quite keen to change its image.

The point of this example is that The League of Health and Beauty was just one of a surprising number of organisations and political groups that

Gertrud Scholtz-Klink (left) and Prunella Stack, Leader of The Women's League of Health and Beauty watch a display by members of the League staged for Klink's official visit to Britain in March 1939.

were very much in sympathy with Nazi ideals. The problem was that some of their members would remain loyal to them even in wartime. There were also many ex-pat Germans and born and bred Britons who were of the opinion that Hitler was truly a great man and some of them would be willing to 'do their bit' for their Führer. Any organised group, club or premises associated with Germany in Britain in the late 1930s was perceived as a potential threat and would often be infiltrated by operatives from Special Branch or MI5. Anglo German Clubs were closed down on the outbreak of war. The German Hospital at Dalston also acquired a particular notoriety for the pro-Nazi sympathies of the staff when it was headed by Otto Bode. Guy Liddell, the head of MI5 B Divsion referred to it as 'A little piece of Nazi Germany in the middle of London,'[6] but when it was reliably reported that Nazi salutes were exchanged in its corridors something had to be done and the German staff were replaced with British ones.

The Nazis never played fair. The good will visits were merely a veneer to cover an operative amongst the group of visiting Germans whose specific remit would be information gathering for espionage purposes. Groups of Hitler Youth on exchange visits taken to see industrial sites and transport hubs would also have been unwittingly taking photographs, gathering maps and business prospectuses that would be of future use to German intelligence. Nazi agents had been operating in Britain since before the Nazi Party obtained power. The Germany Embassy staff and its attachés were all Nazi Party members by the late 1930s. Several of them were exposed for their involvement as recruiters of British people to engage in spying or letter smuggling for the Reich for money. Some of the diplomatic staff and attachés were asked to leave the country when their activities were exposed, others fled by 1 September 1939.

It is not generally realised that the Nazi Party had an overseas branch or *Auslands-Organisation* in Britain. The leader of this organisation was Ernst Bohle who had been born in Bradford, Yorkshire in 1903 to German parents, who had then moved as a family to South Africa in 1906. Returning to Germany as a young man, he was educated in Cologne and Berlin. Bohle

Miss Unity Mitford and her sister Lady Diana Mosley with SS Troops at the Nazi Party Rally, Nuremburg 1937.

Nurses from The German Hospital, Dalston photographed in a train carriage in April 1938. Suspicion fell on the staff of the hospital being Nazi sympathisers and reports were received of Nazi salutes being given regularly in its corridors.

became an early member of the Nazi Party and was appointed Gauleiter of the *Auslands-Organisation* in 1934.

In August 1937 Winston Churchill published an eloquent but critical article in the *Evening Standard* titled *A Plain Word to the Nazis* in which he raised his concerns about the Nazis and called on Parliament to increase scrutiny and surveillance of Germans living in Britain and to deport them if necessary. The article certainly stirred up the Nazi overseas organisation and Bohle wrote to Churchill's literary agent Emery Reves wishing to discuss the article with its author. The message was duly forwarded and Churchill welcomed the opportunity, stating in his subsequent article *Friendship with Germany*:

> *I see Herr Bohle has expressed a wish to talk this over with me. I should be delighted to do so in the most friendly manner, and do anything in the power of a private member to remove this new embarrassment to Anglo–German goodwill.*[7]

Winston Churchill and Ernst Bohle, Leader of the Nazi Auslands-Organisation *in Britain, after their meeting at Churchill's London residence on 1 October 1937.*

The pair met at Churchill's London residence on 1 October 1937. Bohle would recall the meeting lasted more than an hour adding:

> *I had ample opportunity in this thoroughly cordial conversation to describe the activity of the Auslands-Organisation and to dispel his misgivings. At the end he accompanied me to my car and let himself be photographed with me, in order, as he said, to show the world that we were parting as friends.*[8]

Cordial as the meeting may have been Churchill would not be photographed shaking hands with Bohle.

At the time Churchill wrote his article and met with Bohle he was out of office and, being out of favour in political circles, could do very little more than bring attention to the machinations of the Nazis in Britain in his articles. Both MI5 and Special Branch

Restaurant Manager Emilio Rossi's Membership card for the London Branch of Mussolini's Partito Nazionale Fascista, *(National Fascist Party). Every card carried the pledge of the member* 'to carry out the orders of the Duce and to serve with all my strength and, if necessary, with my blood, the cause of the Fascist Revolution.'

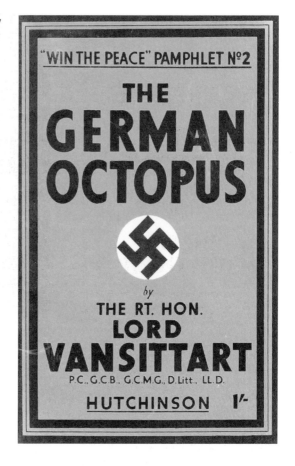

Cover of The German Octopus *by Lord Robert Vansittart (1945). His warnings of the dangers presented by the Nazis, their aspirations for European domination and his opposition to appeasement in the 1930s saw him derided for having 'an inflexible mind' and Vansittartism became a byword for Germanophobia.*

were only too aware if the nefarious espionage activities of the Nazis in Britain, notably that Nazi security services were spying on their own German nationals abroad. Nazi intelligence officials were also not above using coercive methods to get German nationals to spy on other German nationals or use them for the purposes of espionage, but that was not enough. Nazi German authorities issued a decree on 3 February 1938 requiring all German citizens who had been abroad for more than three months to register with their nearest German consulate. Once registered each person would be expected to keep the consulate updated of any subsequent change of address. It was the responsibility of the heads of households to ensure all those residing with them were registered, failure to do so could result in a fine of up to 500RM.

Anyone who knowingly or persistently failed to register would be declared to have lost their German nationality.[9] The official reason given was that this act would unite German nationals abroad and maintain their relationship

WARNING

Thousands of lives
were lost in the last
war because valuable
information was given
away to the enemy
through careless
talk

**BE ON
YOUR GUARD**

*...p mum
...e's not so dumb!*

CARELESS TALK COSTS LIVES

*A wide variety of posters warning of the
dangers of 'careless talk' were displayed inside
and outside offices, public buildings, places of
entertainment, at transport hubs and on our
streets during the war years.*

*you never know
who's
listening!*

**CARELESS TALK
COSTS LIVES**

with the Fatherland, but few were under any illusions, the act was created to enable the Nazis to impose tighter regime controls over Germans living abroad. With fear and coercion, threats of reprisals against family members, seizure of money or property back in Germany all at their disposal, this decree gave Nazi authorities the ability, at will, to apply pressure on any German national abroad to spy on neighbours and/or spy for the Reich. British intelligence was under no illusions that this could potentially create the greatest spy network of all time and it would be at the disposal of the Nazis.

When war loomed the Home Office and security services wanted every Nazi out of the country. Guy Liddell noted on 1 September 1939:

Telegrams for the arrest of German Party members of German suspects in Category I were sent out at 1.30pm. The telegrams for the arrest of persons under Section 18B were sent out between 3.30 and 4.30pm

It had also been agreed by all concerned parties that:

…nobody on our lists of Party members or suspects should be stopped at the ports unless we had very special reasons for holding them.

But still Nazis that were not known to the security services, BUF members and their sympathisers remained at large. As the months passed by, the blitzkrieg unleashed on the Low Countries, Belgium and France knocked allied forces onto the back heel in May 1940 and some of these traitorous individuals gathered at clandestine meetings and drew up their plans to aid the invading Germans to bring about the downfall of Britain.

The War Weekly
of 24 May 1940
graphically warns of
the paratroop menace
that was reportedly
used to devastating
effect during the
German invasion of
the Low Countries.

German occupation troops photographed on the street near The Panthéon, Paris 1940. In the aftermath of German forces invading their european neighbours numerous images were published in various newspapers showing German troops with individuals in civilian clothes the press were quick to not only brand as collaborators but 'Fifth Columnists'.

During the invasion scares of 1940 British newspapers and magazines carried various tips on how to spot and foil 'Fifth Columnists'.

"I think it's silly the way you try to find a perfectly natural explanation for everything I want to report."

A wry comment by the cartoonist Lawrence Siggs on the numerous false alarms over spotting parachute troops, Punch *11 September 1940.*

One of the most ambitious plans for an armed rising by those who could easily be branded 'Fifth Columnists' was revealed by Tim Tate in *Hitler's British Traitors*. It was devised by composer, conductor and expert on the Welsh bardic tradition Dr Leigh Vaughan Henry, a man who was also a rabid pro-Nazi and anti-Semite. Henry and his confederates apparently raised eighteen 'cells' of twenty-five terrorists across London in preparation for an armed coup to pave the way for the German invasion forces landing in Britain.

What Henry did not realise was he had already been infiltrated by two MI5 moles and as Henry began to ramp up his plans he openly shared them with those he thought he could trust. His ideas were very similar to those of Quisling in Norway and on 10 May 1940 Henry's house was raided. The whole sordid story that unfolded was told in the report of Inspector Arthur Cain of Special Branch who executed the warrant:

> *In London Vaughan Henry has organised district 'cells' under 'sergeants' who use code terms and keep in touch with him by telephone. He claims that when all the Government defence authorities in England have been disorganised, his group would come on the streets and assume control.*
>
> *Amongst the documents was a code, which [Henry] stated he had devised for communicating with his wife in Germany. There are also draft plans for a subversive organisation to establish an authoritarian system of Government.*
>
> *The methods to be adopted include illegal printing, a transport section to convey the members in their various activities, an extensive arrangement of accommodation addresses and various aliases for leading members of the organisation. Among Dr Henry's chief associates in these political activities have been Captain Ramsay MP, Jock Houston, Samuel F. Darwin Fox and Norman Hay.*[10]

There was also evidence of serious negotiations for the purchase of weaponry and munitions to arm the group.[11] Vaughan Henry was arrested and would spend the rest of the war interned on the Isle of Man, others would hang for far less under the Treachery Act. Tate suggests a possible reason for his escape from the gallows or even a trial was that Henry's plot included such senior figures from Britain's political and military establishments they could not risk a trial, even in camera, for fear of some or all the names leaking out and becoming known to the public. It could also be argued MI5 would not have wanted to risk the loss of valuable undercover agents who helped to uncover the plot through exposure. The chances are we will never know the truth because the files that name those involved or the exchanges of opinion between MI5 and DPP don't appear to exist any more.[12]

General Edmund Ironside, Commander-in-Chief Home Forces, 1940. One of many senior British armed forces officers convinced of the existence and danger presented by the 'Fifth Column' in Britain.

Another case had also blown up involving Tyler Kent a young employee of the American Embassy who had been caught passing sensitive diplomatic documents to Anna Wolkoff, a known associate of William Joyce the Nazi propaganda broadcaster known as Lord Haw-Haw. Wolkoff also had contacts with access to send diplomatic bags to the continent. She was also known to be part of the 'inner circle' of The Right Club which included Archibald Ramsay its vitrioloic anti-Semite leader. As far as Churchill was concerned enough was enough, something drastic had to be done to cut all those who could potentially rise up as a Fifth Column, regardless of the fall out.

A meeting was arranged with Home Secretary Sir John Anderson at the Home Office on the evening of 21 May. The reason for inaction soon

Detectives arresting a member of the London headquarters staff of the British Union of Fascists, 24 May 1940.

Women 'enemy aliens' leaving under police escort from a London station for detention camps on the Isle of Man, May 1940.

emerged, Anderson had formed the opinion that the BUF was in reality patriotic and he found it difficult to believe that members of the BUF would assist the enemy. Despite some of the underground activities of the BUF, Maule Ramsay and The Right Club, and their close association with Moseley and the BUF being explained to him 'quietly and forcibly'[13] by Max Knight, Anderson appeared unmoved, even when Guy Liddell stressed the urgency of the matter Anderson still expressed his concerns over sanctioning the arrests without solid evidence and due process. Clearly, frustrated by the Home Secretary's stance, Liddell recorded in his diary:

I longed to say that if somebody did not get a move on there would be no democracy, no England and no Empire and that this was almost a matter of days…Either he is an extremely calm and cool-headed person or he has not the least idea of the present situation. The possibility of a serious invasion of this country would seem to be no more than a vague suggestion in Anderson's mind.[14]

Anderson was however, at least in Liddell's opinion, *'considerably shaken by the end of the meeting'*[15] and asked for further evidence of a number of the points brought to his attention for the Cabinet meeting the following night. The meeting and the evidence clearly made an impression on Anderson and the Cabinet decided in favour of the detention of many members of pro-Nazi groups, predominantly members of the British Union of Fascists; a suitable amendment known as 18B (1A) was made to the regulations and the arrests ensued soon afterwards.

Internments under 18B were further extended on 27 May to include 'enemy alien' women who were also to be interned. A concession was made that permitted them to take their children with them. When Italy declared war on Britain on 10 June 1940 Churchill was in no mood for procrastination and it is said he simply barked 'Collar the lot!' and the 4,000 known members of the Italian Fascist Party resident in Britain were arrested and interned along with Italians aged between sixteen and thirty who had lived in the UK for less than twenty years, regardless of their political affiliations.

German map from a 1940 propaganda publication showing a stylised plan for the conquest of Britain.

Chapter 2

Seaborne Agents

After the fall of France in June 1940 Hitler began to draw up plans for the invasion of Great Britain in what would be known as *Unternehmen Seelöwe* – Operation Sealion. Reliable and up to date reconnaissance of the proposed landing areas would be the key to success and the *Abwehr* (German Military Intelligence) chief, Vice Admiral Wilhelm Canaris lost no time entrusting what became codenamed Operation Lena to Colonel Erwin von Lahousen, Head of *Abwehr* II. In turn Lahousen chose Ast Hamburg, under the overall command of *Korvettenkapitän* Herbert Wichmann to see the operation through with Section I-L (Air Intelligence, the 'L' was for Luft) under *Hauptmann* Nikolaus Ritter (aka Dr Rantzau) to oversee agents parachuted into Britain and section I-M ('M' for Marine) under veteran *Abwehr* Officer Hilmar Dierks.

Lena Agents were to be recruited, trained and sent to Britain to gather information about military defences, emplacements, troop concentrations,

An artist's impression based on first hand accounts of what German occupation would mean on the streets of any european country.

Admiral Wilhelm Canaris, Chief of the Abwehr, *the German military intelligence service 1935–1944.*

Obstlt *(later* Generalmajor*) Erwin von Lahousen, Head of* Abwehr *II.*

Hauptmann *Nikolaus Ritter (aka Dr Rantzau).*

Korvettenkapitän *Herbert Wichmann, the officer given responsibility for Operation Lena.*

Abwehr *Radio Centre, Wohldorf, Hamburg c1940.*

and minefields in specific coastal areas to provide invasion planners with the latest information about the areas where invasion forces were being planned. Agents were also ordered to discern what they could of the morale of the British people and to get amongst the population at the moment of invasion. Findings were to be regularly transmitted back via radios using agreed codes and during specific windows of time. There were also to be *Abwehr* groups landed with the specific remit of sabotage of communications and military installations to hinder the efforts of the anti-invasion forces in Britain.[1]

Agents delivered via seaborne landings in the south of Britain were the part of the operation known as *Hummer Süd* (Lobster South) for landings and *Hummer Nord* (Lobster North) was for landings in the north. Four spies landed in pairs on beaches either side of the Dungeness peninsula and the MI5 report, based on interviews with those involved, gives an account of the crossing:

Radio operators at the Abwehr *Radio Centre, Wohldorf.*

Training potential Abwehr *operatives to send and receive coded messages by radio transmitter and receiver.*

In the early afternoon of the 2 September 1940, two single masted diesel engined fishing boats named La Mascott *and* Rose du Carmel, *left Le Touquet for Boulogne where they waited for a favourable tide to cross to England. On leaving Boulogne each boat was taken by a German minesweeper and conducted across the Channel to within a mile or so of the English coast south of Dungeness.*

After sailing some distance in a westerly direction two rowing boats were put out and into these climbed José Rudolf Waldberg [25] and Karl Heinrich Cornelis Ernst Meier [24] from La Mascotte *and Sjoerd Pons [28] and Charles Albert Van Den Kieboom [26] from the* Rose du Carmel. *Poor visibility enabled the rowing boats to approach the shore without being seen. As they drew near the land, Waldberg and Meier sighted a patrol boat in the distance and fearing trouble immediately threw overboard, as previously instructed, a weighted package containing a circular code and two maps. With no further mishap the occupants of the first boat landed in the early morning of Tuesday 3 September, on the beach between Dungeness and Rye and those of the second boat between Rye and Dymchurch.*[2]

The coup of capturing the first enemy agent to land on British shores in the Second World War goes to Private Sidney Tollervey of D Company,

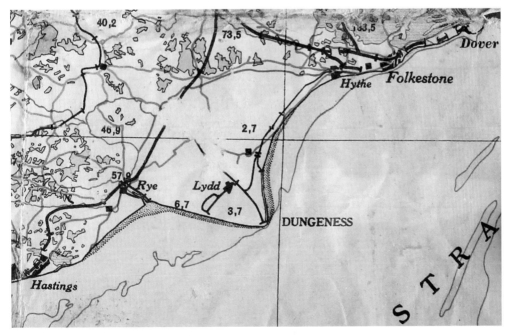

Map carried by the Operation Lena agents who landed by boats on either side of the Dungeness peninsula on 3 September 1940.

Charles Albert Van Den Kieboom.

Sjoerd Pons.

6th Battalion, Somerset Light Infantry who was on patrol at Romney Marsh, Kent at approximately 4.45am. It was still dark when he was near the road at the Dymchurch Redoubt. Kieboom and Pons were in the process of unloading their equipment from their boat and running it into the bushes a short distance away from the beach when Tollervey approached. Pte

The boat used by Kieboom and Pons to row ashore at Romney in the early hours of 3 September 1940.

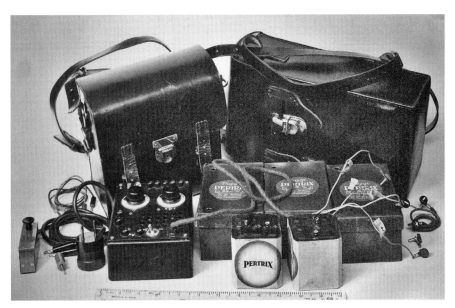

Kieboom's radio transmitter, receiver, morse key, batteries and equipment cases.

Tollervey recalled he heard rustling and suddenly saw the figure of a man silhouetted against the sky as he ran across the road towards the sea wall and flung himself onto it. Private Tollervey challenged the man 'Halt! Who goes there?' and ran down some nearby steps and despite not asking for a password he heard a voice call out 'I do not know your code word.'

Tollervey asked if he had any means of identification to which the man replied he did not understand what he meant. Tollervey told him to advance and be recognised and this the man did with his hands up. He was dressed in civilian clothes wearing white shoes with another pair of shoes slung around his neck along with a pair of binoculars. The man appeared very keen to point out he was a Dutch refugee and asked to see one of Tollervey's officers to whom he would explain his case. He did not know it at the time but Private Tollervey had just earned himself the distinction of capturing the first German spy to land in Britain.[3]

Under questioning the captured spy revealed his name was Charles Albert Van Den Kieboom. He had not landed alone and his fellow spy, Sjord Pons was captured a short while later and their radio equipment recovered from where they hid it. Meanwhile another pair of spies had made their landing at Lydd. They were also soon in custody after one of them walked into The Rising Sun pub on New Street in Lydd and asked for a drink of cider champagne. Landlady Mabel Cole didn't like the look of the man who stood out as a stranger, he was tall, well dressed and she noticed his clothes

José Rudolf Waldberg.   *Karl Meier.*

appeared wet, the drink he requested had not been available for years and the man was clearly not familiar with English opening hours for public houses. She suggested he should go and buy cigarettes at the shop across the road, then visit the local church and return again at 10.00am, which he did.

The stranger duly returned and ordered a drink and biscuits. When Mrs Cole asked for payment she said 'That'll be one and a tanner', slang for one

The boat used by Waldberg and Meier to row ashore at Lydd on 3 September 1940.

shilling and sixpence. The money parlance clearly threw the stranger and he had to proffer the cash in his hand so she could take the requisite coins in payment.

As the stranger eagerly stuffed his mouth with biscuits he had just bought Mrs Cole signalled her concern to local man Horace Rendal 'Rennie' Mansfield, an inspector of the Aeronautical Inspection Directorate (AID) and his friend, insurance adviser Ronald Silvester who had been in the bar a short while before. They had already clocked the stranger and had noticed his rather stange accent, Sylvester recalled:

> *Strangely enough his accent was distinctly American and we were expecting to hear broken English as he had a most Teutonic caste of features. Pocketing his change and with a gruff 'Good morning gentlemen' he made his way to the street, crossed the road and entered a small general store opposite. 'Come on,' said my friend, 'Let's follow him.'* [4]

Mansfield and Silvester followed him outside and watched him visit the shop again. He left having purchased more biscuits and lemonade and walked off

The High Street of the quiet seaside town of Lydd c1940.

down the Dungeness Road towards the sea. Mansfield and Silvester rushed to Mansfield's car and drove along behind the man and after about 400 yards, they passed him, stopped the car, got out and walked towards him. Mansfield mustered up all the confidence he could and producing his AID photo identification, pointed out to the stranger that he was in a restricted area and challenged him to produce his identity card. All the stranger had to offer was a Dutch passport in the name of Karl Meier. He agreed to go with Mansfield and Silvester to Lydd police station. Silvester recalled as he entered the car he said: 'You've caught me I guess and I don't mind what happens to me but I refuse to go back to Germany.'[5]

Meier's fellow spy José Waldberg was captured the following morning, along with his radio equipment in the bushes near Boulderwall Farm, Lydd where he had remained hidden for the last 24 hours awaiting Meiers' return. Waldberg had attached his aerial to a small tree and at 8.30pm he decided to send out his first wireless message, using an emergency code which he had written in his notebook, reporting their safe landing and position and that they had jettisoned some of their papers. He sent a second message on 4 September reporting the arrest of Meier and his own difficult position and requested an aeroplane to be sent on the Friday evening. A third message was ready for despatch when Waldberg was tracked down and arrested. All three messages were found written out in his pocket book with the code when he was searched.[6]

All four spies were soon in custody at Seabrook police station and were then handed over to MI5 and interrogated, the summary noted:

> The demeanour of the spies was such that they were convinced invasion would take place before the middle of September. The spies work in pairs and were provided with food and £60 in British currency for expenses to last fourteen days. There was no German contact in England. The spies gave the information that the contact was unnecessary as the Germans would be here within two weeks.[7]

The signal would be given by waving a handkerchief to approaching German forces. He was then to contact an officer and say 'Ich bin hier mit einem Sonderfrag für deutschen Wehrmann' followed by the password 'Elizabeth'.[8]

The captured spies were charged under Section 1 of the Treachery Act, 1940 and their trial was held in camera before Mr Justice Wrottesley at the Central Criminal Court at the Old Bailey between 19–22 November 1940. The jury found Kieboom, Meier and Waldberg guilty, sentence of death was passed upon them. Pons was acquitted but was re-arrested immediately afterwards. There had been hope within MI5 that Pons would have proved useful to counter espionage but he always proved intractable. Waldberg and Meier were hanged by Stanley Cross, assisted by Albert Pierrepoint and Henry Critchell, at Pentonville on 10 December 1940. Kieboom appealed against his sentence but subsequently withdrew the appeal. This did cause a delay and consequently he was hanged a week later on 17 December at Pentonville by Stanley Cross, assisted by Herbert Morris.

Karl Drücke aka Francois de Deeker.

The next three seaborne Hummer Nord I agents were flown in an X. Fliegerkorps He 115 seaplane from Stavanger, Norway and were set down on the Moray Firth off the coast between Buckie and Portgordon in what was then known as Banffshire, Scotland at around dawn on 30 September 1940.

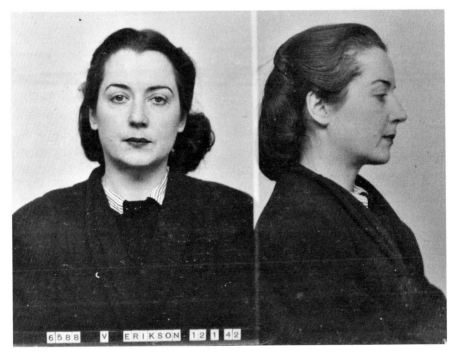

Vera Schalburg photographed during captivity.

The party consisted of Karl Drücke who had been supplied with false documents and a cover story under the name of François de Deeker, a French refugee from Belgium; Robert Petter who was given the name Werner Heinrich Wälti, a Swiss subject living in London; and for the first time a female agent was to be deployed in these operations. She had been one of the pre-war agents active in England, Vera Schalburg (probably known at the time as Vera von Wedel) who, for this mission, would have the cover identity of Vera Eriksen, a Dane living in London. All three of them were experienced espionage operatives and they were not deployed under any coercion.

They had practised launching their 4' x 10' rubber dinghy from a seaplane, getting into it and rowing ashore in a fjord in Norway before they departed. Indeed they had become accustomed to the flights in the seaplane, having prepared themselves mentally and had actually set off to begin their mission on two previous occasions but the aircraft carrying them had to turn back due to adverse weather conditions. Still, it's quite a leap between training and becoming operational and they disembarked onto choppy sea rather than a calm fjord. The bicycles they had been sent with were soon ditched over the

Portgordon, Moray, Scotland. In the foreground is the railway station where Vera and Drücke were captured just hours after they landed.

PORTGORDON LOOKING WEST.

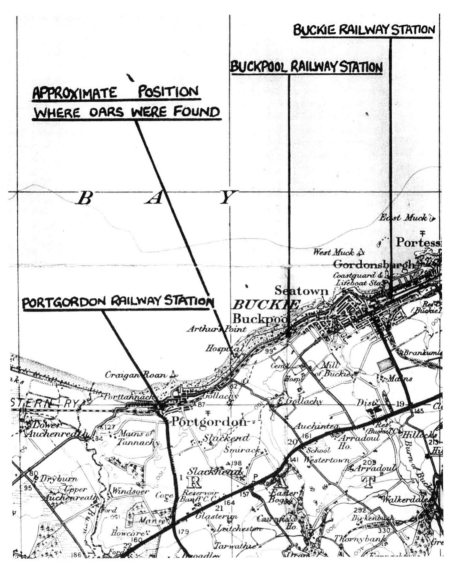

Contemporary map showing the key locations relating to the landing by Drücke, Vera and Walti on 30 September 1940.

side to prevent the boat filling with water and the two male agents rowed for three and a half hours before they came to the shallows at the mouth of the Burn of Gollachy.[9] The three then found they had to get out of the boat and wade some distance through the sea in order to come ashore.[10]

According to Vera, Wälti wanted to go by himself and stayed behind to sink the boat while she and Drücke made their way to a nearby village where they found a station. However, since the sign boards and place names of

Britain had been removed in the face of the invasion threat they had no success in discovering where they were so they walked on and rested under a hedge until daylight.[11]

At about 7.30am they returned to the station and found Stationmaster John Donald in the booking hall. He was approached by Drüke who enquired of him 'What station is this?' to which Donald replied 'Portgordon'. Vera said 'What?' and the name of the station was repeated to her. Drüke claimed he did not attempt to speak to anyone owing to his ignorance of English. In the hope of avoiding suspicion and to not give away their final destination Vera purchased two single tickets to Forres.[12]

Stationmaster Donald recalled how odd it had struck him that someone should be at the station and ask where the station was at such a time in the morning and watched Drüke running his finger down the list of stations from Portgordon to Elgin and on to Forres. The Stationmaster also could not help but notice that the bottom of Drüke's trousers, his shoes and the bottom of his overcoat were soaking wet, as were Vera's shoes and there was a slight deposit of hoar frost on the shoulders of her coat. This and the fact that the man also appeared to be trying to hide his face aroused such suspicion that Donald told Porter John Geddes to keep them talking as he rang the police. He then opened the ticket window of the booking office and Vera purchased the two tickets to Forres.[13]

PC Robert Grieve of Banffshire Constabulary who was stationed at Portgordon was despatched to the station as a result of the call. Arriving shortly after 8.00am he found Drüke and Vera in the waiting room and asked them to show their identity cards which they duly produced. Grieve then asked them their nationality, Vera replied 'He is Belgian, I am Danish'. PC Grieve then asked to see their passports, Vera claimed she had left hers in London, Drüke did not reply but produced his Belgian passport. On examining the document the constable found there was no Immigration Officer's stamp authorising the holder to land.

The summary account of what happened next is in the MI5 file collated for the prosecution of the agents:

They were asked where they came from and the woman said 'we came from London'. The man did not speak. Asked where they had stayed the previous night the woman said 'We stayed in a hotel at Banff'. Again the man did not answer. When asked the name of the hotel in Banff in which they stayed the woman shrugged her shoulders but neither made a reply.

The constable then asked how they had got to Portgordon from Banff, they replied 'We hired a taxi to within a mile of Portgordon and then walked.' The constable being dissatisfied with their explanations then told them he would take them to the police station pending enquiries.

The woman then repeated what the officer had said to the man and he took hold of a small dark blue suitcase with nickel fittings. After arrival at the police station, Grieve communicated with Inspector Simpson at Buckie Police Station and after hearing the constable's conversations she said, 'I told you lies at the Railway Station' and continued 'we landed from a small boat about a mile along the coast, the boat was in charge of a man named Sanderson.' When asked where the boat was she replied 'It has gone back to Bergen.'

Drüke and Vera were taken into custody and escorted to Portgordon police station where they were questioned further by Inspector John Simpson:

He asked the man who he was and the woman said, 'He cannot speak English'. The woman gave her name as Vera Erikson and said she was 27 years of age, a widow and had no occupation. She added that she was a Danish subject born in Siberia. They again produced their Identity Cards and the man his passport. Inspector Simpson observed that Continental figures were on both Identity Cards. When asked how they had arrived at Portgordon the woman said 'We came from Bergen on a small boat called 'Nor Star', the name of the Captain was Anderson'. Inspector Simpson then searched the man and his overcoat pocket found a box containing nineteen rounds of revolver ammunition and when asked if he had a revolver the man replied, 'No'. In addition the Inspector found an electric torch with a blue bulb, bearing the name 'Hawe' and 'made in Bohemia' on the bottom, a watch with the initials 'H.W.D.' engraved on the back a pocket knife, a leather wallet, a Traveller's Ration Book bearing the number C.A. 568263; a piece of flexible material sewn into a piece of blue cloth; a single third class railway ticket from Portgordon to Forres dated 30th September, 1940; £327 in Bank of England notes; a piece of German sausage and other foodstuffs. Later in the man's presence the small suitcase was forced open and the Inspector found a small 'Mauser' pistol containing six rounds of ammunition in the magazine; two circular cardboard discs fastened together with a brass split pin; a sheet of paper bearing a number of place names; a sheet of graph paper; a wireless set...[14]

The game was up and Vera admitted that her National Registration Card was false. The police contacted the Regional Security Liaison Officer who reported to headquarters and instructions were given for the urgent dispatch of the two persons with all the equipment and other possessions found with them to be handed over to MI5. Their claim to have landed by boat was also brought

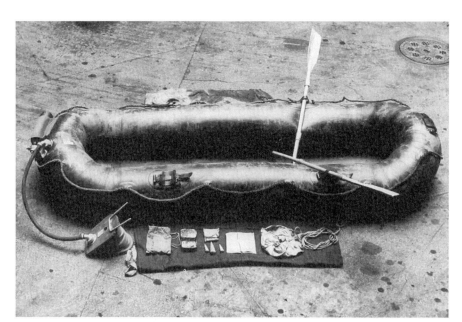

The rubber dinghy used by Drücke, Vera and Wälti repaired and re-inflated photographed with its oars and accessories.

into question when Coastguard James Addison spotted an object in the sea drifting from Portgordon to Buckie at around 11.45am. The Buckie Harbour Master put out in his boat to recover the object. As he approached he picked up the bellows for the inflation of a rubber boat that were floating on the sea. Upon reaching the object spotted by Coastguard Addison the harbourmaster discovered it to be a rubber dinghy that had been rolled up.[15]

Vera and Drüke had not slipped up and given away the third party who landed with them but nonetheless Banffshire Police initiated enquiries to ascertain if any other suspicious individuals had been encountered on the coast that morning in similar circumstances. This dragnet received information from James Smith a porter at Buckpool who had encountered a man at 6.50am who was not sure of where he needed to travel to and spoke with a foreign accent. Smith had directed the man to Buckie Station and there he turned up around 8.00am

Alexander Paterson, a Porter at Buckie Station, had also encountered a man looking at the timetable outside the station who looked rather lost so he had enquired if he had lost his train. The man, without speaking, produced a third class single ticket to Edinburgh from his wallet and was told that his train was at 10.00am. Paterson suspected the man to be a foreigner and remembered that he had with him a suitcase and a dark coloured brief case. Paterson advised the man to put the luggage into the booking office, which he did and at 10.04 a.m. Paterson saw the man board Aberdeen train with his luggage.[16]

Upon receipt of the information that two suspicious persons were believed to be foreign agents Lieutenant Mair of the Scottish Regional Security Officer instigated enquiries conducted by local CID and police at all railway stations, hotels, boarding houses and other likely places. As a result of this appeal Thomas Cameron, a porter at Waverley Station, Edinburgh came forward to say that had attended a man he believed to be the owner of this case, who had arrived off the Aberdeen train at about 4.30pm and spoke with a foreign accent. Cameron was able to identify the case and to say that the owner was returning about 9.00pm to collect it, prior to departing for London. At about 6.00pm a case was traced in the Left Luggage Office at the east end of the station. Upon examination the case was damp and had particles of sand adhering to it.

A report of what happened next is recorded in the MI5 case folder:

Detective Inspector Alexander Sutherland, Detective Alexander McCowan and Police War Reserve James Fair made a search of the case and found that it contained a complete transmitting set contained in a leather case. Also in the suitcase were articles of clothing which were wet. At 6.50pm Lieut Mair telephoned a description of the suspected foreign agent and this tallied with the description of the man who had deposited the suit case. ...In consequence of the find in the Left Luggage Office a watch was kept on Waverley Station.

At 8.58pm that night the suspected agent came from the vicinity of Waverley Steps and after hesitating at the Left Luggage Office he continued to the book stall, some 20 yards distant. A minute or so after he had taken up his stance at the book stall, keeping his eye on the left luggage office Detective Superintendent Merrilees [who had borrowed a railway porter's uniform so he would blend in] *was joined by Thomas Cameron. Just then the prisoner approached Cameron who asked if he wanted his case. The prisoner replied 'Yes' and handed Cameron his cloakroom ticket. Detective Superintendent Merrilees was immediately joined by Detective Lieutenant Cormack, Detective Inspector Sutherland and Detective Sergeant Swan and the prisoner was held. He however made an effort to resist but was overpowered while in the act of trying to put his hand in his left hand trouser pocket.*

He was searched and a Mauser automatic pistol was found in his left hand trouser pocket. He was taken into the left luggage office where Detective Constable McCowan and Police War Reserve Fair were on watch...His articles of wearing apparel were soaking wet. On being arrested, without being spoken to, Walti exclaimed 'I am not German, I am Swiss.'[17]

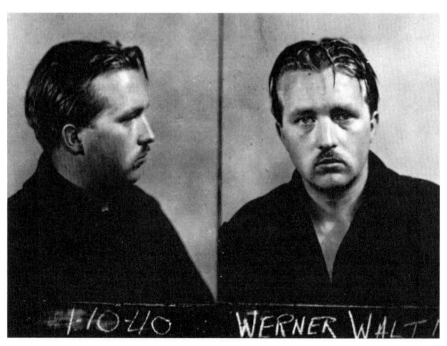

Swiss passport carried by Robert Petter in his cover name of Werner Wälti.

'Werner Wälti' photographed less than 24 hours after his arrest.

Drüke, Vera and Wälti were brought to London under escort and interviewed at Latchmere House. The MI5 report of the interrogations dated 2 October 1940 revealed all three had tried to stick to their cover stories. Vera was first to divulge useful information, but the two men remained uncooperative and anything more had to be derived from the physical evidence of the items found

Mauser pocket pistol as carried by Wälti and other agents on the early boat landings.

in their possession, deduction and the few scraps of information they were prepared to divulge:

> It is however, quite clear that both Erikson and de Deeker are skilled and practised German SS Agents who have been involved in such work for a long time. The exact nature of their mission to this country is not yet clear. It is just possible that Erikson was instructed to proceed to London and it is also just possible that she was to be contacted here by a local German agent. A further interesting fact regarding Erikson is that she has been in this country before, staying with the Duchess de Chateau Thierry at Dorset House, Gloucester Place. The Duchess is well known to this office and Erikson's stay with her confirms previous suspicions that she has been mixed up in German espionage.
>
> From Walti's background story it would appear that he was recruited for the German SS in Brussels. Though younger than the other two (24), Walti had obviously had experience with the German SS and in his possession were found maps detailing the area of the Eastern Highlands of Scotland, Elgin, Aberdeen, Sutherland, Caithness, Ross and Cromarty as well as areas in England which included Norwich and the greater part of Norfolk, Wisbech, King's Lynn, Peterborough and the surrounding country, Bedford and the surrounding country, Cambridge and the surrounding country, Bury St Edmunds and the greater part of Suffolk. It is difficult to account for such a wide area of patrol but it is possible that Walti had to hand some of the maps over to other agents…while varying somewhat in form from the cases of the other six spies recently arrested, the three new ones are clearly directed by the same organisation belonging particularly to the Hamburg end of it.
>
> …It is reasonable to suppose that the two men were intended to carry out espionage similar to that of the previous six on defence works in Scotland

and on the East Coast. The woman Erikson may have had a mission of an entirely different order and it is just possible that she was really intended for London. The wireless sets in the possession of the spies are of a similar type to those previously discovered in the case of the first six. They are capable of transmitting and receiving. The codes are of the type supplied to those parachutists, that is, they are in the form of circular discs. As all three have so far shown considerable composure under interrogation and appear to be reconciled to the inevitable fate meted out to spies, their interrogation presented considerable problems. It is probable that several days more will be necessary before the whole truth can be extracted from them.[18]

The problem for Drüke and Wälti was they had already been 'burned' after national newspapers published the story of a male Nazi spy being caught on Edinburgh station[19] and the whole operation could have been viewed as compromised by their *Abwehr* masters. Drüke and Wälti refused to cooperate with MI5, even after frustrated interrogation officer overstepped their authority and offered Wälti the chance to evade the hangman in return for a full confession, he did not accept the offer.[20]

Drüke and Wälti were tried in camera before Mr Justice Asquith at the Central Criminal Court, The Old Bailey 12–13 June 1941. Like the previous spies they had representation by legal counsel and were convicted under the Treachery Act 1940. The appeals they lodged against the sentence of death were heard by the Court of Criminal Appeal but were dismissed on 21 July. Still arrogant enough to believe they had been betrayed by an informant rather than their own incompetence and misfortune as agents,[21] and undoubtedly bitter at having been convinced they were to be part of a vanguard for an invasion that that had still not arrived, Drüke was left feeling he and his fellow agents were just 'a cargo of meat.'[22]

Jona 'Klop' Ustinov, (the father of the affectionately remembered actor and raconteur Peter Ustinov) was an MI5 operative whose keen perception and genial hospitality was key to 'turning' a number of informants and agents. Perhaps he would be the man to obtain the truth from Vera? His report, based on conversations with Vera during a brief interlude of soft interrogation when she was allowed out of Holloway Prison, drew the conclusion:

The truth seems to be that she and her companions were no more important than the other operational spies who arrived at roughly the same time. They were obviously thrown to the wolves.[23]

A view echoed by Dick White (who went on to become Director General of MI5) when he concluded:

Doubtless the only satisfaction which the directors of the German Intelligence…
obtained from the venture was their ability to report to the High Command
that they were dispatching spies to the United Kingdom in preparation for
the invasion.[24]

Wälti and Drüke were hanged at Wandsworth Prison by Thomas Pierrepoint, assisted by Albert Pierrepoint, Harry Kirk and Stanley Cross on 6 August 1941.

Vera never faced trial, she was not mentioned in any newspaper reports nor in the magazine articles and books published on spies during the Second World War. The reason for the omission was that her presence remained an official secret, but there are a number of possible suggestions for why she did not face trial along with Wälti and Drüke. One suggested in her files is that she was, or at least claimed to be, pregnant. Another is what may seem an old fashioned view now that the British authorities simply did not want to hang a young woman.

Worse still, if she had gone to the gallows the fall-out could have been that Vera became a *cause célèbre*. The outrage over the execution of Nurse Edith Cavell by the Germans for 'war treason' in 1915 had been used to such great effect by the Allies during the First World War, the last thing British authorities wanted to hand the Germans was the propaganda opportunity of the execution of a beautiful woman agent in this war. With all of those possibilities borne in mind the overriding reason for her to be cloaked in secrecy was far more prosaic in that she presented the best prospect of being of use as a double-cross agent and infiltrator than the agents that landed with her.

That, however, did not mean Vera did not present her own problems. Within days of arrival at Camp 020 at Latchmere House Vera was 'showing signs of going on hunger strike' and was removed to Holloway Prison.[25] MI5 seem satisfied with Vera's account of her mission being to reprise her pre-war role as hostess at the Duchess de Chateau Thierry's salon [financed by Ritter with the aim of using the Duchess's contacts to obtain useful information for espionage purposes] at Dorset House, Gloucester Place in Marylebone. Vera gave up the names of a number of those she came into contact with but, very much as Ritter had complained that the Duchess's contacts had been of little use back in 1939, when MI5 investigated them the trails ran cold or the person of interest they were seeking had already left the UK. Those they could trace were mostly already interned or proved to be more Nazi sympathisers in words rather than deeds and would not dream of dirtying their hands by getting involved in actual espionage operations.[26] But there were significant exceptions. Vera did identify a certain My Eriksson as a courier and scouting agent for Ritter. Already interned, Eriksson was questioned on the matter but proved as convincing and as slippery as ever.

MI5 officer Richard Butler had conducted numerous interrogations of suspects and his take on My Eriksson after interviewing her was: '*I am more than ever certain that My is an extremely clever woman, a brilliant actress and a consummate liar,*' he held a similar view of Vera.[27]

The problem with Vera was that it was always difficult to tell when she was telling the truth or not. Lieutenant Colonel Robin Stephens interrogated Vera on several occasions and summed her up well in a report on 6 January 1941: '*she prefers to lie and in order to get rid of us, she not infrequently gives an answer which is calculated to please.*'[28] In a later memo he had clearly lost patience with her dishonest claims and simply described her as 'a prize liar.'[29]

Any plans to use Vera for double-cross work were scuppered in March 1941 after British SIS received intelligence from German espionage centres in Norway that they were aware Drüke, Walti and Vera had been captured. The Director of Public Prosecutions had, however, decided against taking proceedings against Vera under the Treachery Act, in which he recorded:

> So far as her continued sojourn in Holloway is concerned it is felt that since this woman in an experienced and dangerous spy there is no more suitable place for her to be lodged.[30]

After a return to prison an experimental method of soft interrogation was devised by which Vera was taken out of prison. She was bought new clothes in the shops on Oxford Street and went for a sojourn with the Ustinovs at Barrow Elm, Gloucestershire, where she was entertained and shown kindness over the period of a few days during which she opened up and spoke freely in conversation providing valuable insights of a number of her fellow inmates in Holloway.[31]

Vera's candid revelations and participation in what MI5 Director General David Petrie described to Sir Alexander Maxwell, Permanent Under-Secretary of State to the Home Office as a '*somewhat unorthodox course of action, which has been fully justified by the results which have been obtained*'[32] proved to be her ticket out of Holloway. MI5 was not keen for her to return there because those who she would be returning to in prison were '*the very people whom we least desire to known anything of what had taken place.*'[33] So Vera was sent to Aylesbury Prison and was soon transferred to Camp W internment camp on the Isle of Man where she proved useful as a stool pigeon reporting on her fellow prisoners for the rest of the war.

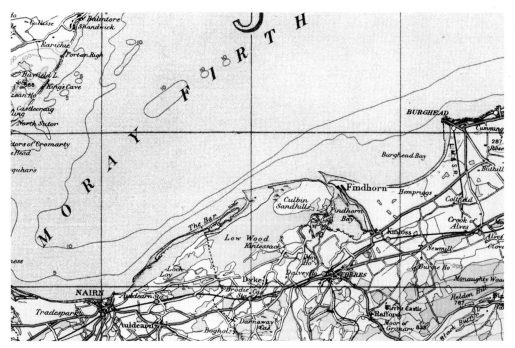

Contemporary map showing the Moray Firth and Culbin Sands where the sabotage team of Edvardsen, Lund and Joost landed on 25 October 1940.

Sometimes events happen in the world of espionage that would be considered too incredible to be included in a spy thriller book. One such event took place on 23 September 1940 when the cutter *La Parte Bien* was found to contain Hugo Jonasson, Gerard Libot, Edward De Lee, all of whom had been recruited by Otto Voight of the German Secret Service as saboteurs. During their crossing from Brest to Le Touquet to collect more agents they had had become so drunk they put into Plymouth by mistake – at least that was the story they all told.[34] They too were given a warm welcome at Camp 020 for the rest of the war.

The next team of Hummer Nord agents flew out from Stavanger on 24 October and landed by inflatable dinghy south of the Moray Firth, about fifteen miles NE of Inverness on 25 October 1940. There were a total of three agents, Legwald Lund, Otto 'Max' Joost and Gunnar Edvardsen. Lund was a Norwegian Master Mariner in his fifties who had threatened a German policeman during one of his drunken binges and deserted his ship. He claimed he had been met by German Secret Service officers who offered him the deal to undertake this mission as the only way he could escape punishment.[35] Otto 'Max' Joost was a German who had fought for the Spanish government during the Civil War and was given a similar option of going on the mission or being sent to a detention camp. The third man was Gunnar Edvardsen a Norwegian journalist who had been conscripted as an interpreter for the German occupation forces in Norway, attached to the Gebirgs (Mountain) Division. He had received some training in espionage and it had been intended for him to be a member of the Drüke, Vera and Wälti group.[36]

This unfortunate trio had been given the mission to bicycle across Scotland cutting telephone lines in an attempt to create alarm and to perform acts of sabotage whenever they presented themselves. The three were told that their operation was in advance of the invasion that would be launched in about three weeks. They would then be expected to join with the invading forces to fight on for the conquest of Britain.[37] Hinsley and Simkins made the observation in *British Intelligence in the Second World War*, '*Of all the spies sent in preparation for the projected invasion, these were the most ill-prepared.*'[38]

They had been despatched with no radio transmitter or receiver so had no way of communicating success, failure, difficulties or observations, with their base. Only Lund had his passport with him but not one of them had an identity card, ration book or any other paperwork to assist their cover and their survival during the mission. In fact according to Edvardsen, the only equipment they seemed to have been issued with to carry out their task were two bicycles, a revolver, a torch, insulated pliers and £100 in notes for each man.[39] The fact that many of the bank notes they had been given were found to have consecutive serial numbers would not have been useful to them if the sabotage group began to be traced.[40]

After rowing for thirteen hours and discovering, as ever, bicycles and rubber dinghies don't mix, they had ditched the bicycles over the side long before they landed at Culbin Sands by Findhorn, Morayshire, Scotland. Once ashore they 'knifed' their rubber dinghy but, according to Edvardsen, all three of them had intended to hand themselves in. They ditched or buried what equipment they had – except the money and Lund's passport – then, feeling cold, wet and hungry they, set off towards the nearest town, which turned out to be Nairn, to try to find something to eat. As they were walking along the main road near the village they were surprised from behind by Inspector Stewart of Moray and Nairn Constabulary and challenged as to who they were. The group spoke very little English but what they had they used to relate their cover story of being refugees from Norway. The story and their demeanour failed to convince and begs the question of whether they really had intended to simply hand themselves in on arrival as Edvardsen would claim. Inspector Stewart arrested the group, took them to Nairn police station and informed the RSLO.[41] After their arrival and initial interrogation

Juan Martinez.   *Silvio Robles.*   *Pedro Hechevaria.*   *Nicolas Pasos-Diaz.*

at Camp 020 'Tin Eye' Stevens would describe this intended sabotage party as nothing more than another *'cargo of meat sent over as part of the jitter war'*.[42] Edvardsen, Lund and Joost were all interned for the duration.

The *Abwehr* were rapidly coming to the conclusion that rubber dinghies nor the row boats of the kind attached to fishing vessels were proving the most covert means of landing spies. Hiding in plain sight was another option, by coercing and bribing the crews of fishing vessels to work for German espionage they could merge in among the fishing fleets that braved the waters around the British isles in wartime to convey agents, sabotage teams and even act as couriers for espionage agents already operating in the countries where they docked.

One such vessel was the fishing smack *Josephine* under Dutch captain Cornelius Evertsen which landed at Milford Haven on 12 November 1940. When asked their business at the port by a naval patrol, Evertsen claimed he was en route from Brest bound for Dublin but one of his passengers, Nicolas

Cornelius Evertsen.   *Arie Van Dam.*   *Peter Krag.*   *Theophile Jezequel.*

Pasos-Diaz, had developed an abscess and required medical treatment. The boat crew and passengers were landed as refugees but sent for further interrogation during which it was soon revealed the vessel had four crew and three passengers, Cubans named Silvio Ruiz Robles, Pedro Hechevarria and Nicolas Pasos-Diaz. The crew soon revealed their three passengers had been recruited by the *Abwehr* as saboteurs and were to have been landed in the Bristol Channel to carry out acts of sabotage around the Bristol area. Reciprocally, the Cuban passengers pointed the finger at Captain Evertsen and crew members Arie van Dam, Peter Krag and Theophile Jezequel claiming they were all in the pay of the *Abwehr*. A search of the boat revealed a hidden Browning automatic pistol and materials for sabotage including explosives hidden in cans labelled 'Green Peas'. Removed to and interrogated at Camp 020, the entire crew were imprisoned and deported after the end of the war with the exception of Pasos-Diaz who died while in Liverpool prison in April 1942.

The final group of spies, that we are aware of to date, that landed on the coast of Britain by rubber dinghy during the Second World War were Norwegians

The rural Scottish fishing village of Pennan when German agents John Moe and Tor Glad landed on 7 April 1941.

Tor Glad and London born John Neal Moe, who were landed by seaplane onto the south of the Moray Firth on 7 April 1941. They rowed ashore and landed near the charming fishing village of Pennan, near Fraserburgh, Banffshire (now Aberdeenshire) with its distinctive row of rustic cottages along its sea front. The primary mission of Glad and Moe was to sabotage food dumps and military clothing stores. Secondly, they were to radio back reports of what they could glean about air raid damage, troop movements, airfields and morale in the Aberdeen and Edinburgh areas.

Neither wanted any part of the operation and they immediately made their way to a cottage near the beach and asked where they should go to give themselves up to local police. Having obtained directions from the cottager they set off, got lost and had to ask for more directions from a man working

A pre-war view of the Harbour and fishing boats Wick, Caithness, Scotland.

in a field. The police superintendent of Banff had already been alerted and had set off looking for the pair encountering them just outside the town. Moe and Glad became double agents for the rest of the war working under the code names of Mutt and Jeff.[43]

That, however, would not be the end of the seaborne agents as the *Abwehr* continued to send fishing cutters out of Norway containing agents as passengers or crew. Two individuals who attracted strong suspicion were, Karl August Hansson and Peder Oien who had landed aboard the MV *Volga* after it docked at Shetland on 6 March 1941. Another was the MV *Taanevik* which landed at Wick on 27 April 1941. This latter vessel was found to contain four men: Bjarne Hansen, Hans Anton Hansen, Henry Torgersen, and Johan Strandmoen, all of whom were found to be in the pay of the *Abwehr*. There were concerns, however, that there were several such vessels containing similar crew and supplies that had gone undetected, as the summary in the MI5 file on Enemy Agent Landings states:

This class is, perhaps, the most difficult of all the German agents to detect, since there is a flood of genuine refugees from Norway reaching this country and there is good evidence that the Germans have penetrated some of the escape organisations. It appears that the Germans are prepared to let bona fide refugees escape to act as unconscious cover for a single agent inserted among them since they do not come with any of the suspicious gear or equipment which has assisted in the detection of other types of agents. It seems that one object of this type of agent is to establish himself among the Norwegian fishing fleet in this country and so exploit opportunities which fishing would offer to act as couriers between here and the Germans in Norway. It is also considered possible that the Germans may intend that a number of agents should make their way into Free Norwegian Forces here, so as to operate as a 'Trojan Horse' in the event of invasion. To date, only four agents of this type have been definitely proved to be such on their arrival here, but there are some others who have been detained because the evidence, not amounting to complete proof, points strongly to their being enemy agents.[44]

All of the suspect crew members of the MVs *Volga* and *Taanevik* were removed to Camp 020's reserve and long term detention centre Camp 020R at Huntercombe near Nuffield in Oxfordshire for the duration of the war and were repatriated to Norway in June 1945.

Gösta Caroli's radio transmitter and receiver in their case.

The code wheel carried by Gösta Caroli.

Chapter 3

Parachute Spies

Against a backdrop of British intelligence services receiving ever mounting numbers of credible intelligence reports of German forces mustering ready for the invasion of Britain along the coast of France and RAF reconnaissance photographs showing barges gathering in French ports, just three days after the landing of the four agents by boat at Lydd and Dymchurch, the first Lena agent to arrive by parachute in Britain landed in a field at Denton, Northamptonshire at around 3.00am on the morning of 6 September 1940. His name was Gösta Caroli and his mission was to report on the area of Oxford, Northampton and Birmingham with particular interest in the air raid damage to Birmingham.[1] Caroli had bailed out at 15,000 feet but as he did so he had been stunned by a blow to his head from his wireless set. His parachute had brought him safely down, but he was discovered lying in a ditch and was rapidly in the hands of the authorities. In 1940 there was a news blackout of the story but like so many tales that were bracketed 'now it can be told' after the end of the war in Europe in May 1945 the *Northampton Mercury* ran the story of the 'Parachute Spy' caught at Cliff Beechener's farm, 'The Elms' at Denton:

At about 5.00pm Mr Beechener was told that there was a man with a suitcase lying in a ditch in one of the fields. It had been seen lying there by Irish farm worker, Patrick Daly. Mr Beechener decided to go and investigate and took his gun 'just in case'. He could see the feet of a man protruding from a bush. As Mr Beechener passed, the man tried to draw himself farther behind the bush but his boots were yellow. Mr Beechener turned sharply and ordered the man out. Mr Beechener found he was carrying a loaded automatic. He forced him to march to the house, which he did in a rapid goose step, and there Mr Beechener set a guard upon him while he summoned the police and Home Guard. The guard had strict instructions to shoot in the event of an attempt to escape and it was sufficiently heavy to be effective – two farm workers armed with Mr Beechener's Home Guard rifle and a .22 rifle and Pat Daly with a shot gun. When police arrived the whole company with their arms and the prisoner went to the spot and searched the kit left in the ditch.

They found a portable radio set in the suitcase, chocolate and whiskey, extra clothing, the parachute on which he had been lying, a compass, maps, clock and other odds and ends. Mr Beechener's opinion is that he might have made a get away but for the amount of equipment. It took three men to carry it. When searched the spy was found to have about £300 in his possession and an identity card with a Birmingham address, but there was a mistake which would have given him away later had he escaped, the address was in continental style, street name first then the number and in addition the date was wrong.[2]

The following day Guy Liddell wrote:

He [Caroli] had been dropped by a Heinkel plane and had embarked at Brussels. He had intended to land at Birmingham and thought that on landing he was somewhere near Stratford-upon-Avon. It transpired he had been in England as late as December 1939 when he stayed with friends at Boughton. He was in possession of a National Registration Certificate. He had been trained at Hamburg. Colonel Hinchley-Cooke took down a statement from him at Cannon Row police station and he was sent on to Latchmere House [Camp 020].[3]

After a few days in captivity Caroli opened up, as Liddell recorded:

[Caroli] is not apparently interested in his own life but merely that of his friend [Wulf Schmidt]. He himself is quite prepared to be shot as a spy and is apparently a student of philosophy. Owing to his German parentage and his admiration of the German regime he joined the German army but was, however, reluctant to become a spy, so having taken the job was prepared to see it through and determined not to give away his friends. Malcolm Frost and Max Knight seem to have succeeded in persuading him that the Germans had given him a very raw deal and had sent him over here ill equipped and under somewhat false pretences. He came round eventually to this view and agreed to work his wireless set, which he had up to then refused to do.[4]

Caroli and Wulf Schmidt had trained together and had agreed to meet up when they both landed in England so a deal had been reached between MI5 and Caroli, in exchange for a guarantee that Schmidt's life would be spared, Caroli would inform them of when and where they should expect him to land. Liddell also spoke with Colonel Kenneth Strong the then Head of the German Section at MI14 (later Major General Sir Kenneth Strong, the first

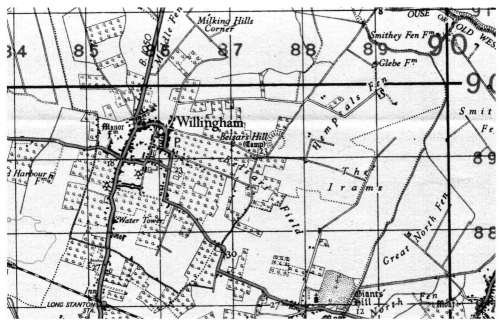

Map showing Glebe Farm, the fields where Wulf Schmidt landed by parachute and the village of Willingham, Cambridgeshire where he was captured on 19 September 1940.

View across the fields near Willingham, Cambridgeshire where Wulf Schmidt landed. Fenland and flatlands between Cambridgeshire and Buckinghamshire provided an ideal and regularly used landing ground for agents dropped by skilled pilots like Hauptmann *Karl-Edmund Gartenfeld.*

Director of the Joint Intelligence Bureau 1948–1964) after he had spoken with Kieboom, Meier, Waldberg, Pons and the newly landed Caroli and noted in his diary:

> *What puzzled him [Strong] was that the Germans, should have given their agents details of their plan of attack. The details they had given more or less agreed with what we had received from other sources and from aerial reconnaissance etc. of the dispositions of enemy forces. This made it difficult to believe that the spies had been sent over here to mislead us. Strong has a great regard for German efficiency and cannot bring himself to believe that they could have been so stupid as to send these men over here without having schooled them properly and worked out plans by which they could be really effective.*[5]

Wulf Schmidt landed by parachute on Fen Field, Glebe Farm, Willingham, Cambridgeshire around midnight on the night of 19/20 September 1940. He believed he had been dropped from 3,500 feet and had even been briefly caught in the beam of an anti-aircraft searchlight battery on the way down. Instead of hitting the ground Schmidt had become entangled on telegraph

Church Street, Willingham, Cambridgeshire as Wulf Schmit would have known it when he limped into the rural village on 19 September 1940.

wires, he managed to extricate himself but sprained his ankle on landing.[6] He then set about hiding his parachute and radio under cover of darkness and then limped off to find the nearest village, Willingham, where he bought some Aspirin to relieve the pain in his ankle and bathed it under the village pump. He had also smashed his watch when bailing out so he bought a cheap replacement at a barbers shop, bought a paper at the newsagents and had some breakfast at a local tea room.

A stranger in a rural village would always attract attention but especially so in war time when his dress, demeanour and foreign accent raised concerns. Schmidt was stopped on The Green and was asked to show his identity card by Home Guard Tom Cousins. Schmidt produced a Danish passport and a forged British Identity Card but when he could not easily explain his presence in the village he was taken to Three Tuns pub kept by Willingham Home Guard Platoon Commander Major John Langton who questioned Schmidt. Not being satisfied with the answers he received he called the police. By lunchtime Schmidt was at Cambridge Police Station under the personal charge of the Chief Constable with Captain Dixon the Regional Security Liaison Officer.[7] The anticipated guest had arrived and Schmidt was transported to Camp 020 at Latchmere House on 21 September 1940.

Schmidt was persuaded to become a double agent and was willing to reveal the location of his wireless transmitter which he had hidden in the field near where he had landed so he was transported back the the site by car to recover it. The problem was that in their excitement and haste MI5's B Division did not inform Cambridgeshire Police nor the Regional Security Officer that they were doing this. The local constabulary and Home Guard had been searching for the set for the previous forty-eight hours and encountered members of the public who alerted them to 'some mysterious diggers' that had come down in a car and had removed what appeared to be a wireless set. It was only after urgent further investigation that they had been informed that these people were officers of MI5. Cambridgeshire Constabulary were less than pleased, MI5 Deputy Director Jasper Harker had ended up having to make a frank apology over the telephone and Charles Butler (Harker's deputy) kindly offered to go over personally to smooth things over the following day.[8]

Both Schmidt and Caroli were initially held at Camp 020 but were removed to 'safe houses' from which they sent regular messages back to their controllers. Caroli was given the MI5 code name SUMMER and Schmidt was dubbed TATE, the latter name because he bore a likeness to the popular music hall comedian Harry Tate. The situation, however, weighed heavily with Caroli and on 11 October he attempted to commit suicide.[9] After

Wulf Schmidt, aka double agent TATE and his transceiver radio.

recovery he was released to MI5's 'Home for Incurables' (those who would not be turned to become double cross agents or were no longer trustworthy or able to carry on in the double agent system) at The Old Parsonage, Hinxton in Cambridgeshire.

On 13 January 1941 Caroli was left alone with only one guard and he seized the opportunity to try and make his escape. He knocked down the guard and attempted to strangle him. He then tied him up, got hold of a motorbike that belonged to one of the other guards, and lashing a 12ft canvas canoe from a nearby barn on one side and a suitcase on the other he sped off in the direction of Newmarket. After a number of falls from the bike as he attempted to reach the coast when it spluttered to a halt Caroli handed himself in to the authorities at Newmarket Police Station.[10] If Caroli had got back to occupied Europe and his Nazi spymasters there was a risk was that he could expose the fact we were turning agents and could have destroyed the whole double cross system. Liddell was clear about his future after the incident: '*Clearly SUMMER can never be allowed to use his wireless transmitter again and will have to remain under lock and key.*'[11]

A course of action was decided upon:

We had a long discussion this morning about SUMMER's future and that of the other people with whom he has been associated. We have all come to the conclusion that somehow or other SUMMER must be eliminated… If therefore we report that he has been captured the Germans may think that the whole organisation has been compromised. Various ingenious suggestions have been made. The best I think is that BISCUIT should report that SUMMER is on the run, that he has put his wireless into the cloakroom at Cambridge station, and sent the key to BISCUIT. Later we could say that he has been picked up by the police for failing to register.[12]

Caroli was left to sit out the war incarcerated and in radio silence, he was repatriated to Sweden in August 1945.[13]At least one agent from every group landing, even if they were uncooperative or had come to the end of their time as an effective double-cross agent, would not be sent to the gallows or firing squad. The reasoning behind this was provided by Masterman in his book *The Double-Cross System in the War of 1939–1945* originally compiled and written in 1945:

…the Security Service always opposed execution except when no other course was possible. A live spy, even if he cannot transmit messages, is always of some use as a book of reference; a dead spy is of no sort of use. But some had to perish, both to satisfy the public that the security of the country was being maintained and also to convince the Germans that the others were working properly and were not under control. It would have taxed German credulity if all their agents had apparently overcome the hazards of their landing.[14]

TATE was a very different matter and he became one of the longest running double cross agents. In October 1940 Liddell wrote:

It has been decided that TATE is to pose to the other side as Harry Williamson, a British subject educated in Denmark. As a result of failing to establish contact he had almost given up hope and had resigned himself to living here for the rest of the war and had accordingly not gone to the trouble of obtaining information for which he had been sent over. Now he has established contact he will set out his job and is awaiting instructions.[15]

TATE continued communications with Germany throughout the war and participated in the Operation Bodyguard deception that misled the Germans about the date and time of the Normandy landings. He was never found out, indeed he was considered a valuable agent to the very end and was even awarded an Iron Cross. After the end of the war TATE continued to live Britain and kept a low profile working as a photographer in Watford under his cover name of Harry Williamson which he retained until his death aged 80 in 1992.[16]

The third of Ritter's parachutists landed on fields near Easton Maudit, south-west of Wellingborough, Northamptonshire on the evening of 3 October 1940. He was not spotted on his way down and did all he should have done as per his espionage training, cutting up his harness and parachute and stuffing them down rabbit holes, stowing his equipment under bushes and changing into civilian clothes. However, the weather was inclement and he took shelter in farm buildings on the Grendon Road, Yardley Hastings where he was discovered by market gardener, Thomas Leonard 'Len' Smith.

The problem for the lurking stranger was that the area was particularly alive to the reality of German spy parachutists, Caroli had landed only a shot distance away at Denton less than a month earlier. It had not made the newspapers but news travels fast in the countryside and the Civil Defence, Home Guard and Observer Corps in the area had been briefed to be extra vigilant. When Smith challenged the stranger about what he was doing he tried to make the excuse he had been sheltering and 'It is a bit finer now, I think I will be going.' When Smith asked where had he come from the stranger could not tell him but in good English, he explained he was staying at a nearby farm house, but could not remember its name. Smith asked to see his identity card and the stranger obliged. The card, in the name of Philips, A. with the address of 20, Grange Road, Southampton looked genuine, but something was just not right and it struck Smith that it looked too new to be genuine, so Smith said he would walk with the man back to where he was staying to establish his identity.

Smith was at his gateway when neighbouring farmer Percy Keggin was driving along the road in his car, Smith signalled him to stop. Smith didn't know what to do with the stranger so Keggin also checked his identity card and suggested they drive up the road together to see if they could find the farm where the stranger was staying and they could sort the matter out there. Failing to find the farm, the three went to Keggin's home where they talked over the names of local farmers to see if they could jog the stranger's memory of where he was staying and he seemed to recognise the name of Mr Penn so Keggin telephoned him.

Walter Penn just happened to be head air raid warden and Section Leader of the Easton Maudit Home Guard. Taking Robert Ingram with him, the two men went to Mr Keggin's home where Penn asked to see the stranger's identity card. The newness of the card also aroused Penn's suspicions as did his demeanour so he marched him (some accounts say at the points of an agricultural fork) to the Police House at Bozeat, home of PC 23 John William

Forth. PC Forth checked the stranger's identity card and when he asked the man where he came from he told him he had come from Bedford to Yardley Hastings by bus and was heading to Kettering where he hoped to find work as a waiter. During the conversation the constable detected the man spoke with a foreign accent and his clothes looked both new and foreign in style. PC Forth telephoned his police divisional headquarters at Wellingborough who dispatched Inspector Sharman.

As they awaited the arrival of the Inspector the stranger was kept under close watch. PC Forth's wife simply saw a scared and hungry man who kept nervously playing with the fringe of his scarf and would remember he was polite and expressed his sincere gratitude for the scrambled eggs she cooked for him.

Inspector Sharman arrived at 8.00pm and it was only then that the stranger was searched and a number of identity cards and a small pistol were discovered about his person. The stranger then admitted he had landed by parachute near a pumping station, his mission had been to collect and transmit weather information back to Germany. He was then handcuffed and taken to the pumping station at Hollowell Plantation at Easton Maudit where he took his bearings and led Inspector Sharman and PC Forth to where he had hidden his parachute, harness and equipment. He was then removed to Wellingborough Police Station where he was taken into custody.[17]

Removed to Latchmere House, examination of his Identity card revealed that although there were no continental characteristics to the writing, it had been incorrectly filled in. Instead of Phillips, A. it should have had the full Christian name, Philips, Alfred. Under interrogation by Robin Stephens it appeared that the agent was willing to co-operate and revealed his name as Karl Goose (although this may not have been his real name either). According to Guy Liddell MI5 were had already been made aware of Goose from TATE. Goose was adopted by the double-cross programme under the codename of GANDER – who says MI5 don't have a sense of humour! Liddell noted:

He has a one-way set of maps of the Liverpool area. His instructions were to hike about and and report on morale (or as he puts it morals), road blocks, weather conditions etc. He is going to work his set and we propose to run it as a very obvious double cross in order to enhance the value of SUMMER and company.[18]

Karl Goose should have been ideal for the role of agent in enemy territory, he had been a soldier in the elite Brandenburg Lehr Regiment but it appears he had never wanted to be a spy. In his interrogation at Latchmere House he claimed it was only shortly after he joined the Brandenburgers a sergeant asked who spoke English and, eager to please, he put up his hand and before he knew it he was in espionage training.[19] A story perhaps given some credibility by his obvious nerves and the fact the uniform and overalls he had parachuted in were spattered with his faeces.[20]

Attempts were made to send messages via Goose's set but as it could not receive messages and there seemed to be no intelligence from Germany that his messages were being received, GANDER was stood down as a double cross agent transferring to Camp 020R (Huntercombe) and spent the rest of the war in captivity.

Prime Minister Churchill had been asking since early October 1940 why some of the spies that had been caught in Britain had not been shot. Lord Swinton, Chairman of the Home Defence (Security) Executive, a position his Lordship, according to Liddell: '*seemed to think made him head of MI5 and to some extent SIS*'[21] continued to press for an example to be made and in 1941 he got his wish.

The prospect of an actual invasion of Britain by German forces may have been fading fast in the minds of German military commanders, but in Britain there were renewed fears of invasion in the spring of 1941 and accordingly a raft of new leaflets would be issued to the British public by central Government and local councils urging the population to 'Stand Firm' and offering methods for beating the invader. Undoubtedly the *Abwehr* were aware of these concerns and perhaps they decided to capitalise on them with some scare tactics, such as sending a few spies over.

At around 8.20am on 1 February 1941 smallholders Charles Baldock and Harry Coulson both from Puddock Drove, Warboys were walking across farmland at Dove House Farm near Ramsey in Huntingdonshire when they heard three pistol shots. They looked to see where they were coming from but could not spot anyone, so they kept walking. Further shots were fired so they looked around again and about 150 yards away spotted a man lying on the ground. Mr Baldock approached first, holding up his hand he told him not to shoot, and would recount what happened next in a statement:

The man then put his hands up and we went across to him. The man was lying on his back and when we got to within 15 yards of him he threw a revolver [actually a Mauser pistol] into a steel helmet which was lying close to him. When we got to him I could see a camouflaged parachute covering him. I asked him what he was up to and he said 'Solo flying'. I asked him where he

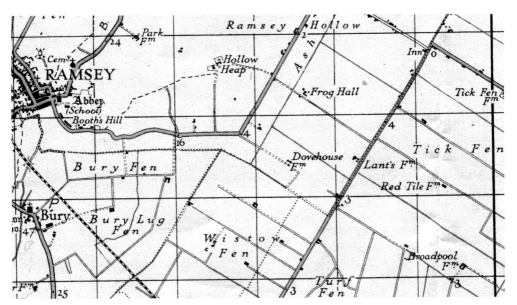

Contemporary map showing Dovehouse Farm near Ramsay, Huntingdonshire where Josef Jakobs landed on the night of 31 January/1 February 1941.

came from and he said 'Hamburg, I am in no war.' He pointed to his leg and said 'Broken.' I stayed with him and sent Coulson for assistance. He told me he was a Frenchman sent from Hamburg and handed me a small cardboard box containing some rounds of ammunition.[22]

Coulson found Harry Godfrey, a volunteer in the Ramsey platoon of the Home Guard who rang the police then returned with Coulson and a horse and cart. They were soon joined by Captain William Henry Newton, Officer Commanding E Company, 1st Huntingdonshire Battalion, Home Guard who had been called by the local police to attend the scene who was accompanied by Lieutenant John Curedale. Captain Newton took charge of the man's pistol and ammunition. They then helped him up as he could not walk unaided. He was still wearing the flying overalls and the parachute helmet he had jumped in but on his feet he seemed to be wearing low boots and spats. Underneath the flying overalls he was wearing civilian clothes.

The man was searched by the Home Guards and a wallet containing a blank ration book and two identity cards, one black and the other completed, were found along with a wad of money to the value of £498 in £1 Bank of England notes. Beneath him was a case buried in the ground with one corner sticking up. A map of the local area was marked with the location of a local aerodrome and a triangle indicated the area where the man had landed lay nearby and an amount of ripped up cardboard (this was code wheel the man had tried to destroy) was scattered around the area along with a small bottle of brandy, some sandwiches and a piece of German sausage. The case was also removed from the ground and the man taken to Ramsey Police Station. Once there he handed over the key and the case was opened to reveal a wireless set with headphones, dry batteries, insulated wire and some sheets of paper.[23]

The police were soon on the scene and the parachutist was delivered by Detective Sergeant Thomas Mills of the Huntingdonshire County Constabulary to Major 'Tar' Robertson and John Hayes Marriott at Canon Row Police Station (part of the New Scotland Yard building) in the late afternoon on 1 February. Pronounced fit for questioning by the police doctor – although in great pain and discomfort – he was first interrogated by Robertson and Marriott and only afterwards was then taken to Brixton Prison Hospital Infirmary for treatment for his broken ankle.

When interviewed by Robertson and in due course by Lieutenant Colonel William Hinchley-Cooke the parachutist freely gave his name as Josef Jakobs. He confirmed he was a German citizen and stated his mission had been to send reports back regarding weather conditions. He also explained to how he came to be found in the field:

When I was ready to jump out of the plane they opened the trap-door in the floor of the plane. I put my foot through the aperture but my parachute got jammed because the aperture was very small and owing to the pressure of the wind I broke my right ankle before I was able to get clear. I got clear in the end and came down by parachute. I landed in a soft freshly ploughed field where I lay all night...[24]

Two portraits and one profile photograph taken of Josef Jakobs while in captivity.

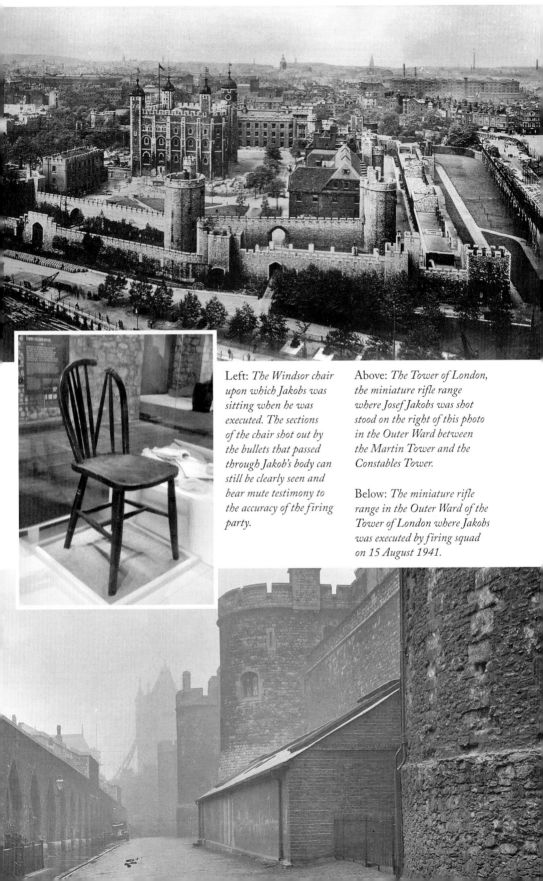

Left: *The Windsor chair upon which Jakobs was sitting when he was executed. The sections of the chair shot out by the bullets that passed through Jakob's body can still be clearly seen and bear mute testimony to the accuracy of the firing party.*

Above: *The Tower of London, the miniature rifle range where Josef Jakobs was shot stood on the right of this photo in the Outer Ward between the Martin Tower and the Constables Tower.*

Below: *The miniature rifle range in the Outer Ward of the Tower of London where Jakobs was executed by firing squad on 15 August 1941.*

Jakobs' fracture required hospital treatment and he was removed to Dulwich Hospital on 3 February. Released to Latchmere House on 26 March he was returned to Brixton Prison Infirmary after a relapse a few days later and remained there until 15 April when he was returned to Ham Common. On 23 July Jakobs was placed in the hands of the Military Police at Wandsworth Prison where he was charged under Section 2(1)(b) of the Treachery Act, 1940 on 24 July 1941. Hinchley-Cooke read over the charge to him in German and Jakobs replied '*I have nothing to fear.*'[25]

Josef Jakobs was tried in camera before a General Court Martial held at the Duke of York's Headquarters, King's Road, Chelsea on 4–5 August 1941. Found guilty as charged, Jakobs was removed to the Tower of London. There he was held in a cell at Waterloo Barracks until the morning of his execution when he was escorted to the Miniature Rifle Range that stood at that time in the Outer Ward between the Martin Tower and the Constables Tower. Seated in a brown Windsor chair, a piece of cloth was pinned over the area of his heart as a target and he was shot by an eight man firing squad drawn from members of the Holding Battalion, Scots Guards at 7.12am on Thursday 14 August 1941.

Josef Jakobs was buried in an unmarked grave at St. Mary's Roman Catholic Cemetery, Kensal Green.[26]

The night of Wednesday, 14 May 1941 was a dark one and a lorry driver and his co-driver were driving through an unfamiliar part of the country at a time when all the road signs had been taken down to help foil enemy invaders and had lost their way to the North. Shortly after 10.00pm they were passing through London Colney in Hertfordshire when they spotted a man by the roadside and stopped to ask him directions. The replies the man offered soon made it clear he was not a local and only spoke very broken English, but what he did manage to explain was that he was sick and wanted to find a hospital. At 10.20pm War Reserve Constable 106 Alec John Scott of Hertfordshire Police was on duty on the North Orbital Road near the Roundabout, London Colney when he encountered the lorry drivers on the footpath. They asked him for directions and he was happy to help them, they also mentioned the man now standing at a telephone kiosk about 10 yards away who 'appeared to be a foreigner' and wanted to go to hospital.

Constable Scott approached the man who in answer to his his initial enquiries claimed to be a Czechoslovakian subject on his way to Cambridge but felt ill and wanted to go to hospital. He produced his identity card and repeated he wished to be directed to a hospital. Constable Scott telephoned his police station and Sergeant Palmer instructed him to detain the man until

Mug shots of Karel Richter taken shortly after his capture.

he arrived. When Sergeant Palmer arrived he requested the man to produce his Aliens Registration card but he failed to do so. Instead he offered an identity card in the name of Fred Snyder, 14, Ducket Street, London EC1. When asked where he had come from he replied 'Ipswich'. He also claimed he had been to Cromer, Norwich, Cambridge and Bury St Edmunds and wished to return to Cambridge.

Not satisfied with the bona fides of the man Sergeant Palmer conveyed him to Fleetville Police Station, St Albans. While here the man produced a Czechoslovakian passport in the name of Karel Richter. Upon examination there was no endorsement showing where he had landed in the UK. Richter was then searched and found to have on his person a wrist compass, a combination knife of German manufacture, a portion of a map of East Anglia showing the coastline of Norfolk, Suffolk and Essex, a pipe, two packets of Dutch tobacco, a pink ration book and some £552 in English treasury notes, 2/7d in English coins, 1400 American dollars in tens, twenties and fifties and four Dutch notes. He was also carrying a safety razor, shaving stick, mirror, fountain pen and pencil, a packet of cigarette papers and some broken chocolate.

A telephone message was sent to the Regional Security Liaison Officer Major C.E. Dixon who was based in Cambridge and Richter was removed to the Hertfordshire Constabulary Headquarters in Hatfield. During his first interviews Richter initially claimed he had landed at Cromer with two others in a small ship in January 1940. He subsequently claimed he had been transported by motor boat from Amsterdam and had landed at Cromer on the North Norfolk coast at about 5.00am on 10 May 1941, he then claimed he had got a lift by lorry from Ipswich, but after that his story stalled and he could offer no account of how he got to where he had been arrested. When asked why the details on the ration book found on him had not been filled in or that the names on the indentity card and his passport did not match, he claimed they had been bought on the black market in Holland and had not had time to fill in his details. He emphatically denied any suggestion that he had arrived by air or that he had brought a radio transmitter with him.

Richter was removed to Camp 020 with his story of landing by sea undemolished, unfortunately for him Josef Jakobs had provided a description of a parachute spy who would be following him in the not too distant future. Commandant Lieutenant Colonel Robin Stephens recalled:

> He [Richter] arrived here in reasonable good health and unreasonable frame of mind. He showed no anxiety to make a confession. He was quite convinced that the Germans would soon launch a successful invasion of Britain. He felt, and said, that soon he would be sitting on the right side of the interrogation table. His obstinacy and disputatiousness were soon overcome, though not without trouble. The facts about himself revealed by Jakobs were produced for his discomfort; and when Jakobs, carefully groomed for his reluctant role, was brought into the room for confrontation, Richter slipped and began gradually to break.[27]

Richter finally admitted he had dropped by parachute from a plane flown by the highly-skilled and experienced special operations pilot *Hauptmann* Karl-Edmund Gartenfeld from Schipol in Holland at 0315 on 12 May 1941 But, as Stephens would point out it would take seventeen hours of interrogation (and a spell in the cell termed and believed among the inmates to be 'the condemned cell'[28]) before he would reveal the place where he had hidden his equipment.[29]

On the afternoon of 18 May 1941 Richter was taken under escort to the area where he had actually landed by parachute and he guided the officers with him to find the things he had hidden there. Among those present were senior MI5 officers Lieutenant Colonel Robin Stephens, Lieutenant Colonel William Hinchley-Cooke and Camp 020 Medical Officer Dr. Harold Dearden. Superintendent Sidney Reeves of Hertfordshire Police who had carried out the initial interviews with Richter at police headquarters was also present and reported:

Karel Richter, under military escort (wearing a long civilian coat and trilby hat), shows senior MI5 officers where he had hidden his parachute, food and radio near the field where he landed at London Colney in May 1941.

Search of the district was made with his [Richter's] aid. Going towards Hatfield from London on the right hand side about 350 yards along a small land we entered a corn field where in the hedge was found a camouflaged (green and brown parachute) together with a leather knife holder, a parcel of food, a steel helmet and a small trowel which had earth adhered to it.

The prisoner pointed out a spot in the field where he had descended by parachute. A search was made of the field but the sheath knife could not be found. We then came towards Hatfield and about 200 yards west we entered another field beside the main road where in the ditch an automatic pistol, a wireless transmitter and a torch were found. The pistol was loaded in the magazine but not in the breach.

All these articles had been secreted by digging out small holes in the bank of the ditch. The whole of this property was taken in possession of by the Army Authorities.[30]

In Stephen's account of the search of the area with Richter he recalled:

A few feet away from this activity was a small picnic party. It included a very small girl who, in piping voice, enquired of Mummy what those soldiers might be doing over there. Mummy scarcely looked up 'Never you mind, dearie; you never known what the military are up to next.' And the little girl never knew…[31]

Richter eventually admitted he was a 29-year-old Sudaten German who had been recruited for the mission by the German secret service. When awaiting deployment abroad he was taken to Amsterdam where he was given lodgings at the Viktoria hotel from where he was driven to Delfzijl where he set off at 7.00pm 9 May 1941 in a 22ft motor launch, with two other agents he named as Fritz and Piet, intending to land on the English coast in the vicinity of Cromer in the early hours of the following morning. According to Richter, the launch got within eight miles of the shore but the sea swell was too heavy to allow a successful landing so the mission was aborted and they returned to Delfzijl. After a brief return to Hotel Viktoria, Richter was then taken to Schipol, flown over and dropped by parachute on the night of 11/12 May 1941. His pilot, Gartenfeld, informed him that they were near Cambridge, an area he had known from the previous agent drops, and that Richter would probably land between Cambridge and Bury St Edmunds. Richter would recall he was pushed with force through the trap door of the aeroplane, the parachute ripcord was attached to the aircraft to avoid fouling the opening of the parachute. He felt a sudden jerk as it opened and then found himself floating through the clouds. When he could finally distinguish the countryside beneath him he saw he was directly over some small houses. It was only due to a sudden gust of wind that he was able to avoid them and made a safe landing in a nearby field.

Richter had landed near London Colney and immediately hid his parachute in a hedge and then found a suitable place to hide his food supplies, then as the sun began to rise, he went into hiding in a nearby wood. While there he lost his nerve and remained there for two days and three nights, too frightened to make the five minute walk back to where he had stashed his food, he chose to eat some damp grass instead.[32]

Hunger got the better of him and ditching his flying overalls he finally emerged from hiding wearing his civilian clothes at around 10.00pm to go in search of food. He followed the nearest road which led to London Colney, around fifteen minutes later he encountered the lorry drivers and was arrested shortly afterwards. Richter had not moved more than half a mile from where he had landed.

His mission was to hand a spare radio crystal to a man who would contact him at the Regent Palace Hotel in London on 15, 20 or 25 May 1941. The man he was to contact was Wulf Schmidt the spy who had been parachuted in back in September 1940 who turned double agent and was given the code name TATE. He had been sending misleading reports that had been carefully crafted by British military intelligence back to his masters in Hamburg as if he was still carrying out his mission. Richter was to meet with Schmidt under the guise of delivering a radio crystal to him and check his reliability because his recent messages had given rise to the suspicion Schmidt was either under control or had been substituted by another man. Richter was then to use his own transmitter to send back meteorological reports, details of the electrical grid system in England and general intelligence including controls on roads and at railway stations. At least, that was the gist of it. As Lieutenant Colonel Robin Stephens bemoaned in one of his interrogation reports: 'Richter has lied to such an extent that modifications in reports are necessary from day to day.'[33]

Richter was found so unreliable he was not considered a suitable candidate for double cross and thus his fate was sealed. He was tried in camera before Mr Justice Tucker at the Old Bailey under the Treachery Act 1940. After a four day trial that ran from 21–24 October the jury found Richter guilty and he was executed at Wandsworth by Albert Pierrepoint on 10 December 1941.

Of all those Pierrepoint hanged during the war, including Nazi War Criminals, Richter would particularly feature in the executioner's memoirs.

Pierrepoint vividly recalled how when he entered the condemned cell he was used to having the condemned seated in a chair with their back to the door, they would rise, Pierrepoint would pinion their wrists with a restraint strap which was fixed in place with a buckle, rather like a trouser belt. The condemned would follow him to the execution chamber with warder escorts on either side.

Executioner Albert Pierrepoint.

Richter, had positioned himself standing on the far wall of the cell and as Pierrepoint entered Richter charged, like a bull, headlong at the wall apparently intent on smashing his own head in. It took five warders to restrain him enough for Pierrepoint to get the restraint strap on his wrists. With apparent order restored as the hangman headed to the execution chamber he heard another scuffle and was called back again. The powerfully built Richter had used all this strength to bust out of the wrist restraint, in fact he had split it from eye hole to eye hole. Pierrepoint had to return to the ensuing melee, dug his knee into Richter's back and pulled the strap tight to the intact hole for the buckle. The warders manhandled Richter over the trap doors the spy struggling all the way. The noose and ankle strap were applied but as Pierrepoint stepped across to push the lever that would release the trapdoors, Richter, even with his ankles strapped together managed to jump to the side.

The trap doors fell open and Richter still plunged down but as he disappeared through Pierrepoint saw Richter had dislodged the noose by jumping and it was slipping. Fortunately it caught half way up his face, just below the nose and it still did its job. To the great relief of all present the rope was strait and still. The medical officer that examined Richter's body noted the severance of the spinal cord had been perfect and could declared 'A clean death. Instantaneous'. The legacy of this incident was the rubber retaining claw grip washer that would hold the loop of the noose in place (originally been designed by Albert's uncle Tom Pierrepoint several years earlier) was adopted as standard for all future Home Office execution ropes.[34]

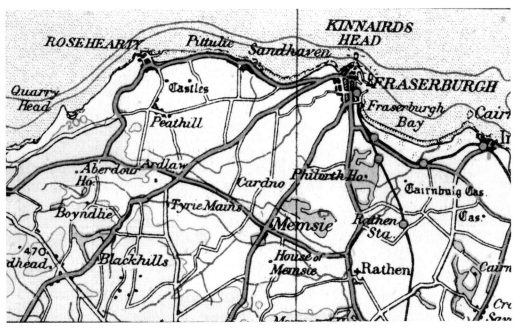

Contemporary map showing Boyndlie, Tyrie, 10 miles from Fraserburgh, Aberdeenshire, Scotland where Nicolay Hansen landed by parachute during the night of 30 September/1 October 1943.

Nicolay Steen Marinus Hansen, the last known German agent to be parachuted into Britain during the Second World War.

After a gap of over a year the last known parachute spy to land in Britain arrived landing in the Den of Boyndlie, Tyrie, 10 miles from Fraserburgh, Aberdeenshire during the night of 30 September/1 October 1943. A few minutes after his descent Hansen found a roadside and signalled a passing lorry with his torch, he was soon in the hands of the local police and was quickly removed to Camp 020. The man openly identified himself as Nicolay Steen Marinus Hansen, a Norwegian national. Hansen arrived wearing civilian clothes under a boiler suit. He had with him a German radio receiving and transmitting set in a sealed container. In addition another wireless and transmitting set of the type used by the British Special Operations Executive (SOE) was dropped by parachute from the same aircraft shortly after Hansen bailed out and was found hanging from a tree.

The initial report on Hansen noted that he knew very little English but he did manage to explain how he got to be there and honestly stated that another set had dropped nearby.[35]

MI5 B Section head Guy Liddell recorded the event in his diary on 1 October 1943:

> At 4.00am today a man calling himself Hansen, apparently a Norwegian, was dropped by parachute near Frazerburgh. He said that he had come from Farstadt and was a stevedore or labourer who had been in jail for stealing cigarettes and had then been contacted by German Intelligence to send to this country. He had attempted to come last Monday but the weather had been too bad and the aircraft had returned. The aircraft left Norway at 10.55 yesterday evening and was to have landed Hansen at Ellon…The man had two wireless sets, one of which was dropped separately. His instructions were to give himself up with one wireless set after he had buried the other. He was then to express the desire to join the Norwegian forces and in 2 or 3 months he was to return to the other wireless set and start operations. He carried £60 in £10 and £5 notes. This man is presumably identical with an ISOS character who was mentioned some weeks ago as being trained in Norway for a journey to this country.[36]

It initially appeared that Hansen had given full disclosure but on 3 October Camp 020 Commandant Robin Stephens contacted Liddell to inform him Hansen had disclosed his codename as Heini. He also related how when he had asked Hansen if he had brought any secret ink he had admitted that he had, but could not remember where it was. He finally admitted it was concealed in one of his teeth. A dentist was summoned and the ink was recovered in a tiny rubber cover that had been placed in a hollow tooth and cemented over). He was then asked if he had been given an address to write to. Hansen said he would only be given the address once he was in wireless communication and would only use the ink in the event the wireless becomes damaged.

Stephens urged him to think again. Hansen finally offered an address in Stockholm to which he said he had been instructed to write. His excuse for not offering this sooner was that he was afraid MI5 would 'make a mess of things' and his wife would be punished.[37]

It was soon decided at MI5 that they really could not use Hansen for purposes of double cross or espionage. The case was passed to the Director of Public Prosecutions as per routine but it was not recommended as one suitable for prosecution. Interned for the rest of the war in Europe, Hansen was deported to Norway in June 1945.

An Artillery spotter from 4th Field Battery, 1st Polish Corps keeps a watchful eye out for enemy intruders by air or sea atop an anti-tank block on the beach at St Andrews, Fife, Scotland, May 1941.

Chapter 4

Spies Undetected

Any officer doing a thorough job in counter-espionage should regularly consider the question 'What have I missed?' The unique problems presented by wartime demands were pulling field officers left right and centre with regular reports of enemy parachutists being spotted making a landing in one place, someone signalling to the enemy by flashing a light in another, and reports of 'suspicious' behaviour, which although well meaning and sincere usually turned out to have some innocent explanation. Consequently, under such pressures and with only limited staff and resources (remember this is decades before the likes of computer databases and CCTV) meant spending any great amount of time contemplating anything that did not immediately present itself during an investigation was something of a luxury. Even promising leads could peter out as blank after blank was drawn during investigations. There was always a suspicion in the intelligence services that enemy agents were slipping through what 'net' they had.

MI5 was confident it had been on top of the Lena spy landings in Britain thanks to Arthur Graham Owens. In the years before the war Owens had worked as an electrical contractor in British and German shipyards and had dabbled in some espionage for SIS (Secret Intelligence Service) providing them with information about German shipyards where he had worked, until he was found also to be reporting to the *Abwehr* without the knowledge of his British handlers. On the outbreak of war he saved his skin by striking a deal with MI5 to turn double agent. He was accepted and given the codename SNOW.[1]

There were concerns, however, that the Lena agents that had been caught had been apprehended too easily. Once they were interrogated it soon became clear they had only been given limited training and a number of senior members of MI5 expressed concerns that the agents they had apprehended to date had been sacrificial personnel deployed as distractions while more covert arrivals of other agents were being made elsewhere.

Several possible candidates for who the undetected agents in Britain might be emerged during the interrogation of captured German agents Waldberg, Meier, Drüke, Schalberg and Wälti. For example, there was an athletically-built German Army NCO Peter Schneider who was also at a lecture given when a number of the agents were present. They shared an understanding that Schneider was destined to come to the south coast of England 'clandestinely by boat, with another German NCO. He was a member of a special assault company and trained in pontoons and mines work.'[2] Others that were mentioned in interrogations were Oberleutnant Paul Koch, who was 'destined to be dropped by parachute in Norfolk or Suffolk'. José Waldberg also mentioned German soldiers Walter Pfeiffer and Paul Schneider (cousin of Peter Schneider) who he believed were both destined to spy in the UK.[3]

The one figure that they had all independently mentioned had been one of their instructors, Oberleutnant Werner Uhlm. Originally a member of Ast Wiesbaden and later Ast Hamburg, Uhlm was lauded for having made a successful clandestine reconnaissance mission to England in 1940. It was claimed he had been parachuted into Norfolk where he reconnoitred some of the defences along the coast and the Wash, and then made his exit by boat off the coast of Cromer where he was picked up by a sea plane.[4] MI5 B Division director Guy Liddell sceptically declared this was 'obviously an untrue story,'[5] but it remains unclear how or if this claim was investigated at all and if Liddell had been aware of an unaccounted ship's life boat being washed up on the shore around the time Uhlm was supposed to have made

A ship's lifeboat washed up on Cromer beach, March 1940. Was it a genuine loss from a shipwreck or a means by which German spies had come ashore?

East Gangway, cliff and beach, with the mysterious ship's lifeboat on the promenade by Joyce's Cafe, March 1940.

his exit from Cromer. Perhaps it was just considered 'old news' by the time Uhlm was brought to his attention and they had far more current 'live' cases to investigate.

In mitigation it must be remembered that throughout the war coastal communities around Britain became accustomed to seeing rubber dinghies washed up or drifting offshore which had been used by British or German aircrews whose aircraft had been brought down in the sea. If the aircrew were rescued or sadly had been washed overboard the boat would simply be left at sea and could be carried on the current and washed up on beaches many miles away.

Throughout the U-boat campaign in British coastal waters, and especially in the wake of the Dunkirk evacuation, the lifeboats of vessels that had been sunk would also be washed up on our shores, found adrift by fishermen and in numerous incidents the coastguard and lifeboat crews were alerted to the presence of the boat just in case there were crew aboard in need of help. If the boat was found empty of personnel, ascertaining where it had come from or whether it had been used for the comings or goings of enemy agents was difficult to discern.

A typical example was recorded in the MI5 B Division Intelligence Summary of 30 January 1941. A rubber boat containing paddles, an inflating pump, uniform side hats, a blue tunic, letters, a Christmas card and an identity disc bearing the name of Karl Schmidt were discovered after being washed ashore on a beach near Shorncliffe on the afternoon of 21 January 1941. At 9pm that night an unidentified person was spotted and challenged by a sentry, a shot was fired and he or she disappeared into the darkness. The following night another individual was challenged by a sentry at a nearby location, more shots were fired but the intruder eluded capture. Regional Security Liaison Officer, Major Cyril Grassby wrote up his findings:

> *The rubber boat was found unoccupied at 4pm when it was first seen but this does not necessarily mean that no-one came in it. It may be that the person landed further along the coast and pushed the boat out to sea. This would have been an easier and more effective method of getting rid of all papers of identification than by tearing them up and strewing them along the beach. Furthermore, the reports of two sentries on two different dates of the appearance of a stranger who was fired at strengthens the supposition that someone might have been in the locality. Both soldiers could not have suffered from hallucination...* [6]

The problem was the local military (XII Corps) headquarters had not been informed of the boat until 23 January, it was also some time before the Kent police were informed and consequently a search of the area for traces of the person or persons who arrived by the boat was not conducted while the discovery was still fresh. Subsequently a yellow life preserver with eight air pockets was washed ashore at Sandgate. There was no further update about the rubber boat or its passengers published in the later intelligence summaries. [7] This is not surprising, with alleged sightings of enemy parachutists still being reported, along with a resurgence of reports of Fifth Columnist activities after 'thousands of enemy aliens' had been released from internment, and the flashing of lights supposedly signalling to the enemy. These all needed to be investigated and the unidentified boats were just one more item added to the already crammed to-do list of the local police, military intelligence officers and MI5's regional security liaison officers in coastal areas. [8]

A possible female agent was revealed after her photograph with a loving message signed Clara on the reverse was discovered on Josef Jakobs when he was searched following his capture. When the question of the woman's identity was put to Jakobs during his interrogation by Stephens at Latchmere House he identfied her as his mistress, Clara Bauerle, a tall, 36 year old

German cabaret singer Clara Bauerle, a suspected Nazi agent earmarked for a mission to England in 1941.

Ulm-born cabaret singer who toured with the Bernard Ette Orchestra. Jakobs insisted she had never visited England. Searches of Home Office records and investigations conducted by both SIS and Special Branch eventually revealed a Klara Sofie Bauerle had visited Britain in 1930, perhaps touring with an orchestra, and had departed from Warwickshire in June 1932.[9] A subsequent interrogation of Karel Richter revealed he had also known Clara Bauerle through Jakobs. In July 1941 the breakthrough came in a covertly recorded conversation between Richter and Jakobs at Camp 020 during which it was revealed Clara was due to follow them to England. Jakobs would also reveal he had been aware Clara was training to become an agent and had been given instruction in wireless communications in Hamburg. Jakobs did add, however, that in the last letter he had received from Clara she said she would only come if she received word from him, because no news of him had been received she would not come to England.[10]

Perhaps having realised he had let slip about Clara, Jakobs was attempting to create what smoke screen he could for her imminent arrival. No conclusive evidence has emerged to date to prove if Clara ever landed in Britain. Perhaps the whole story was a sham to tie up more of the precious time and resources of the British security and intelligence services.

A bizarre twist to this story appeared in *The Independent* newspaper in March 2013 in an article that suggested the skeletal remains of a woman that had been found in a Wych elm at Hagley Woods near Stourbridge in Warwickshire in April 1943 were those of Clara Bauerle. This infamous unsolved murder dubbed 'Bella in the Wych Elm' after the cryptic graffiti 'Who put Bella in the Wych Elm?' that was scrawled nearby six weeks after the remains had been discovered has been the subject of conjecture for decades. Newspaper articles and books have made claims since the 1950s that the body was that of a Nazi agent. The 2013 article published in *The Independent* by Alison Vale was the first to suggest the remains were those of Clara Bauerle. The theory falls down on a number of points, the most significant being that the skeletal remains were assembled and measured during the original pathologist's examination and were recorded as having belonged to woman who would have stood a little over 5 feet tall[11] whereas Bauerle was a statuesque 6ft.[12]

Giselle Jakobs, one of the granddaughters of executed spy Josef Jakobs, has carried out considerable research into Clara which she has published on her execellent *Josef Jakobs 1891–1941* website. She has traced Clara's appearances as a supporting artiste in films during the 1930s and her appearances on gramophone record recordings released between 1940 and 1942. They certainly pose the question, was there even time for Clara to have trained as an agent and to have carried out a mission during the relevant period? Giselle has also uncovered Clara's death certificate which states she died of a lung infection caused by *Veronal* (a popular sleeping aid) poisoning at the Königin Elisabeth Hospital on 16 December 1942. As she quite rightly points out, there is no suggestion of whether the poisoning was due to an accidental overdose or murder.[13] Then again, if she really was an operative of the secret service it was not unknown for deep cover agents, wherever Clara may have been, to simply need to disappear or her untimely death while on an espionage operation be explained away with a banal death certificate.

There is however one agent, that we know for sure, went undetected. Under the cover of darkness between 31 October and 2 November 1940 an enemy parachutist landed near Haversham, Buckinghamshire. Owens/ SNOW had given no warning of his arrival. Guy Liddell noted the discovery in his diary on 5 November:

> *An enemy parachute landing was reported today. A complete parachute with harness, overalls and flying helmet was found neatly folded and placed in a hedge beside a bridle path on Hill Farm…The parachute was wet but the clothing inside dry and it appears that it may have been dropped during the past two or three days. Inside the parachute was a paper wrapping for chocolate made in Belgium and a packet containing a white tablet, probably concentrated food* [on examination it was found to be Aspirin]. *The packet had recently been opened and contents consumed. The parachute had without doubt been used and the parachutist landed uninjured and is still at large.*[14]

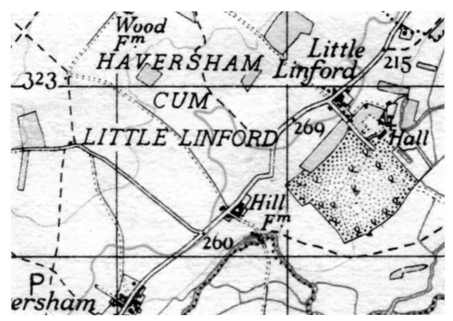

Contemporary map showing Hill Farm, Haversham, Buckinghamshire where a parachute with harness, overalls and flying helmet were found neatly folded and placed in a hedge beside a bridle path on 3 November 1940.

The parachute had been discovered at around 12.00 noon on 3 November. On receipt of the report, and confirmation of the discovery of the parachute and harness, Buckinghamshire Police contacted the local Home Guard Battalion Commander who immediately mobilised his men, they continued observation and searched through the night for the parachutist or any of his equipment. Special Branch was also informed along with Air Intelligence, Field Security, local military units, searchlight and RAF units. Neighbouring constabularies in Bedford and Northamptonshire were also put on alert and enquiries were made at shops, hotels, railway stations and other places that may have been used by the parachutist. At dawn on the morning after the discovery a thorough search of all woods and outbuildings was carried out with the aid of military units from Bletchley, Stony Stratford, Whaddon, Windlow, Lathbury, Hanslope and Cold Brayfield.[15]

Enquiries with the Observer Corps revealed enemy planes had been plotted over Haversham district on the evenings of 30 October and 1 November. The Radio Security Service were also on the case and it appears some signal was intercepted and on 5 November they reported: '*it seems likely that there is*

'Station X' the Government Code and Cypher School (GC&CS) at Bletchley Park c1939. Particular concern was raised because this top secret facility was only around 10 miles away from where the parachute had been found and an enemy agent was still at large in November 1940.

at least one wireless set being operated in the country.[16] The problem was that the equipment available at that time was not sophisticated enough to detect exactly where it was being sent from.

Concerns over national security had also been aroused by the fact that the parachute had been found less than ten miles from Station X the top secret Government Code and Cypher School (GC&CS) at Bletchley Park. There was a newspaper blackout on any news of the landing or the search for the missing spy. From previous experiences hopes were high that the spy had injured himself and would soon be tracked down or would give themselves away by some basic error. Despite the concerted efforts of military authorities, police and MI5 personnel they drew a blank and this agent, probably more by luck than judgement, had just walked away into the darkness.

In his pocket the man carried a passport and identity card in the name of Jan Willem Ter Braak. He had arrived in Cambridge on 4 November 1940 and was operating under the cover of being a Dutch national who had served in the Dutch forces, had escaped to Britain at the time of the Dunkirk evacuation and was now engaged with the Dutch Free Press that had its head office on Pall Mall. Braak rented a back bedroom at 58 St Barnabas Road, Cambridge, the home of Mr and Mrs Sennitt. He was usually seen leaving the property about 10.00am and returned between 9.30 and 10.00pm each night. He was sensible enough to purchase new British clothes in Cambridge and Peterborough so he blended in well. He seemed a nice enough gentleman and would often sit in the evening after his return from work with the Sennitts playing cards, darts or other games. He never seemed short of money and had even got Mr Sennitt to change American dollars into British pounds for him at the Lloyd's Bank on Mill Road. On 31 January 1941 Braak told Mr Sennitt he was leaving for London. Some weeks later Mrs Sennitt saw Braak in Cambridge and asked him to call and collect the remainder of his clothes which he did a few days later.[17]

Braak was now staying at 11 Montague Road in another small back bedroom in the home of Miss Greenwood. He had never been any problem to her, he had retired to bed when she went up and she never heard anything of him during the night. On Saturday 29 March he left the house with two cases and told her he was going to join the Dutch forces on the coast but would return. He headed for Cambridge Railway Station where he deposited his cases at the Parcels Office.

At around 11.00am on Tuesday, 1 April 1941 an electrician entered a public air raid shelter on Christ's Pieces, Cambridge to complete an installation and discovered the body of Ter Braak lying on his right side, his head in a pool of congealed blood, a Browning Automatic pistol was lying nearby. Dr Donald

The body of Ter Braak photographed as it was found in a public air raid shelter on Christ's Pieces, Cambridge 1 April 1941.

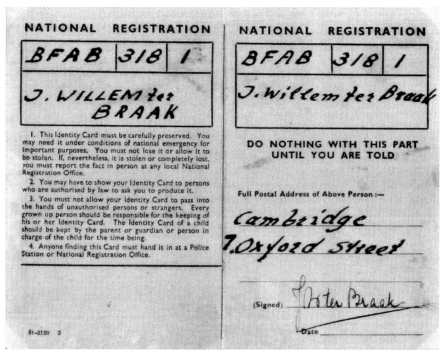

Jan Willem Ter Braak's forged identity card bearing the the non-existent address of 7, Oxford Street, Cambridge.

Ter Braak's radio that he deposited at the Parcels Office at Cambridge Station before committing suicide.

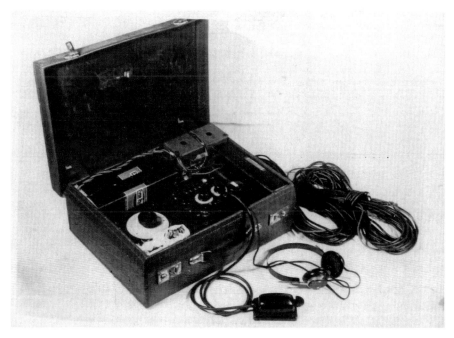

Cameron was called to examine the body and declared it was in an advanced state of rigor mortis, he had been dead for around twenty-four hours. Braak had shot himself in the head.[18]

Liddell recorded:

> *There is no doubt that he was the parachutist who was reported to have come down near Bletchley. We have obtained the wireless set which was in the cloak-room of Cambridge Railway Station. The joke of it is that in spite of our instructions to the police Ter Braak has been living within 50 yards of our RSLO in Cambridge. It seems the landlady did report his presence to the local police who merely said that they expected he would register before long. The man had been trying to get a ration book having run out of food and money, he presumably decided to shoot himself.*[19]

The Coroner, Mr W.R. Wallis agreed to hold the inquest in camera and it was impressed upon him that it was of paramount importance that no report of any kind should be published of the proceedings.

Despite thorough investigation by MI5 the only communications that could be found from or to Braak were the correspondence over the replacement of his ration book.[20] The batteries in his radio were found to be run down but it was not thought he communicated at night and tests revealed he would not have been able to obtain contact during the day because the frequency of his aerial was unsuitable.[21] There were also bus tickets found in his clothes that indicated that he had been to London, but nothing more.

The name on his Dutch passport, identity card and papers, the name he lived and was known by while in Britain was Jan Willem Ter Braak. Only in recent years after research by a family member has his real name been revealed as Engelbertus Fukken who had been born in The Hague in 1914 and had been recruited to the *Abwehr* by Rittmesier Kurt Mirow of Ast Brussels.[22] He was buried in secret and still lies in an unmarked grave in Great Shelford cemetery, about four miles south-east of Cambridge.

The undetected spy, Jan Willem Ter Braak (real name Engelbertus Fukken).

J.C. Masterman reflected: '*It is not altogether fanciful to speculate how much more happy and more useful his career might have been if he could have fallen into the hands of the Security Service and become a double agent.*'[23]

Then there was a certain Wilhelm Mörz aka Werner Mickelsen, clearly he had been a person of interest to SIS for some time when they compiled their report on him in July 1939. It noted he had been a captain in the Hamburg Gendamerie but claiming he was an opponent of the Nazi regime and having narrowly escaped arrest by the Hamburg branch of the Gestapo he had fled and arrived in Prague in 1935.

Mörz assumed the name of Werner Mickelsen and along with another man he would have known as Wilhelm

Wilhelm Mörz aka Werner Mickelsen the Nazi agent who evaded the manhunt for him across Britain in 1940.

Steiner, (real name Georg Schwarzloh or Schwarzlow, a member of the Social Democratic Party in Germany in the 1930s who had been detained by the Gestapo and had fled to Czechoslovakia immediately after his release) were both taken under the wing of Dr Caspari, the former leader of *Schneidemuehl* (Social Democrat Party) who made the right introductions to Czech authorities and both men became members of the Counter-Espionage Section of the Czechoslovak Ministry of National Defence.[24] Initially Mörz appeared to be a first class agent loyal to his employers, indeed he was described as one of the best men they ever had, but the problem with Mörz all along was that he was a ruthless and 'dangerous double-crosser.'[25] SIS listed the instances of concern as:

A. *On many occasions Gestapo agents in Prague were pointed out to Mörz for arrest. These men were warned by Mörz and managed to flee the country.*

B. *Mörz enticed two German military officials to the Czechoslovak border, obtained information from them, which he sold to the Czechoslovak authorities. He denounced his informants to the Gestapo, which resulted in their being shot.*

> C. *Through his connections with emigrant groups, Mörz obtained the addresses of German opponents to the Hitlerian regime and his denouncing them resulted in their arrest.*[26]

It was also independently corroborated that Mörz had been involved in money laundering, shady arms deals and revealing Czech military secrets to the Gestapo .[27]

Mörz himself was arrested when German forces entered Prague but very soon afterwards he was taken by German army car to Holland where he maintained his claim that he was anti-Nazi. He was also known to be spending time in France and Switzerland where he was in direct contact with a Dr Max Spieker, with whom Dr Franz Fischer was also known to be in direct contact.[28] The same Franz Fischer that instigated the first meetings between British intelligence officers Captain Sigismund Payne Best and Major Richard Stevens and the supposed rebel German officers that culminated in their abduction at Venlo on 9 December 1939. Both Fischer and Mörz were known to be operating in The Hague at the same time. Liddell recorded a view held by a number of those who had served in the Netherlands that Mörz was: *'believed to have been responsible for the Venlo incident.'*[29] There was only circumstantial evidence Mörz was involved in the abduction of Best and Stevens[30] but SIS regarded him still being at large in Holland *'as a tremendous danger to the Allied Intelligence Service there.'*[31]

The curious twist to this tale is that SIS were trying to enact their own Venlo style sting on Mörz by attempting to entice him to France, but with no success and it was noted in the internally published minutes of a meeting dated 11 March 1940 that Allied Intelligence Services were then working on a plan to entice him to Britain. On hearing this Dick White was asked if Mörz did actually come would it be possible to guarantee he would be locked up for the duration to which White responded: *'I rather rashly answered yes to this and feel strongly that this is a pledge which we shall have to honour at all costs.'*[32]

On 12 March Guy Liddell recorded in his diary: *'We are trying to get Morz over here and intern him…He will be a good bargaining counter for Best and Stevens.'*[33]

Mörz arrived in Britain the following month, the problem was, apparently, that no security service appears to have arranged his arrival or nor did they know how he had arrived here. Mörz remained undetected until the afternoon of 25 May 1940 when a former member of the Czech Intelligence Service who had known and worked with him in Holland and was living under MI5 protection in London spotted Mörz purely by chance as he was getting into a taxi on Regent Street and warned his MI5 contacts of the sighting.

Even though MI5 did not have extensive files on Mörz, after consultation of what they did have the potential danger he posed was clear and MI5 requested the Metropolitan Police Special Branch to commence search and enquiry to find him at once. Armed with a description and the photograph MI5 had on file, officers began the man hunt at all London hotels in an endeavour to effect his arrest.[34]

MI5 Deputy Director Jasper Harker was only too aware of the threat Mörz posed and would state in a letter to Special Branch Head Albert Canning at the height of the investigation:

We have reason to know here that the capture of Mörz would be a matter of the greatest significance at the present time. He is undoubtedly one of the cleverest secret agents the Germans have at the present time and after tremendously successful action in Belgium and Holland he has, no doubt, been drafted to this country to take charge of Fifth Column activities here. If Mörz could be captured it might mean that we should obtain thereby the means of breaking up a large part of the German network before it had a chance to operate.

Shaftesbury Avenue from Piccadilly Circus in London's West End, one of the popular haunts of Wilhelm Mörz in 1940.

Special Branch was mobilized onto the trail of Mörz and officers were sent out to enquire at all possible hotels. One of the early enquiries found the night receptionist clerk at the Cumberland Hotel recognised the wanted man as one who had stayed there in late March and who had sent a cable which Mörz had signed in the name of Novak. Other staff also recognised the man and recalled during his stay he went by the name of Wilhelm Novak. Another receptionist at Mount Royal Hotel, Marble Arch identified Mörz as a man he had seen six weeks previously in the company of 'Dawn' Karland, a dance hostess at the El Morocco Club on Albemarle Street.

Karland was soon traced and when interviewed by Inspector Hunt, Special Branch. Despite giving the impression she was willing to help, she agreed she might have met him but said she saw so many men she could not remember him at Mount Royal. As plausible as she was MI5 were not pleased when they learned she had not been followed in case she went to warn Mörz.[35] Another club hostess, Mrs Glen Coutts at Murray's Club, also came forward and a picture soon emerged of Mörz as a man who liked West End restaurants and night club life.

The *Police Gazette* Special Notice was circulated nationally and enabled MI5 to track the movements of Mörz across Great Britain based on positive sightings and hotel registers. From 21–31 March he stayed at the Royal Hotel, Edinburgh, the County Hotel, Newcastle on 1 April and then on to The Queens Hotel, Leeds. In early May he had been to The Hague and back. A case note on his file dated 29 May 1940 stated confidently:

> *Owing to the plans we have made it should be impossible for Morz to leave this country by any way of the ordinary channels and escape discovery. A wide search was carried out throughout the whole London area and a hundred photographs were circulated at points where it is possible he may appear.*[36]

On 8 June 1940 another foreign agent exiled in London who had known Mörz and had provided information on him to MI5 spotted him on Tottenham Court Road, even though his hair had been dyed chestnut brown. Mörz saw and recognised him too and immediately got on a bus. The agent got into a taxi to follow but to no avail, Mörz slipped away again.[37] Two Scotland Yard officers were employed continuously for nearly two months pursuing enquiries and keeping watch on the restaurants, cafes, night clubs and hotels of Knightsbridge, Kensington and the Tottenham Court Road.

Despite his description and photograph being supplied to many transport hubs Mörz simply departed from Croydon Airport for Basle under the name of Wilhelm Novak, a Czech engineer, one of his known aliases on 15 June

1940. He even filled in his traffic card index honestly stating he had been staying at Lexham Garden Mansions Hotel in Kensington,[38] a hotel where it was soon discovered he had stayed in April, May and June 1940. By the time this was discovered he was long gone.

In one of the concluding minutes on Mörz MI5 file Dick White offered his theory of how Mörz had evaded capture:

> 'experience has shown over three months' search for him, Mörz personal appearance conforms to a fairly common type. Working entirely from the photo, I thought myself I had seen him in a waiter at the Chinese Restaurant at Piccadilly Circus. The likeness was almost exact. Nevertheless, on examination, the waiter did not turn out to be Mörz... the police detained and questioned about a dozen people in the belief that they had caught him. Nevertheless if he is here, he still eludes us...He is in fact one of the cleverest agents the Gestapo has.[39]

Finally, on 7 August 1941 Dick White wrote to the Deputy Commissioner Special Branch with a heavy heart to state MI5 had no objection to the description of Mörz being removed from the *Police Gazette* because '*There appears to be no longer any hope of tracing him in this country.*'[40]

Chapter 5

The Black List

With the thousands involved in the internments of May and June 1940 most internees were initially held in designated prisons, often in old wings that were especially re-opened to cope with the numbers. They were then removed to various detention camps, in some cases tented camps surrounded by barbed wire fences, at various locations across Britain. Thousands of internees were removed to detention camps converted from old hotels, on the Isle of Man the men were at Peveril Camp, Peel and the women and children were held in Rushen Camp at what was usually the summer resort of Port Erin in the south of the island. Many would spend months or even years behind barbed wire as tribunals sat and those who were judged 'of least concern' were gradually released.

The infamous German *Sonderfahndungsliste G.B.* (Special Search List Great Britain) otherwise known as the 'Black List' of British people the Nazi security services would wish to track down and arrest on the grounds they were considered likely to be subversive to the Nazi regime has become the topic of numerous books and articles over the years. Less known was the German 'White List' of those who they considered would be likely to collaborate in the event of an invasion. Almost unheard of is the British 'Black List' or to give it its correct title, the: *List of Suspected persons who might be disposed to assist the enemy in the case of invasion, prepared in accordance with a Home Office circular of 24 August 1940.* Fears of a 'Fifth Column' existing in

Prime Minister Winston Churchill took a personal interest in the establishment of Suspect Lists.

One of several posters created during the war to urge the Britsih public to quash lies and defeatist speech.

Britain had rumbled around press and public rumour since the late 1930s. A list of some eight hundred names of German suspects had been compiled by MI5 before the war but the majority of those named on the list avoided arrest by leaving Britain before the outbreak of war in September 1939.[1]

The problem was that, by its very nature, the Fifth Column was a secret and shadowy network of spies, collaborators and saboteurs, so nobody was sure who its members were although there were plenty of likely candidates known to the police, Special Branch and military authorities. However at that time no formal lists collated all of these people. The military personnel of Eastern Command started to take matters into their own hands. Guy Liddell noted:

THIS IS NOT BIG-HEARTED ARTHUR, NOR IS IT OLD STINKER---OH, NO! IT'S THE DONKEY THAT'S BRAYING FROM HAMBURG, LORD HAW-HAW, HEE-HAW,- HAW, HEE-HAW!

A wartime postcard mocks German radio propaganda broadcast's most infamous presenter dubbed 'Lord Haw-Haw' because of his sneering, haughty voice.

Some of the units appear to have prepared a kind of Black List of their own. When the balloon goes up they intend to round up or shoot all these individuals. The position is so serious that something of a very drastic kind will have to be done.[2]

When these lists were brought to the attention of Prime Minister Churchill he was not prepared to pussyfoot around when dealing with those of questionable loyalty and replied by enquiring why these people had not been arrested already. A Home Office circular duly followed on 24 August 1940 which authorised all regions to undertake the compilation of their own Suspect List. The process was to be carried out by all Chief Constables who would then submit their lists to their Regional Commissioner. Some regions certainly embraced the idea with gusto, the Region 11 Headquarters in Edinburgh was sent returns from Chief Constables in their area that amounted to some 1,700 names but after discussions between Regional Commissioner and the Chief Constables approximately sixty names were entered on the Suspect List for Scotland.[3] After the first submissions, sifts and due consideration of each case the twelve Regions of Great Britain ended up with between 46 (Region 3 HQ Nottingham) and 104 (Region 2 HQ Leeds) names on their lists.

Regional meetings of Police Security Officers had been established under Colonel Brook HM Inspector of Constabulary in July 1940. These gatherings would usually include the regional inspector, a police staff officer and Chief Constables and Detective Superintendents from the various constabularies in the region (in 1940 there were still City, Borough and County Police in many counties) there would also be representatives of officer rank from military units based in the locality (usually the Intelligence Officer) and similar from both fixed and mobile military defences, a field security officer, Field Security Police, the Regional Security Liaison Officer (MI5), RN and RAF Security Officers and the Security Control Officer for Ports. By the time the Suspect Lists were established the Regional Security meetings had also found their feet, the Suspect List was added to the agenda and the forum would discuss additions and deletions and update the group of any persons named on the Suspect List who had moved in or out of their area.[4] It was also suggested Chief Constables should circulate photographs of enemy aliens who they consider might return to Britain as parachutists.[5]

Many of those whose names appeared on the Suspect List were those who had been released from internment. However, significantly, there were also individuals named on the list who had not been detained because there had been the lack of sufficient evidence against them, but their outbursts of anti-British and pro-Nazi speech and/or their suspicious behaviour had been reported to the police, and brought to the notice of MI5 or Special Branch.

All walks of life could be found on the Suspect Lists, young and old, from retired British Army officers, civil servants and businessmen to teachers, publicans, shopkeepers, housewives, domestic servants, roundsmen, factory workers and farm labourers. Some had German or Austrian parents, many more were born and bred British nationals. Every suspect on the list would be submitted by the Chief Constable of the area they resided in with a brief case report, although some of these ran over several pages for particularly active Fascists. There were, of course, the obvious suspects, such as those who had been members of the BUF who were described as 'being of the thug type' who had absolutely no regrets for being active and committed members of the BUF. Then there were those considered 'a dangerous liar' who tried to mask their associations when interrogated but continued to spout their pro-Nazi and anti-Semitic beliefs while they were in detention or even those who saw it as an opportunity to get rich quick, who would not shirk anything for

In every country occupied by the Nazis there were both men and women who sought a better or easier life by collaborating.

money. Phrases such as 'a dangerous person to be at large should an invasion of this country take place' and known to express 'subversive and anti-British views' were frequent comments on the Chief Constables' case reports.

If Churchill had needed any justification for Suspect Lists literally the same day as the Home Office circular to authorise the regions to start the compilation of their lists was published an MI5 undercover agent was penetrating a Leeds BUF terrorist cell. What was uncovered would give Churchill all the reasons he needed. At one of the group meetings the main speaker was one Sidney Charnley, brother of a senior BUF officer from Hull who had been interned. Charnley was keeping the BUF alive for what he would simply refer to as 'The Day' when German forces would invade Britain. He also spoke of the existence of a shadow organisation which would come into being when the occasion arose. The leader of this shadow organisation, he claimed, was the senior BUF officer Major General J.F.C. 'Boney' Fuller. Charnley added: 'if the object was to bring off a revolt and challenge the Churchill Government by force, then he felt that every Blackshirt in the North would obey any order issued by Fuller whether it came from a shadow organisation or not.'[6]

With regard to Major General Fuller, the MI5 report on the Leeds cell commented hopefully:

Fuller has for some time been the subject of close investigation by this office, but he is extremely cautious and astute. We are not yet in a position to say anything regarding the nature of his activities, but we shall probably have obtained valuable information from quite another source within the next week or so.[7]

Fuller was a leading light of the British Union of Fascists and his activities drew suspicion throughout the war. He would be named in more than one coup plot but still he was never arrested as other senior officials of the BUF had been in May 1940. Even Mosley expressed 'a little puzzlement' that 'Boney' had not ended up with him in Brixton.[8] It has been suggested that Fuller was protected because of his close associations and perhaps what politically compromising knowledge he may have had about other senior officers, notably Field Marshal Edmund Ironside, the man who had been Commander in Chief Home Forces until July 1940.[9] Fuller's detailed entry from the Suspect List appears on pages 152–155.

On a practical level procedures also had to be drawn up to activate the arrest of those named on a regional Suspect List in the event of an invasion. An order applying Regulation 18B (1B) would be sent to the Regional Commissioner by the Relay Dispatch-Carrying Scheme. Chief Constables then would be notified by the Regional Police Staff Officer (RPSO) by use of a code word, (in the North East Region it was 'Meccano', in other regions they would have had their own code words to minimise the chances of the order being given in error) and the arrests would be made. Police would then transport the arrested persons to the Collecting Centres (often a large military camp with a secure stockade) or prison in their region. Security Officers were asked when advising the Regional Security Liaison Officer of any suspects whom it had not been possible to arrest, to give particulars of any action taken to trace the missing persons. Arrangements were also made to circulate the description (and photographs where available) of missing suspects through the RPSO and Police Forces.

Some of those named on the Suspect Lists would not have been taken into any sort of custody. In the event of invasion each Patrol of the Auxiliary Units (Britain's secret resistance organisation) knew their duties only too well. Each unit had been entrusted with a sealed envelope and had been issued with one excellent quality hunting rifle complete with scope. Inside the envelope was a list of names of people – perhaps three or four names, undoubtedly drawn from the Suspect List held by their local Civil Defence Commissioner and Chief Constable – of those in their local area that were considered to pose the greatest threat in the event of an invasion and would have to be eliminated. There was no explanation on the note as to why those listed had been selected, just a name and an address. Under their solemn oath they would not open the envelope unless they had received warning invasion had actually taken place.

During the invasion scares some Auxiliaries opened their envelopes, others looked at them at the end of the war. Those who would comment on the names they saw never named them directly. One of them did comment that although not a close friend of the man he did know him and he 'seemed quite a nice bloke really'. When the veteran Auxiliary was asked 'Would you have carried out your orders?' He gave his answer very matter of factly: *Well if they were not on our side we would have had no choice, they would have to be eliminated.*

Suspect Lists were maintained and updated across the Civil Defence Regions until late 1944 when the fear of invasion finally passed after the success of the campaigns for the liberation of North-Western Europe.

The following are edited transcriptions of the surviving case papers submitted to and approved by the Regional Commissioners of Eastern and Southern Region for inclusion on their Suspect Lists of persons considered to be of doubtful loyalty likely to assist the enemy in the case of invasion 1940–1944.

Note: Many of those who had been detained for extended periods with some concern still remaining over their reliability were released subject to restrictions. This would usually mean that the individual concerned would not be permitted to enter any Aliens Protected Area without police permission, they must notify changes of address and make weekly reports to the police. If they resided in the Metropolitan Police District (MPD) they may not leave it without consent of the Commissioner. Those living outside the MPD would be subject to a ten mile limit of travel.

Alken, Henry Wilfred Seffrien 52, Norres Road, Didcot, Berkshire. Removed from the Isle of Wight after his wife wrote to the Under Secretary of State saying her husband hated England and wanted to get to Germany via Holland to take part in anti-British broadcasting.

Ambler, Mrs Antonia (38) 'Firsbrow', Ravine Road, Canford Cliffs, Parkstone, Dorset. Co-Director, with her husband, of Speedy Clean 1935 Ltd 177–179 Old Christchurch Road, Bournemouth. Born in Germany, described as 'a true Prussian type' anti-British, suspected of 'being in contact with persons in Germany and that she was assisting that country.'

Ambrose, John Desmond 'Thatched Cottage', Hindlesham nr Wokingham, Berkshire. Activist member of the BUF.

Armstrong, Appollonius Aurelius George 'The Little House', Northway, Headington, Oxford.
  Born in Moscow in 1903 of a Russian mother and a father who was British subject of German extraction. Armstrong is a staunch Roman Catholic and shortly after coming to England in 1939 engineered an introduction to Father Miller of St Augustine's Mission, Hendon. He asked Father Miller to help him send money and goods into Germany. He also called on Father Schnitzler of the German Catholic Church and asked permission to lecture to members of Father Schnitzler's congregation. Father Schnitzler was unfavourably impressed by Armstrong and suspected him of being a German agent. He also came to the notice of Special Branch for his violent anti-Semitic views. He was also reported by a number of witnesses for his anti-British and pro-German outbursts.

Ashby, James George 5, Salisbury Road, Southsea. Clerk at the Portsmouth Labour Exchange. Pro-Nazi and active member of the BUF.

Ashworth-Jones, Thomas Jabez (34) 14, Onslow Gardens, London N10 and later Digswell Park, Welwyn, Hertfordshire.
  This man was born on 22 October 1909. He was detained under DR 18B in January 1940. Shortly before his arrest his premises were searched and

among other things were found two diaries which contained entries such as the following:

7 May 1940: There is little to record. Last night went to the Nordic League – now called by some other name, but it is the same as before. It is good to have the entry to a real 'Fifth Column' organisation and I must go as often as possible in the future.

27 May 1940: At last! Of this evening's occupation I dare not write even in this private book. I am now where I have wanted really to be in relation to the war.

26 June 1940: To Shepherd's Bush this evening, and to Gladys Fortune's place. Eddie there too and we chatted optimistically; listened to Bill Joyce from Bremen and toasted the day of liberation – 'Der Tag'. I am honestly not worried about air raids. I know that 'Uncle' is not trying to harm me. Only the Yids and their dupes need to be afraid! Some of us white folk will be hurt by accident no doubt, but it would be wrong to either fear, lament or curse such a just and welcome deliverance from vile bondage. Heil Führer – und Juda Verrecke.

Ashworth Jones was reported to be a section leader in the Fascist movement. His group leader was said to be Dr Leigh Vaughan Henry.

Ashworth Jones appeared before the Advisory Committee in June 1941. With regard to his political history, he admitted to having been an active member of the British Union for some 18 months. He attended meetings of the Nordic League and had met Vaughan Henry there. His continued detention was recommended in April 1941. In February 1943 he was released subject to restriction. His behaviour while in detention was extremely eccentric. He read voluminously, mainly on political subjects, and appears to have taken a great interest in anarchism.

Since his arrival in London Ashworth-Jones has been present at meetings of the 18B Detainees (British) Aid Fund and the Fascists meetings at Hyde Park. In view of the fact that he is known to be easily influenced by his acquaintances, it seems likely that he may soon take an active part in the present underground Fascist movement.

Atrill, Sydney, 98, Dickens Road, Portsmouth. Skilled labourer employed at HM Dockyard, Portsmouth. Reported for making Pro-Nazi and anti-British comments such as 'All bastard Englishmen should be strung up and thrown into Spithead.' He also visited Germany on several occasions before the outbreak of war.

Auerbach, Ernst 20, Longcroft Avenue, Harpendon, Hertfordshire. Reported for making pro-Nazi statements.

Austin, Jack 'St Kilda', Blackbrook Park Avenue, Fareham, Hampshire. District Leader East Bristol BUF

Avery, William Frederick 39, Victoria Road, Emsworth, Hampshire. County Propaganda Organiser for South Hampshire BUF.

Baikaloff, Anatole Vasilievitch (Born 1887 in Russia) 'Rhodalin', West End, Stoke Poges, Buckinghamshire. Journalist.

Ball, Frederick Andre, Ashe Close, Wootton St Lawrence, Basingstoke, Hampshire. Former District Leader, Epping BUF.

Banyard, Daisy Ethel Agnes 'Windrush', Eve's Corner, Danbury, Essex. Reported for making pro-Nazi statements.

Barnes, Joseph, 'Redthorne', Rownhams, Southampton. Ardent supporter of the BUF, reported for making anti-British and anti-Semitic remarks and was suspected of holding private Fascist meetings at his house. By December 1940 larger clandestine BUF meetings were believed to be held at the Shirley Billiards Club on Church Path which was run by Joseph Barnes.

Barrett, Mrs Wilhelmine née Theis, 12, Collingwood Avenue, Didcot, Berkshire. British by marriage, formerly German. Her husband works in Central Ordnance Depot Didcot, her brother is German soldier in the SS and he came to visit her when he was on leave summer 1939. Reported for voicing pro-Nazi sentiments.

Bates, Cyril (28) 88, Northcourt Avenue, Reading, Berkshire. Garage proprietor. Keen and active member of Reading Branch BUF. Stood as Fascist candidate in the Reading Municipal Elections.

Bates, Percy, 88, Northcourt Avenue, Reading, Berkshire. Chief Organiser and speaker of Reading Branch BUF. In May 1940 Bates was still making public speeches on behalf of the BUF. He was detained under DR 18B(1A)

in June 1940. When his premises were searched a large amount of Fascist propaganda, literature and sticky-back labels, as well as photographs of Hitler and Mosley were found. Two black shirts were also found, which Bates stated had been put away 'in readiness for the day'. On leaving his home with the police Bates gave the Fascist salute and said 'Hail Mosley'.

Baumann, Hans, 'The Old Forge' Flaunden, Hertfordshire. Unreliable loyalty.

Beaumont, Percy W., 34 Culver Street, Colchester, Essex.

This man carries on a good class hairdressing business and is reported to have been instilling pro-German and defeatist views into his customers. He is alleged to be always praising Hitler and to have said 'You can't prove to me that he is not the reincarnation of Christ.' When interviewed by police he stated that he was in favour of and believed in the policy of Germany and Italy because their policy stands for progress and that the policy of the British Government was all wrong. He is generally considered to be very bitter and antagonistic to this country and a strong supporter of the enemy and all they represent.

Beckett, John (born 1894) c/o Dr Robert Forgan, Meadow Place, Kelvedon Common, Brentwood, Essex removed to 29, Chenies, Buckinghamshire.

Beckett is a British subject, who was born on 11 October 1894. From 1914 until 1917 he served in the army, and was discharged owing to war disablement. From 1918 to 1920 Beckett was chairman of the National Union of Ex-Servicemen, and from 1920 until 1922 he was secretary of the Southern Divisional Council of the ILP He was Labour MP for Gateshead from 1924 to 1929, and for Peckham from 1929 to 1931. In this latter year he voted in favour of a memorandum put forward by Sir Oswald Mosley who until then had been a member of the Labour Party, and was forced to resign from the Labour Party for failing to obey the Party Whip. It was at this time that he achieved notoriety by removing the mace from the table of the House of Commons.

In 1933 Beckett joined the British Union of Fascists soon after its inception. He became a frequent speaker at BUF meetings, and one of Mosley's chief henchmen, In 1935 he was appointed Director of Publicity, and in 1936 he became editor of the Fascist paper *Action*.

In March 1937 Beckett and William Joyce (Lord Haw-Haw) left the BUF as a result of internal differences and intrigues in this organisation. Subsequently Beckett wrote a letter to one Dr Bauer, who was a German agent (Beckett denies that he knew this at the time), saying that he and Joyce were 'most anxious that our German friends should know the truth about their split with the BUF.'

Later in 1937 Beckett and Joyce founded the National Socialist League, with objects similar to those of the BUF. The League did not make much headway, and in September 1938 Beckett left it as a result of a difference of opinion with Joyce. Beckett immediately became secretary of the British Council against European Commitments; one of the main objects of this Council was to advocate non-intervention in the cause of Czechoslovakia. Shortly after the Munich settlement the Council ceased to function as a propaganda body, but its President, Lord Lymington (now Earl of Portsmouth) arranged to publish a monthly journal called the 'New Pioneer', of which Beckett became assistant editor. Many of the contributors to this journal were ex-member s of the BUF.

In April 1939 the British Peoples Party was formed with Beckett as honorary secretary and the Marquis of Tavistock (now Duke of Bedford) as president, Ben Greene as treasurer, and John Scanlon, former BU Member, as Press secretary. A.K. Chesterton, a noted writer on BU Policy, later joined the BPP. Soon afterwards a Peoples' Campaign against War and Usury was launched by the BPP.

In September 1939 the British Council for Christian Settlement in Europe was founded, with Lord Tavistock as chairman, Beckett as secretary, and Captain R. Gordon-Canning, a former BU official, as treasurer. However, the BPP continued in being, and in December 1939 the BPP published a book called 'The Truth about this War', the sole object of which was to prove how right Germany was, and how wrong this country was about the treaty of Versailles, the Austrian Anschluss, the Munich crisis and the Danzig trouble which led to the outbreak of war.

In February 1940 Beckett and his wife, who shared his political views, began to issue a weekly sheet called 'Headline News Letter'. These publications advocated a negotiated peace with Germany, put forward anti-British propaganda, made personal attacks on members of the government, and alleged that prominent persons and institutions were making material profits from the hostilities. Since his detention Beckett maintained that its anti-British propaganda was intended to put before the British public the German case, and justified this on the ground that he believed that peace should be negotiated with Germany, and that therefore it was his duty to try to combat the atrocity stories, etc., with which the British Government were trying to enlist and maintain support for their war. However, the following examples of the contents of the newsletter hardly bear out this claim: (i) the publication of an Italian report that the SS *Athenia* has been sunk by British destroyers, (ii) the quotation of lengthy extracts from the German White Book on Poland, and (iii) the allegation that this country was responsible for the invasion of Norway and Denmark by the Germans.

Beckett was detained under DR 18B order made by the Home Secretary on 22 May 1940. Since then Beckett did not changed his attitude towards the war and Germany, although at about the time of his detention he was beginning to realise that it was no longer wise to advocate a negotiated peace in public. Early in 1941 or thereabouts he made the following entry in the autograph book of a detainee: 'To one of my good German friends in anticipation of the new and glorious Europe for which they fight and we can only pray.' During his detention he developed a particularly violent hostility towards Mr Churchill and Mr Morrison.

Beckett's detention order was suspended by the Home Secretary on 23 October 1943 on grounds of ill-health, and he was released subject to restrictions. He went to stay with a Dr. Robert Forgan in Essex, who was at one time a member of the BUF and had since been in sympathy with Beckett's political views.

On 10 November 1943 Beckett applied to the Chief Constable of Essex for permission to stay with Ben Greene's mother in Battersea for two nights, and also to go on a visit to Cairnsmore, Newton Stewart, Wigtownshire, one of the Duke of Bedford's residences. Permission was refused.

On 28 February Beckett left Essex and moved to Chenies, Bucks, where a house had been put at his disposal by the Duke of Bedford. The Home Secretary imposed restrictions on Beckett which forbade him to change his residence in Chenies without the Home Secretary's consent, and forbade him to travel more than five miles from his residence without the permission of the Chief Constable of Buckinghamshire.

The Chief Constable of Buckinghamshire and MI5 were of the opinion that in the interests of public safety and the defence of the realm it would be necessary to re-detain Beckett in the event of invasion under DR 18B.

Beer, Mrs Lina. 157, Kynaston Road, Didcot, Berkshire. Born 1911 in Germany, her father, mother and brother were all still living in Germany whom she regularly visited, the last occasion being on 6 August 1913, from which she arrived back in England the day after war was declared. Reported for making Pro-Nazi statements on a number of occasions.

Bell, Alexander, Mill House, Mill Lane, Colinbrook, Buckinghamshire. Employee at Langley Alloys. Reported for Pro-Nazi speech. Suspected to have been a member of the BUF, Fascist literature was found in his property when it was searched.

Bell, Mrs Lucy Margaret, Mill House, Mill Lane, Colinbrook, Buckinghamshire. Reported for Pro-Nazi speech. Suspected to have been a member of the BUF. Fascist literature was found in her property when it was searched.

Bellamy, Richard Reynell, (born 1901) 796a Christchurch Road, Boscombe, Hampshire. Former National Inspector and Director of Propaganda at BUF headquarters, subsequently District Leader Canterbury.

Bennett, Mrs Anna née Ringnortner (25) West End Lodge, Sir William's Lane, Aylsham, Norfolk.

In July 1937 this woman arrived in this country and registered as a domestic servant. Although her good looks and smart appearance show that she is not the peasant girl of the domestic servant class which she represents herself to be, she is, in fact a very intelligent young woman, who carries herself with confidence and self possession.

On 3 July 1938 she was employed by William Howes of the International Serum Company. This man is regarded with a certain amount of suspicion as for many years he has traded with and visited Germany regularly and his sister-in-law, Mrs Hermann Busch still lives with her husband, a former member of the German Secret Service at Kiel.

In September 1939 Howes evacuated from Norwich to Aylsham brining Anna Ringnortner with him. Aylsham is the centre of three aerodromes and is surrounded by defences of every kind. On 16 October 1939 she was exempted from internment and special restrictions on enemy aliens.

During the winter 1939–40 she was taught to drive a motor car by a garage boy named Harold Bennett, the son of William Howes' gardener, although aliens were prevented from driving motor cars. On 7 June 1940 as a result of the Aliens Protected Areas No 4 Order Miss Ringnortner had to leave Aylsham and went to live at the YMCA, 90 Sutherland Avenue, Maida Vale W9. Howes immediately made representations to the Deputy Chief Constable asking that she may be permitted to remain.

On 19 June Harold Bennett went to London to see this woman and on 20 June married her, William Howes being one of the witnesses, thus having acquired British nationality and a British name, she was able to return to Aylsham. The police came to the conclusion that this was a marriage of convenience which had been engineered by Howes and this woman in order that she might return to Aylsham. Howes admits that he connived it and expedited the wedding.

Since her return to Aylsham she has been acting as chauffeur to Howes and Howes has discharged his own chauffeur whom he had employed for 12 years. Howes by his inquisitive curiosity and his suspicious connections has attracted the attention of the police and is still the subject of enquiry. In all the circumstances, it is considered that this woman is of doubtful loyalty to this country and would assist the enemy in the event of an emergency.

Benter, Louis Hardy William Vas, 59, Southampton Street, Reading removed to Coppice Bungalow, Kelvedon Common, Essex. Civilian M.T. Driver RAF Milton (dismissed). Pro-Nazi and Anti-British.

Berger, Elizabeth Winifred, 39a, Pelham Street, South Kensington SW7. Secretary of the Kensington Branch of the Imperial Fascist League. Unreliable loyalty.

Berndt, Mary Antonia, 14, Walton Road, Norwich, Norfolk. Born 1914. Shorthand Typist. Reported for making pro-Nazi statements.

Bird, William, 16, Bridge Street, Maidenhead, Berkshire. District Leader of the Maidenhead Branch of the Imperial Fascist League and a member of The Link. When his premises were searched police discovered two rugs with swastikas woven into them, two swastika car mascots, knuckle dusters, revolvers, twenty-eight copies of Mosley's *Tomorrow We Live* and numerous Fascist, Nazi and anti-Jewish books, pamphlets etc. Bird visited Germany in 1935, 1936 and 1937. The first visit was a tour organised by the IFL. In 1938 and 1939 Bird had a young German, who was a member of the Hitler Youth, to stay with him in Maidenhead.

Birks, George J., Regal Cinema, Southampton. Reported for making pro-Nazi statements.

Blind, Harold (50) 36, London Road, Maldon, Essex. Former District Inspector of Chelmsford, Maldon and Colchester District BUF.

The suspect joined the BUF in 1933, but states that he resigned from the Party in 1938 when he held the rank of District Inspector for Chelmsford, Maldon and Colchester districts. He is in possession of a passport which shows that he visited Germany in 1936 with the British Legion. He was a member of

'The Link' and assisted to form a branch of that organisation in the Maldon district. He speaks fluent German and has entertained Germans in his house. He owns a motor boat which is anchored in the River Blackwater. On 17 July 1940 his house and motor boat were searched but nothing subversive was found. He is not now active in the BUF but he is thought to be of the type who would assist the enemy in the event of an invasion.

Bliss, Mrs Eda, 'Silverdale', Wimborne Road, Staplehill, Wimborne, Dorset. German by birth and acquired British nationality on her marriage to Ernest Bliss who was killed in the First World War. She has a sister who lives in Hanover who is said to be married to a German official and has other relatives in Germany. A nephew from Germany visited Mrs Bliss in June 1939. Mrs Bliss was reported for expressing pro-Nazi views. Among a number of reported incidents she said if invasion did take place and a German soldier came to her for food, she would give it to him.

Blunk, Mrs Ena. Reported for making pro-Nazi statements.

Boesen, Alfred Jens Peter aka Alfred Buison, (44) 'Wayside', 35 Wymondley Road, Hitchin, Hertfordshire. Resident in Britain since 1926, in 1932 he formed a partnership with a British subject as the Acme Vacuum Flash Manufacturing Co. In 1933 he becme naturalised.

Between May and July 1940, both Boesen and his wife were the subjects of constant reports to the police. These reports alleged that they were both violently pro-Nazi, that they were friendly with Ribbentrop and that they made no secret of their approval of Hitler and the Nazis. In addition it was stated that they still had relations in Germany one of whom is clearly an ardent Nazi.

The Boesens were both interned in July 1940. They were released subject to regulations in February 1941. Since he has been at liberty it has been noted that Mr Boesen has become particularly friendly with Fritz Ernst Reichenbach, who is the subject of considerable suspicion and whose name is also on the Suspect List. In view of his hostile origin and of the suspicion which he has aroused it is felt that Boesen is of doubtful loyalty.

Boesen, Maria Louisa née Rossa, (38) 'Wayside' 35 Wymondley Road, Hitchin, Hertfordshire. This woman who was born in Munich, is the wife of Alfred Boesen whose name is also on the Suspect List. Between May and July 1940 her name was coupled with that of her husband in numerous reports alleging that she was violently pro-Nazi and a fanatical admirer of the Nazi leaders; furthermore she is stated to have relatives still living in Germany. In July 1940 she was interned with her husband. In February 1941 they were released subject to regulations. In view of her hostile origin and the suspicion surrounding her it is felt that she should be arrested with her husband in the event of an emergency.

Bolton, Mrs Katherine, (Born in Germany) 40, Foster Road, Portsmouth. Reported for expressing pro-German sympathies. Her brother is in the German Army. Before the war she visited Germany each year with her husband and her brother visited her in Portsmouth. Since the outbreak of war she has communicated with her brother through the Red Cross.

Boothby, Cyril, 28, Marshall Road, Holloway Road, Cowley, Oxford. Unreliable loyalty.

Bornheim, Anthony Joseph. 18, Ferguson Avenue, Hornchurch, Essex. Furrier. Unreliable loyalty.

Borra, Ezia (24) British subject with Italian parents lining in Southampton. Ezia Borra joined the Partito Nazionale Fascista and in 1938 she was a member of the Fascio Femminile di Southampton, in which she played a prominent part. Her father was interned and her mother and sister had to leave Southampton when it became a 'protected area'. She was reported for regularly talking to members of the armed forces asking their regiment, where they were based and if they are mechanised.

Borra, Livio Nella (24) British born to Italian parents, Hotel Russell, Russell Square, London WC1, removed to Civilian Camp, Ambrosden near Bicester removed on release to Arlscot, Windmill Hill, Alton.

Borra was educated in England, France and Italy. He was working as a waiter in Stuttgart until just before Germany's invasion of Poland, and returned to England via Switzerland at the end of September 1939. On his return he was found in possession of drawings and details of guns and aeroplanes which gave rise to some suspicion.

Borra was member of the Fascist GILE organisation in Italy, but he denied any connection with the Fascio in this country. Borra's fiancée Erna Fabbro is described as an undoubted Nazi, his father Luigi and sister Ezia were members of the Fascio in Southampton.

Borsdorf, Emile Heinrich aka Bradley, 12 Goldington Road, Bedford. Reported for making pro-Nazi statements.

Brenninkmeyer, Willibrordus Cornelis (Dutch) and **Brenninkmeyer, Mrs Anna** (Dutch) Oldfield Furze, Longbottom Lane, Beaconsfield, Buckinghamshire. Mr Brenninkmeyer is the Managing Director of C&A Modes Ltd. MI5 received reliable information from more than one source that Brenninkmeyer and his wife had Pro-Nazi sympathies and it was believed that information from Britain that would of value to the enemy reached Germany via their business interests in Holland.

Brewer, Ronald Geoffrey, (Born 7 March 1914), 55, Cardiff Road, Luton, Bedfordshire. This man, who comes from a good family and who received a good education joined the BUF in October 1932. He soon allowed his membership to lapse and it was not until 1936 that realising war with Germany was possibility he revived it 'in order to keep England out of the war'.

In September 1939 he arrived in Bristol and police soon formed the opinion that he was an active fascist. In February 1940, in company with a number of other fascists, he created a serious disturbance at a meeting at Colston Hall addressed by the late Sir Kingsley Wood.

In August 1940 one of the leading Bristol Fascists Raymond Luxford died. Shortly before his death Brewer removed from his house a large number of Fascist uniforms and a quantity of other Fascist material. From this action it would seem fair to assume that he intended to take over party leadership in Bristol.

In September 1940 Brewer advised a young woman to listen to the New British Broadcasting Station. He also told her he was attempting to recruit people who were against the war and to spread the idea that this country had no quarrel with Germany. The young woman concerned further reported that in addition Brewer instructed her how to spread details of wavelengths and programmes of the New British Broadcasting Station without arousing suspicion.

In November 1940 Brewer sent a birthday letter to Sir Oswald Mosley:

Dear Sir
My friends and I in Bristol cannot let the occasion of your birthday go without sending our loyal greetings and many sincere wishes. We hope you are in the best of health and we shall be seeing you soon. Yours still in Union,
R. G. Brewer, on behalf of your friends in Bristol.

In 1941 he was reported as attempting to raise doubts in the minds of his workmates as to the wisdom of carrying on with the war. As a result of further enquiry, it was found that he had a rubber stamp reading 'Mosley for Peace' which was used to print sticky-back labels for attachment to buildings in Bristol, that he was prepared to give food and shelter to German parachutists, that he was trying to pass material for propaganda to William Joyce (Lord Haw-Haw) and that he was anxious to produce a pamphlet demanding an immediate peace and overthrow of the present Government.

Brewer was detained under 18B on 10 April 1941. At the time of his detention he had in his possession a BU badge and membership card, a Fascist signet ring and a BU Diary containing a list of people in the Bristol area whose sympathies were known to be Fascist. In addition correspondence was found which confirmed the view that he was an ardent and active Fascist and a disseminator of Peace Chain letters:

Two sheets of paper were found on each of which were printed the following words:

Join the Peace Chain
It's better to live for England than to die for Churchill
If you want to stop the war copy this out and send it without your name to six other people

Brewer admitted in a statement that he listened to NBBS and made notes on what the speakers said concerning the forming of a propaganda unit and that the wording of the peace chain letter was taken down by him on one such time and had written several peace chain letters in order to post them to people.

Brewer was released under conditions on 19 November 1943. In view of his past history and contacts his name was included on the Suspect List for arrest in the event of invasion.

Brock, Charles William (46) 30, Temple Road, Ipswich, Suffolk. Cranfield Dock Roller Mills employee.

This man married his present wife a German girl about eight years ago and is now employed by Messrs Cranfields Brother Ltd, Dock Roller Mills, Ipswich. Statements have been given by various employees that before the war Brock had been very pro-German. These statements further alleged that he continued his pro-German talk at every turn, even breaking into conversations with it. He is regarded as being openly in love with Nazism and is causing much resentment at the works.

Brock, Eliesabeth Henriette, (née Wiedom) (39) 30, Temple Road, Ipswich, Suffolk. Wife of Charles Brock. This woman is German by origin. She is alleged by a neighbour to have told her in May 1940 that if German parachute troops landed anywhere near her house she would go and welcome them. She is believed by the same person to have influenced her husband by her views.

Browne, Patrick, The Mint, Godalming, Surrey. Member and activist of the BUF.

Bridger, Kenneth Marston (born 1913) 144, Marlborough Road, Oxford. Radio service engineer. District Leader, Sevenoaks BUF.
    In April 1940 Bridger volunteered for the RAF. He was called up and placed on deferred service. A certain Mr Fairland, worried at Bridger joining the RAF reported to the police that Bridger hated the English and had applied to the German Embassy for a permit to go to Germany. Fairland added that he believed Bridger 'would do all in his power to wreck any work, and to cause all the trouble he can'. A Detention Order under DR 18B against Bridger was made on 2 July 1940 and he was removed to detention camps on the Isle of Man. Bridger was released in November 1943. A report compiled from Peveril Camp described Bridger as 'a BU partisan whose sympathies with Germany appear deep rooted.' Bridger was believed to be 'as bitterly anti-Jewish as might be expected of a man who looks upon the Jews as the root of all evil'. His determination not to give any help to Britain in the war was thought to be unabated.

Bruning, Guy Anthony, (37) (German) Living at 8, Walmer Gardens, Ealing with Ronald Bruce Cutler and his wife. Removed to 221 Pear Tree Avenue, Southampton, He and his two brothers Maurice, Joseph and Clement were all members of the BUF. He was for a short while a member of the Police War Reserve but was dismissed in January 1940. Bruning then returned to assisting at BUF HQ and at the Silvertown by-election.

Budd, Captain Charles Henry Bentinck, Manor Farm House, Dummer, Hampshire. Elected member of West Sussex County Council. Deputy Administration Officer, West Sussex BUF. A member of the British Union as early as 1933 when he came to notice as Deputy Administration Officer for the West Sussex Area BUF.
    In May 1934 Budd was reported to be an enthusiastic worker for the movement, and to be attending meetings practically every evening. In

October 1933 he was summonsed for Riotous Assembly in company with Sir Oswald Mosley and William Joyce.

In December 1939 Budd was acting as adjutant of 12th Division, Royal Engineers, at Gravesend Barracks. At this time he was reported by a relation of his to be an ardent Fascist, to have obtained information from secret documents in the possession of his Commanding Officer and to have imparted some of this information to other members of the BU. Later it was reported that on 13 January 1940, Budd had a long conversation with Raven-Thomson, Deputy Organiser of the British Union and that Thomson subsequently disclosed the fact that Budd had given him important information. There seems little doubt that the information passed to Raven-Thomson by Budd was that obtained from the confidential documents referred to above. The chief document was one dealing with Communism and Fascism in the Armed Forces and was therefore of considerable interest to BU headquarters.

It is also believed that during the early months of 1940 Budd conveyed similar information to Sir Oswald Mosley, for when he saw Mosley in March 1940 he handed him a document which was subsequently returned in an envelope marked 'Private' and addressed in Mosley's own handwriting.

During the early months of 1940 Budd is known to have been in contact with Archibald Ramsay as well as Mosley and among his other contacts is believed to have been Lord Tavistock (Duke of Bedford). In May 1940 a relative of Budd's saw a letter written by him to his wife in which he said that when Hitler won the war he would negotiate direct with Mosley, that the Duke of Windsor would return as King and under no circumstances would the present form of government be tolerated.

Budd was one of those detained in 1940 under the Home Secretary's 'Omnibus Order' and as a consequence he brought a successful writ of Habeas Corpus against the Home Secretary, and was released in May 1941. He was re-detained under a fresh order on 6 June 1941.

Budd made three appearances before the Home Office Advisory Committee, and only after his third appearance was his release recommended. Besides seeing Budd himself, the Committee questioned a relative of his, not the informant referred to above, who stated that Budd is mentally unstable and at time almost irresponsible. He was badly wounded in the head during the last war, and this injury is believed to have affected his mental block.

Budd was released in July 1943, subject to restrictions requiring him to report his address and changes thereof, and to report monthly to the police and limiting the employment which he might take up. After remaining in London for a few months Budd who is believed to retain his Fascist views, has now moved to Dummer, Hampshire, where he has started a business of agricultural contractors. He is employing in his business one Ernst Keller, another released BU detainee of German origin, whose case is also being submitted for inclusion on the Suspect List.

In view of Budd's record as a BU official and Fascist sympathiser, and the uncertainty of his reactions to any crisis, MI5 are of the opinion that, in the interests of public safety, he should be re-detained under DR 18B(1B) in the event of invasion.

Burdett, Mrs Olive Alice Kate née Hawks, 298, Well Hall Road, Eltham, Kent removed to 'Chalfont', Longfield Drive, Amersham.

Mrs Burdett was a well-known member of the Headquarters staff of the British Union under her maiden name of Olive Hawks. She joined the movement in 1933 at the age of 16 and in 1935 became a confidential typist at the Headquarters. She was at one time employed by Captain Bryan Donovan, Assistant Director General, Mrs Anne Brock Griggs, Chief Women's Organiser and Raven-Thomson, Director of Policy, all prominent officials at the BU Headquarters.

Two days after the outbreak of war Olive Hawks married F.E. Burdett, also a well-known member of the BU and within a short time the two of them became well-known for their defeatist statements and their perpetual advocation of a negotiated peace. Mrs Burdett was also active as a speaker for the BU and it has been suggested that she spread the defeatist opinions mentioned above with the intention of undermining the morale of this country and so hastening the negotiated peace which she thought was so desirable.

Both Burdetts were detained on 23 May 1940 and when their rooms were searched a large quantity of BU literature was found as well as uniforms and membership cards.

Mrs Burdett was detained in Holloway prison and a report obtained from the Governor said that she appeared to be an ardent fascist and as late as August 1941 in the same year, when she was in the Isle of Man, she wrote to Raven-Thomson commenting on Oswald Mosley's move from Brixton to Holloway and sympathised with detainees in Brixton for having lost 'the inspiration of OM's presence'. When she herself was in Holloway she did secretarial work for Lady Mosley. The Governor stated, however, that although such an ardent Fascist, Mrs Burdett would not be the type of person to make a good leader and it was considered she had no real depth of character.

Olive Burdett after being arrested at the British Union of Fascists headquarters in London on 23 May 1940.

Throughout her detention she communicated regularly with Raven-Thomson and both their letters confirmed the opinion that they remained convinced Fascists.

Mrs Burdett made two appearances before the Home Office Advisory Committee, the first in July 1940 and the second during May and June 1942. She gave the impression on both occasions that she was quite unshaken in her loyalty to the British Union and that she was incapable of realising that such loyalty might conflict with her patriotism; she insisted that her whole attitude was dominated by the BU slogan 'Britain First'.

Although she had been trained as a speaker for the British Union, Mrs Burdett seems to have no grasp of international affairs and persisted in telling the committee that Britain was only justified in entering this war to defend her own territory and that there need be no difficulty in that she describes as 'an honourable peace of course, no truckling or crawling or giving them anything'.

A similar attitude is shown in a camp report received from the Isle of Man in April, 1942 which says that Mrs Burdett is definitely whole-heartedly British and says that she shows nothing and cares nothing about Germany so long as it is beaten; the report, however, goes on to say that she showed no willingness at all to help this country's war effort. In September 1942 Mrs Burdett told her father who was visiting her in prison that she did not want to be released before the Leader; that every great nation had a Leader born to lead the people and that England would never be a fit country to live in until Sir Oswald Mosley was released and had led the people to freedom.

After her hearing in June 1942, the Home Secretary decided that her detention should be continued and she was only released in August 1943 after the Home Office had reviewed her case again.

Towards the end of 1943 Mrs Burdett submitted to E.D. Hart, a member of the 18B Publicity Council and former BU official, a long and rather disjointed manuscript abut conditions in Holloway Prison with the idea that it should be printed by the Council as a pamphlet. The manuscript is based on Mrs Burdett's own experiences as well as those of Mrs Goody, Mrs Elam and the Misses Link who were also detained in Holloway. Mrs Burdett also recently paid a visit to Henry Williamson, author of 'Tarka the Otter' etc and former BU member in Norfolk.

Mrs Burdett developed a great admiration and affection for Raven-Thomson when she was working for him before her detention in 1940, and this developed during her detention. There is reason to think that she now hopes eventually to marry Raven-Thomson who is still detained, although he, like Mrs Burdett, is married to someone else at the present time.

MI5 are of the opinion that in view of Mrs Burdett's strong Fascists sympathies and devotion to cause of the British Union, she should be re-detained under DR 18B(1B) in the event of invasion.

Bush, Sheila Margaret (24) 40, Fairlop Road, Leytonstone E11 removed to Harold Wood Hall, Romford, Essex.

During January 1941 Miss Bush wrote a letter to Olive Hawks (BU member) detained at Holloway Prison under 18B. The letter contained such passages as 'Give my love to Lady Diana and the others. I was lucky to get a letter from my old District Leader Ernest Forge. I know that the great ideals that I work for will be fulfilled', and it was obvious from the contents that the writer was a member of or sympathiser with the BU.

Enquiries by Special Branch showed the writer was Miss Sheila Margaret Bush, born at Leytonstone on 28 September 1920 residing with her parents at 40 Fairlop Road, Leytonstone E11. She left school at the age of 14 and for a number of years was employed as a factory hand by the City Knitwear Ltd 806, Lea Bridge Road E10. During the end of 1940 and the beginning of 1941 she was employed as a clerk by her father who is Secretary to M. Abbot & Co Ltd coal merchants, St Anne's Wharf, Burdett Road E14 but owing to the necessity for a reduction of staff he was obliged to dispense with her services. She then obtained a position as wages clerk with I. Miller & Co Ltd Tresham Works on Tresham Road E8 engaged on the manufacture of army clothing.

She has an elder sister and a younger brother, both of whom received a fairly good education. Family finances however did not run to much in the way of schooling for Sheila. She was put to work as a factory hand at the age of 14 and this in conjunction with her lack of schooling, has made her consider that she has had an unfair start in life. In consequence, she had a grievance which made her an easy prey to Fascist propaganda. Her views had caused considerable trouble to her parents who did not share her sentiment.

When interviewed by police during March 1941 Miss Bush stated that she was formerly a member of the Salvation Army but owing to a dispute left this body during the summer of 1939 in a very disgruntled frame of mind. She was then apparently at a loose end for some time and gradually made the acquaintance of Miss Orrin who was selling *Action* and other Fascist literature in Leyton Street. In September 1939 she became a member of Leyton Branch of the BUF in September 1939. She added that her activities were confined to attending classes for speakers held at headquarters, Great Smith Street, SW1 under the instruction of Olive Hawks and Mrs Elsie

Steale (both interned) and occasionally selling Fascist literature at meetings. She admitted that she continued to believe in the principles of BU policy and was obviously anti-Semitic but she gave no grounds for believing that she was not in favour of the prosecution of the war.

On 27 March 1941 Mr I. Miller, a director of I Miller & Co Ltd, Tresham Works E8 called at Hackney Police Station and stated that he had recently dispensed with the services of Miss Bush owing to her ardent Fascist views. He added that she always wore a locket containing Mosley's photograph round her neck and had openly boasted to other employees that police had been making enquiries at her address.

In BU circles she was received with every consideration. This made her a loyal and devoted, if never very distinguished, member. Amongst the early friends she made was Sarah Constance Orrin. When the latter's rooms were searched a letter from Sheila Bush (dated January 1941), was found which gave ample evidence that the writer was in touch with Lady Mosley and other distinguished Fascists, that she was engaged in typing and distributing propaganda and that she was pro-German. The discovery of this letter led to the search of Sheila Bush's home, where a miscellaneous collection of Fascist literature together with her membership card and some correspondence with various known Fascists was found.

In June 1941, Sarah Constance Orrin was sentenced to five years imprisonment for suborning members of HM Forces. Amongst her possessions were two letters from Sheila Bush, both of which testify to her continued Fascist convictions. 'I have decided to get another job…I do not have anything to do with the works but I feel that even working in the office is helping in this war.'

In June 1941, to commemorate the anniversary of Lady Mosley's detention, she sent to the 'Leader' a fountain pen and to Lady Mosley a telegram: *'One year today we will be the victors of tomorrow who are the victims of today.'* In consequence, she was interviewed once more by Special Branch to whom she stated that she was still a staunch adherent of BU policy and that she would do nothing to further the war effort.

A police report from July 1941 stated:

Her anti-Jewish feelings were clearly evinced at one period during the interview when she was almost in tears with rage whilst asserting that Jews were allowed to go scot free after vilifying the King and Queen, whereas she was dismissed from her employment (I. Miller) for expressing Fascist views which were quite loyal to the King. She stated she was not in favour of the continuance of the war and that there should be a negotiated peace.

Miss Bush is an extremely obstinate, intolerant and sullen person, who is suffering from a bitter sense of grievance at the alleged persecution of British Union, and it was only after considerable persuasion that she would discuss her views with me…I am of the opinion however, that in view of her frame of mind and fanatical belief in the tenets of British Union policy, that she should be detained in the event of an invasion of this country.

From then until February 1942, apart from a letter which she wrote to the Home Secretary, she did not particularly bring herself to notice. However, her Fascist convictions remained and in February 1942 she registered for National Service as a conscientious objector. In November she appeared before the tribunal, giving the usual anti-Semitic objections to war service. Her application was turned down but subsequently in January 1943 the Appellate Tribunal allowed it subject to her undertaking full-time work on the land or in a war nursery.

In July 1943 she obtained a position as an assistant in a day nursery under the West Ham Borough Council. In December she sent a Christmas card to

Women aliens arrested under Defence Regulation 18B leaving a police 'Black Maria' to go into their first place of detention.

Sir Oswald Mosley and Lady Mosley. In February 1944 she was discharged to her present employment with the Essex County Council Harold Wood Children's Home.

Butzer, Paul, (born Germany) 'Cloebury', Pine Avenue, Parkstone, Dorset Employee of the Loewy Engineering Company at Branksome, Dorset. Firm works on Government contracts but regarded with uneasiness by police and MI5 owing to the number of people with Nazi sympathies connected with it. Pro-Nazi. Member of the Arbeitsfront.

Butzer, Wilhelmine (born Germany) 'Cloebury', Pine Avenue, Parkstone, Dorset. Unreliable loyalty.

Buuren, Adrian Diederik van, (41) (Dutch) Bottrells Close, Chalfont St Giles, Buckinghamshire. Interpreter for the Dutch Nazi leader Mussert on his visit to Mussolini in 1934. Arrived in Britain after fall of Holland, May 1940. Director of an export company suspected of espionage activities by Dutch authorities.

Buuren had acted for the Italian Legation in The Hague and had accompanied prominent Dutch Nazi leader Anton Mussert to Italy and acted as interpreter during a conference Mussert had with Mussolini with a view of obtaining funds for the Dutch Nazi Party back in 1934. File records showed he 'had certain business interests and on the German invasion of Holland in 1940 he was one of three directors of a Dutch firm with considerable German interests, some of whose employees were suspected by the Dutch authorities of espionage activities on behalf of Germany', but it was not possible to state definitely that Van Buuren was implicated in these activities. He arrived in UK at the time of the invasion and was interned on 15 July 1940 on the strength of the above information. Released on 20 November 1940 although both MI5 and the Dutch Security Services were of the opinion he should have remained in internment.

Once released Van Buuren worked at a company connected to his Dutch firm with his office at 16 Finsbury Square, London EC. MI5 kept an eye on him and noted one of his known associates, a certain Gaston Brezet had obtained a week's trial as Works Superintendent for Electric Sound and Television Patents Ltd. The day after his engagement he was discovered alone in the office examining a drawer containing confidential signal drawings of tank electrical equipment. The following day he was seen examining five books of drawings of electrical equipment and later opening a drawer containing contracts for projectiles, signals and bombs and further confidential documents. He then asked for time off and was seen to enter Van Buuren's office at Finsbury Square. There was little doubt that he was visiting Van Buuren. Brezet was found out and discharged from Electric Sound and Television.

The report concluded 'Although it may be that the incidents can be explained by the unscrupulous business technique of van Buuren and were not actually attempts to damage the interest of this country, they show that no faith can be placed in the integrity of Van Buuren and in view of the evidence of Van Buuren's hostile associations serious doubt exists with Van Buuren's loyalty to the Allied cause. MI5, therefore, are of the opinion that in the interest of Security it is necessary that Van Buuren should be detained under DR 18B in the event of invasion.

Carnegy, Mrs Valentine, 41, St Mary's Mansions, St Mary's Terrace, Paddington, London W2. Housewife. Reported for making pro-Nazi statements.

Carroll, Cola Ernst, White Cottage, Tilehurst, Reading, Berkshire. Journalist. Carroll was born in Tasmania in 1896, and was educated at the Universities of Zurich and Basle. His father was a British subject of Swiss origin. Carroll's first wife was German born, and his two sons by this marriage, his mother-in-law and his three sisters in law are living in Germany. His first wife died in 1936, and Carroll was married again shortly after the outbreak of war to a British woman who was his secretary.

In June 1926 Carroll obtained employment as a journalist with Wilhelm Schredler of the *Transocean Nachichtendienste*, Berlin. He was assisted in obtaining that employment by a German journalist in London called Glimpf. Carroll gave up this job in 1929, and later became editor of the Journal of the British Legion. This post was terminated in 1934, owing to a disagreement over Carroll's conduct of the paper.

In 1935 a proposal was put forward on Carroll's behalf that he should be employed by the British intelligence authorities as an agent to supply information on German military, political and economic matters, but Carroll was not accepted for this work.

In 1936 Carroll got in touch with Schwedler again with a view to starting a paper to be called the *Anglo-German Review*. Carroll told Schwedler that Fitzrandolph of the German Embassy was interested in the idea. Carroll also contacted Otto Karlowa the Acting *Landsgruppenleiter* of the Nazi party in London, and obtained a promise of assistance in getting subscribers for the new Review among the German community in England. He also wrote to

E.W. Bohle, Gauleiter of the *Auslands-Organisation* in Berlin, asking Bohle to bring the Review to the notice of German residents in other parts of the British Empire.

In March 1937 the Review had been started and in this month K.F. Durckheim, who was working in the Ribbentrop Bureau in Berlin, wrote to Karl Markau of the German Chanber of Commerce in London, expressing satisfaction with the way the *Anglo-German Review* was being produced; it was, he said, the first paper which published 'the truth in our sense'.

Later in 1937 'The Link' was founded and the *Anglo-German Review* became its official organ. In June 1938 the office of the *Anglo-German Review* took over the running and organisation of 'The Link'.

From intercepted correspondence between Carroll and the Ribbentrop Bureau it is clear that in the months before the outbreak of war Carroll was receiving regular financial payments from Germany for the running of the *Anglo-German Review*. The *Review* was almost entirely devoted to articles extolling the Nazi regime, and no criticism of anything in Germany or of any reaction of the German Government was allowed in its pages.

Aliens and other suspect individuals en route to an internment camp leave from a London station under armed military escort, June 13, 1940.

'The Link' and the *Anglo-German Review* were closed down on the outbreak of war. But in September 1939 Carroll was one of those who attended a meeting at the London flat of Gordon Canning, a prominent member of the BU and a Germanophile, the outcome of which was the founding of the British Council for the Christian Settlement in Europe, which favoured peace with Hitler and was supported by Fascist and pro-Nazi sympathisers.

In January 1940 Carroll offered his services to the British Intelligence authorities and suggested that he should undertake a mission to Germany with a view to probing the minds of leading Nazis to whom he considered he could easily gain access. Carroll's motive for this offer appeared to be to establish a channel through which peace negotiations between England and Germany could be conducted.

In May 1940 two witnesses reported Carroll for praising Hitler and the German people in their presence. He was detained under DR 18B in July 1940. Carroll appealed to the Home Secretary against his detention in November 1940 and again early in 1942 but the detention order was confirmed on each occasion. Carrol's detention order was suspended in November 1943 but he was only released under a restriction order whereby he was not permitted to travel any more than ten miles from his home.

Cassirer, Heinrich Walter. Corpus Christi College, Oxford. Unreliable loyalty.

Catford, Alfred John Buffette (25) Poole, Dorset. Hotel Worker. Catford has a number of convictions for crime. He is a worthless type of individual who has had opportunities to go straight but has failed to take them. Arrested in Plympton, Devon after posing as an Italian and trying to register as an enemy alien Italian named Danti Zinero Barletti. A map was found in his possession showing vulnerable points in the locality. MI5 took part in the case and it is understood that Catford knew a number of Italian Fascists in the Portsmouth area.

Chubb, George, Twyford, King's Road, Sherborne, Dorset. Member of the Worthing Branch, BUF.

Clark, Harry (55) 49, Roman Road, Colchester, Essex.
This man who is by trade a door to door salesman has resided in Colchester for a number of years. Prior to the proscription of the BUF he was an enthusiastic member and acted as local branch Secretary. On 17 June 1940

his premises were searched and a large quantity of Fascist literature was found as well as a register containing the names of the local members of the BUF. In January 1941 his home was searched again as there was reason to believe that he was still active in the furtherance of the BUF. Nothing of importance was found. In spite of these searches Clark still continued to give the Fascist salute openly to callers at his house.

On 12 May 1941 a reliable informant reports that Clark made the claim 'I'm a Fifth Columnist and they haven't caught me yet.'

Clegg, Mrs Eugenie Victoria, (41) Mount Pleasant, Bury Road, Branksome Park, Dorset. German born, reported by numerous people for expressing strong Nazi views. She was known to have visited Germany on a number of occasions before the outbreak of war and kept a copy of *Mein Kampf* and a book of Hitler's speeches in her bedroom. She also displayed an autographed photograph of Hitler she claimed had been given to her personally by the Führer.

Cloche, Miss Christine, (Born 1897) 'Marksbury', Shaw Hill, Newbury, Berkshire. Father French, mother of Danish descent. Reported for her pro-Nazi statements.

Coldwells, Mrs Isabel, (Born 1880) Downside, Niton, Isle of Wight. Keen and active BUF member.

Mrs Coldwells came to the notice of the Isle of Wight police as a result of a search of the premises of Edward Carl Davies, Isle of Wight District Organiser, BUF. Letters from Mrs Coldwells to Davies dated April 1940 showed that she was a keen and active BU member who was willing to hold meetings on the island for the purpose of 'converting' villagers to the Fascist cause. When Mrs Coldwell's house was searched in June 1940 a considerable amount of Fascist literature and propaganda was discovered.

Cole, Alfred Ernest, The Street, Kingston near Canterbury, later 43, Queens Road, Thame, Oxfordshire and subsequently 'The Caravan', Emmington, Chinnor, Oxon. Reported for defeatist talk and listening to German news broadcasts. Cole and his wife Laurie were very strong supporters of Hitler and Mussolini and were anxious England should be smashed in the war. When their premises were searched by the police on 12 June 1940 a very large quantity of Nazi and Italian Fascist propaganda was found.

Cole, Mrs Elizabeth, (Born in Germany) 27, Foster Road, Portsmouth removed to c/o Mrs Fryer, 30 Lansdowne Avenue, Widley, Hants. Reported for expressing pro-Nazi sympathies.

Cole, Mrs Laurie, (Wife of Alfred) 43, Queens Road, Thame, Oxfordshire. Reported for defeatist talk and listening to German news broadcasts. Unreliable loyalty.

Colenutt, Mrs Helene Klara Auguste (Born 1902 in Germany) Berryll Bank, Mitehill Avenue, Ventnor, Isle of Wight. Pro-Nazi and known associate of others on the island who share pro-Nazi sympathies. She is suspected of using Red Cross letters to send messages that are in fact codes to her family in Germany.

Collins, Harry Benjamin, Reported for making pro-Nazi statements.

Condren, Donald Michael, 'The Haven', Mardley Hill, Welwyn, Hertfordshire. Reported for making pro-Nazi statements.

Cowlishaw, Mrs Johanna Katherina Elisabeth (née Hartman) Cowlishaw's Stores, King George V Road, Bovington, Dorset.
Mrs Cowlishaw is German by birth, having been born on 17 July 1895 and her relations are still living in Germany. She married her husband William Cowlishaw who is a British subject, when he was serving in the British Army of Occupation on the Rhine and they returned to England in 1922. About 1926 they set up business in Bovington until 1938 when they separated and Mrs Cowlishaw carried on the business alone.

During 1940 it was reported to the police that Mrs Cowlishaw had stated that Hitler would be coming to this country and we should all be under Nazi rule, and that she felt it was not worth going on and doing anything about it. On 3 September 1942 a reliable informant of German origin, who during the summer of 1942 saw a lot of Mrs Cowlishaw, but whose identity it is necessary to conceal, was interviewed by an officer of MI5 and gave the following information:

At their first meeting Mrs Cowlishaw asked the informant whether she was happy and on what kind of work she was employed. Later the informant attended several small parties which Mrs Cowlishaw gave either in her shop or in the rooms behind the shop and to which she invited the NCOs from the Royal Armoured Corps camp at Bovington, and the informant was struck by the way in which Mrs Cowlishaw discussed with the NCOs matters concerning their military duties.

Apart from her interest in such matters Mrs Cowlishaw's behaviour in the presence of the NCOs was in no way subversive, but when she was alone with the informant Mrs Cowlishaw did not hesitate to express anti-British and pro-German sentiments. The informant allowed Mrs Cowlishaw to think that she also was to some extent pro-German and Mrs Cowlishaw expressed to her, her strong admiration for Hitler. Mrs Cowlishaw told the informant that she knew a great deal that would be of use to Germans in the war against England and that some day she might be able to put this information at Germany's disposal. She asked the informant whether her work put her in possession of any information which might be of value to Germany.

Mrs Cowlishaw told the informant that she was very well thought of in the neighbourhood and that she was on good terms with the police. Although Mrs Cowlishaw always showed herself to be completely pro-German, when alone with the informant she was extremely careful to give no indication of her real views when in contact with English people. She did in fact warn the informant against letting fall any pro-German views when in the presence of English soldiers, but her final words to the informant when the latter left the Bovington district were 'Well, never mind. Very soon we will have our [German] flag flying over England.'

The informant described Mrs Cowlishaw as a woman of some intelligence and of potential courage. Although she has not been to Germany for many years, she is an ardent disciple of Hitler and would be prepared to do anything to assist the German cause.

Creasy, Ronald Noah, (30) Cranley House, Eye, East Suffolk. District Leader, Eye Division, Suffolk BUF.

Prior to his internment on 4 June 1940 Creasy had been a very active District Leader for the Eye Division. He used to distribute Fascist literature and arrange meetings in furtherance of the movement, one of which was addressed by Mosley at Eye in 1939. Creasy frequently advertised his farm in *Action* [the BUF newspaper] as a place where BU members could stay in a National Socialist atmosphere. Although never caught he was strongly suspected of painting and chalking Fascist slogans and signs on walls, bridges and roads in the neighbourhood.

On 26 August 1939 Creasy was concerned in an ugly incident when distributing Fascist handbills and a few days later he was roughly handled in a public house for doing the same thing. On 8 April 1940 he wrote to the Chief Constable demanding police protection to enable him to sell *Action* at Stowmarket on 13 April as he had previously been ill-used when engaging in this activity. He is alleged to have taken every opportunity of thrusting his political views on others, or criticising the Government and praising the Nazi regime.

He was released from detention on 23 November 1940 but it was noted 'it is felt that in the event of an Emergency his loyalty will not be beyond doubt.'

Mrs Rita Creasy, (35) Cranley House, Eye, East Suffolk. Women's District Leader, Eye Division, Suffolk BUF.

This woman is the wife of Ronald Noah Creasy whose extreme sympathies with and activities on behalf of the BUF caused him to be interned in 1940. She was Women's District Leader for the same Division as her husband was District Leader and publicly boasted of it as late as April 1940 and was present on various occasions when her husband was distributing Fascist literature. It was in April 1940 that she was enthusiastically upholding Hitler to such a degree that a reliable informant reported her as pro-German.

After the internment of her husband in June 1940 she went to live with her mother, Mrs Harris, in Ipswich where her close association with members of HM Forces gave rise to considerable suspicion. Frequent parties were given to officers at this address which used to continue to early hours of the morning when those present dispersed the worse for drink. On these occasions Mrs Creasy was strongly suspected of attempting to collect information which would be of value to the enemy.

As recently as 31 December 1940 she attended a party at a neighbouring aerodrome in company with her husband. A brawl ensued as a result of Mrs Creasey expressing defeatist and unpatriotic views. It is felt she is of doubtful loyalty and likely to assist the enemy in the event of an emergency.

Critchley, Colin William Ashton, Colehill near Wimborne, Dorset. Came to the notice of the police because of his endeavours to contact Army officers and engage them in conversation about troops. He claimed he was a retired captain of the RAF, a retired naval captain and a retired captain of the Royal Naval Air Service and that he came to the Wimborne district in 1939 from France…His wife told a reliable informant that her husband was very pro-Nazi.

Another reliable informant heard Critchley say that the army was completely useless and our searchlights likewise; the air force would land at Weymouth and Falmouth and the Germans were going to take Ireland and invade England on the West coast…Germany will win the war, in fact, he hoped they would so so. He admitted he was a Fascist and claimed he was 'one of the men who could save informant's children' because the Germans knew their friends in this country like Lady Mosley and her husband.'

The report concluded: 'Up to present there is no actual evidence of subversive activities available, but Critchley is regarded with considerable suspicion locally. In view of his comments to informants it is considered that he is not the type who should be allowed to remain at large in the event of invasion or other grave emergency.'

Dallas, Mary Elizabeth, (58) 25, Clarence Road, Windsor. Language mistress at the Clapham County Girl's School which was evacuated to Windsor. Pro-Nazi, she holidayed in Germany and was an official guest at the Nuremberg rally in Germany (I suspect with Pitt-Rivers in 1937) and a known associate of prominent Fascists such as Captain Pitt-Rivers. She is said to have visited Hitler at Berchtesgaden. When war broke out she was in South Africa accompanied by prominent Fascists Captain Pitt-Rivers and Mrs Lance Taylor. For many years she spent her holidays in Germany and associated there with persons whose hostile feelings towards this country are well known. Correspondence found in her possession substantiated this. Amongst other property found was an address book containing numerous addresses of people both in Germany and Great Britain, many of whom were suspect.

Miss Dallas was detained on Saturday, 22 June 1940. On 29 June 1940 in consequence of a communication from the Secretary of State she was released and served with a restricted movement order which in turn was revoked by the Home Office on 29 August 1940. She was, however, placed on the Suspect List. 'In view of her activities and utterances, she would appear to be a person who, in the event of an invasion, it would be a danger to have at large.'

D'Arcy, Michael Patrick 148, Queen Street, Portsmouth. A native of southern Ireland he made no secret of his pro-Nazi views and preached the benefits of Fascism. Called for service in the Royal Navy with the rank of Petty Officer, his conduct was brought to the notice of naval authorities. Steps were taken to remove him from the service: this was facilitated by the fact he suffered from diabetes and he was invalided out of the Navy. After release he continues to boast that he is a Fascist.

Davies, Albert Charles (50) 'Crossbank', Sunset Road, Totton, Hampshire. Lived on Isle of Wight before the outbreak of war where he was BUF District Secretary and Organiser. He knew William Joyce and he had stayed at Davies' bungalow on IOW. Employed until the beginning of 1940 as a draughtsman at the Ordnance Survey Office, Southampton. He then entered the RAF and in August 1940 he was stationed at Poling, near Arundel, Sussex. Davies came

*Internment Camp
Headquarters and Hospital
in the former Hydro Hotel,
Port Erin, Isle of Man,
1940.*

*Internees of the Women's
Camp engaged on farm
work outside their camp on
the Isle of Man.*

*Internees from the Married
Camp working in the camp
cobblers shop. A number of
trade and craft skills were
taught and practised in the
internment camps on the Isle
of Man.*

*Children from the Women's
Camp on the Isle of Man
taking part in organised
exercise on the sands.*

under suspicion at Poling because of the tone of his conversation. He showed strong anti-British feelings and sympathy with the Nazis and Germany; he agreed with everything the Germans had done including the sinking of a ship containing evacuee children. He was discharged from the service and returned to work for Ordnance Survey. In May 1941 the Hampshire police reported that Davies and his mother, with whom he lives, listen in regularly to the German wireless news and to Lord Haw-Haw in particular. On these occasions Davies usually has large maps spread out on the table which he studies carefully.

Davies, Edward Carl 'Pip', 71, Newcombe Road, Southampton. District Leader Isle of Wight BUF. Davies is aged about 50, and is a writer and journalist by profession; he also has a very considerable knowledge of wireless matters. He had lived on the Isle of Wight for some time before the outbreak of war where he was well known for his energetic leadership of the local BUF.

Davison, Thomas William, 256, Southchurch Road, Southend-on-Sea. Member of Southend Branch BUF.

Dewhurst, Captain Charles R. (60) 'Limberlost', Poy Street Green, Rattlesden, Bury St Edmunds, Suffolk.
Captain Dewhurst is the son of a former manager of the Stowmarket Branch of Barclay's Bank. He served as a captain in the Royal Engineers during the last war. He is now employed as a wholesale agent and representative for East Anglia by Messrs Clayton Engineering Engineering Co. Prior to October 1939, Dewhurst resided at Watford and in the summer of 1940, a report was lodged with the Hertfordshire Police that before he left the district he was known to have expressed pro-Nazi views. Further enquiry by the West Suffolk Police elicited the information that shortly after his arrival at Rattlesden, Dewhurst had remarked to a neighbouring farmer, 'It does not matter if the Germans do win, we should be better off.'

Dewhurst lives with Mrs Elizabeth Swann who has been reported for pro-Nazi views. She is alleged to have said that Dewhurst was a friend of Captain Archibald Ramsay of the Right Club.

In March 1942 Dewhurst contacted the British National Party, a new Fascist movement which is bitterly anti-Semitic and ardently advocates peace negotiations with Germany. It has been reported from a reliable but delicate source that Dewhurst entirely endorses these views. In his own words, 'Though I shouldn't like to say it openly, I don't care a damn whether we win or lose. We shan't gain anything if we win and if we lose we might get rid of the Jew element quicker.' He is also known to consider Hitler the greatest man that Europe has ever seen and to have described Margaret Bothamly, who is the female counterpart of Lord Haw-Haw a 'splendid woman' and 'very loyal to this country' who only broadcasts from Germany because of her intense hatred for the 'horrible foreign influence that's got into us – like a cancer.' It appears prior to the outbreak of war Dewhurst attended anti-Semitic meetings at Miss Bothamley's address in Cromwell Road, London. William Joyce, better known as Lord Haw-Haw, is also in Dewhurst's opinion a first class radio announcer.

In view of this information it seems clear that Dewhurst's anti-Semitism leads him to condone active assistance to the Germans on the part of others and might well lead him to personally assist the enemy in the event of an invasion of this country.

Domvile, Admiral Sir Barry Edward KBE, CB, CMG, Shalden Lodge, Shalden, nr Alton, Hampshire. Founder of 'The Link'.

Admiral Sir Barry Domvile was born in 1878, he had a distinguished career in the Royal Navy. He was the Director of Naval Intelligence between 1927–1930 and finally retired in 1936. In 1916 he married the daughter of a German diplomat named Van der Heydt.

In 1935 Admiral Domvile met a Swiss subject named Anton Water de Sager, who seems to have had useful contacts with Himmler and other prominent Nazis and who invited Admiral Domvile to visit Germany. Admiral Domvile accepted this invitation and, in addition to meeting Himmler and several German naval authorities visited the Dachau concentration camp. In 1936 Admiral Domvile visited Germany again and, at Hitler's invitation, attended the Nazi party conference where he met Himmler, Ribbentrop and members of Ribbentrop's *Dienstelle*. In this year he also went to Rome where he witnessed an inspection of young Fascists by Mussolini.

On his return to England in 1937, Admiral Domvile was approached by C.E. Carroll, Editor of *The Anglo-*

Admiral Sir Barry Edward Domvile, KBE, CB, CMG.

German Review with the suggestion that he, Admiral Domvile, should form 'The Link' for the purpose of fostering friendly relations and understanding between England and Germany. There is evidence to show that Carroll's approach to Admiral Domvile was made with the support and approval of the Nazi propaganda authorities. Admiral Domvile was sympathetic to Carroll's proposal, and agreed to found 'The Link', which he has described as 'a perfectly genuine association to carry out which should have been a most laudable object.'

An examination of the activities of 'The Link', from its foundation by Admiral Domvile in 1937 to its dissolution in 1939, shows that, in his efforts to understand the German point of view and interpret it to his fellow countrymen, Admiral Domvile came more and more to regard things from the official Nazi standpoint, and many of his speeches and writings during this period reproduced exactly official Nazi propaganda.

Admiral Domvile kept in touch with members of Ribbentrop's *Dienstelle* during 1937–39, and he and Carroll, who became secretary of 'The Link', discussed the affairs of 'The Link' with them and with Fitzrandolph of the German Embassy in London. It is also worth noting that the Nazi Party in England showed considerable interest in 'The Link' during this time, e.g. on 8 December 1938 Otto Karlowa, the acting *Landesgruppenleiter* of the NSDAP in London, sent a circular letter to the five leaders of the NSDAP in this country inviting them to a gathering of 'The Link' which was to take place the following week; in this letter Karlowa wrote: 'I have promised Admiral Domvile that we will take part.' The branches of 'The Link' at Glasgow, Doncaster, Sheffield, Liverpool and Hull were also all started with the co-operation of the NSDAP, and one E. Lehrmann, *Stutzpunkleiter* of the NSDAP, wrote to Admiral Domvile as follows:

'It is with great pleasure that I acknowledge receipt of your letter......I have heard of "The Link" through Herr Karlowa and I had the pleasure if meeting at my office Mr Pilling from Southport who I believe has established a branch of "The Link" in that city.....I would like to assure you of my cordial co-operation in your efforts to establish a branch in Merseyside...."A further example of the value attached to "The Link" by the German Government is that in April 1939 one, Herr Piert, who has been selected by the German Government to act as guide and host to a "Link" party which was visiting Cologne, informed one of the party that the Germans regarded "The Link" as one of the best channels for propaganda in foreign countries.'

Although Admiral Domvile has consistently denied since 1939 that 'The Link' was an instrument for the dissemination of German propaganda, copies of the *News from Germany*, which was published by Rolf Hoffmann of the *Reichspressedienst* (Nazi Press Bureau) in Germany, were included in letters which were sent by 'The Link' to new members at the end of 1937 and during the early part of 1938. Furthermore, it is known that in May 1938 a hundred propaganda leaflets dealing with the Sudeten German question were sent from Germany to 'The Link'. In June 1939 it was reported that *News from Germany* was distributed at meetings of 'The Link' in London. In August 1939 Hoffmann suggested to a member of 'The Link' that she should duplicate copies of *News from Germany* and distribute them, as he suspected that the British Government might try to prevent copies being sent from Germany through the post reaching persons in England.

In May 1939 Professor Laurie, who was a member of 'The Link', wrote a glowing panegyric of Hitler called 'The Case for Germany'. He was unable to find an English publisher for it, but the Germans paid him £150 for it, and it was published by the Reich Propaganda ministerium. Admiral Domvile contributed a preface in which he said:

> 'Professor Laurie writes of the National Socialist Movement with knowledge and with great sympathy. The particular value of this book lies in the fact that it is written by a foreigner who cannot be accused of patriotic excess in his interpretation of the great work done by Herr Hitler and his associates. I recommend this book with confidence to all people who are genuinely impressed with the desire to understand one of the greatest and most bloodless revolutions in history.'

Admiral Domvile has since admitted that 'The Case for Germany' was sheer Nazi propaganda, and has tried to excuse his praise of it by saying that he had not had time to read the book when he wrote his preface, and that he could not be held responsible for Professor Laurie's sentiments.

Although 'The Link' was not officially anti-Semitic, Admiral Domvile himself was fanatically anti-Jewish. In January 1939 he said: 'The situation in Europe was never so peaceful, apart from the trouble which the Jews are trying to stir up. They are endeavouring to push us into war with our best friends the Germans.'

After the outbreak of war Admiral Domvile wrote: 'Those hard-luck stories of lying Jews have been kept in cold storage since the beginning of the war.' In April 1940 he wrote: 'There is nothing to be done until the general clean up comes – we have sunk to such depths of degradation and depravity under our Jewish teachers that nothing can surprise me.'

Admiral Domvile first met Sir Oswald Mosley in 1933 or 1934. Subsequently he wrote two articles for *Action*, the BUF paper. He has stated that he was in general sympathy with the foreign outlook of the British Union, though he knew little of their home policy. On 9 May 1938 he wrote to Gordon Canning, a prominent BU official, saying he would like to attend one of the BU meetings and hear Mosley speak. BU and Imperial Fascist League literature was distributed at 'The Link' meetings.

When the war broke out in September 1939, Admiral Domvile closed down 'The Link', but he remained bitterly opposed to the war. On 5 September 1939 he wrote to Luttman Johnson, a well known Fascist in Scotland: 'Alas today the King's enemies are our enemies and "The Link" is no more….I can never regret having done my small best to stop this craziness, but the forces acting against us are too strong…the real enemies of the British Empire are the people in this country, who have brought this catastrophe upon their ignorant countrymen.'

On 7 September 1939 he wrote to one Olive Baker, an English school-teacher, who had regretfully returned from her beloved Germany: 'After all, you and I did not make this unnecessary war.' On 24 September he wrote to Lutmann Johnson again: 'No voice was raised in H of C against war except Lansbury, Maxton and Gallagher….I should have liked to hear a few more sensible men opposing this ghastly folly so opposed to all the interests of our Empire.'

In May 1940 the Director of the Star and Garter Home for ex-Servicemen at Richmond reported that Admiral Domvile, who was a governor of the Home, had told the inmates that Hitler was going to win the war and would soon be in this country, but that there was no reason to worry about it, because he would bring the Duke of Windsor over as King and conditions generally would be much improved. Shortly before, on 1 April Admiral Domvile wrote to Olive Baker: 'Do you listen to the New British BBC? Short wave 50.6. 5.30 and 9.30 Sundays, 9.30 and 10.30 weekdays. It is grand. Ramsay asked questions in the House and gave it a good adv.' (In July 1940 Olive Baker was sentenced to five years penal servitude for advertising this German propaganda wireless station.)

In the months following the outbreak of war Admiral Domvile kept in touch with a number of persons, mostly of Fascist sympathies, who were opposed to the war and were working for a negotiated peace under the auspices of the British Council for Christian Settlement in Europe, e.g. Gordon Canning, Ben Greene, C.E. Carroll, John Beckett, etc. He also attended private meetings called by Sir Oswald Mosley. On 12 October 1939 he wrote to Lutman Johnson: 'I am having some very interesting negotiations with O.M. (Sir Oswald Mosley), Ramsay (Captain Ramsay, MP) and Norman Hay.' Norman Hay was a fascist sympathiser who ran an organisation at this time called 'Information and Policy', whose meetings Admiral Domvile attended and to whose paper he subscribed. On 20 January 1940 Admiral Domvile wrote: 'I work in close touch with Sir Oswald Mosley – just awaiting events – I do not know how long it will take to reach the crisis.'

In February 1940 Lord Tavistock, now the Duke of Bedford, visited Dublin for the purpose of contacting the German Legation and exploring the possibility of a negotiated peace. On his return an invitation was sent to a number of prominent persons to attend a private meeting to discuss the results of Lord Tavistock's approach to the German Legation. Among those who accepted this invitation were Admiral Domvile, Gordon Canning, Ben Greene and General Fuller. When asked about this meeting after his detention, Admiral Domvile said that owing to his deafness he had been unable to hear anything that was said. However, Admiral Domvile's attitude towards Lord Tavistock's attempt to achieve a negotiated peace is shown from the following extract from a letter he wrote on 5 May 1940 to John Beckett, who was working closely with Lord Tavistock at this time:

'I have the greatest admiration for your Führer (i.e. Lord Tavistock) and think he showed great courage over his Peace Proposals. I only wish that all the people working on the same direction would get together – there are literally dozens of movements. "Workers Unite" should be their motto.'

It is known that Admiral Domvile attended meetings of extreme Right Wing leaders in London in November and December 1939 and February, March and April 1940, the purpose of which was to co-ordinate the activities of the various Fascist and quasi-Fascist movements in existence at that time, and to organise a campaign for a negotiated peace. The meetings in November, December and April took place at Sir Oswald Mosley's house in London. It is also known that Admiral Domvile attended a political lunch party at the Ladies Carlton Club on 9 December 1939 at which Lady Mosley, Norman Hay and Mrs Whinfield, an ardent BU Member, were present, and on 1 March and 26 April 1940 Admiral Domvile attended luncheon meetings at the Criterion Restaurant for members of the London Administration of the BU There is no doubt that during the first nine months of the war Admiral Domvile's association with Sir Oswald Mosley and the BU leaders became increasingly close, and on the day that Mosley was detained in May 1940, he is known to have stated that he had begged him to keep quiet for the present, because he was too invaluable a man to get himself into trouble at that time.

Admiral Domvile and his wife were detained under DR 18B on 8 July 1940, and his son, Compton Domvile, on 10 July. Lady Domvile was released on compassionate grounds on 28 November 1941 and Admiral Domvile in July 1943. From correspondence written by Admiral Domvile during his detention it is clear that his anti-Semitic views are as strong as ever, and that he blames the 'Hidden Hand' for his misfortunes.

Since his release Admiral Domvile has been living for the last twelve months in his house at Roehampton. He is known to have been in touch during this period with Gordon Canning, Arnold Leese, formerly of the Imperial Fascist League, C.E. Carroll, and John Beckett, and to have been present at a luncheon in London in January 1944, which was also attended by General Fuller, Major Harry Edmonds and Rex Tremlett, all of whom are former Fascists. It was reported that all those present at this luncheon showed their admiration for the Germans and their hatred of Jews and Americans; they were convinced that the war was entirely due to the influence of International Finance, that the British Empire was finished, and that our only hope for the future was to unite with Germany and the rest of Europe.

On 30 June 1944 Admiral Domvile left London and took up residence with Mrs Whinfield at Shalden Lodge, Shalden, Hampshire. Lady Domvile also left London, but she went to stay with friends elsewhere.

Of those persons mentioned above John Beckett, C.E. Carroll and Mrs Whinfield are residing in Region 6, and are included on the Regional Commissioner's Suspect List. MI5 are of the opinion that, in the interest of public safety and the defence of the realm, Admiral Domvile should be re-detained under DR 18B in the event of invasion.

Donovan, Mrs. Heather F., Bloomfield Hatch Farm, Three Mile Cross, Berkshire. Women's District Leader, Westminster BUF.

Dreibholz, Albert Erich, (40) York House, Norwich Road, East Dereham, Norfolk (German born). Doubtful loyalty.

Dreibholz (née de Rochebrune), Elizabeth Christina Frederique, (38) York House, Norwich Road, East Dereham, Norfolk. This woman was born in Ginneken, Holland and married her husband in 1926. She has been residing in East Dereham with her husband since 1932 and in 1938 acquired British nationality when she became naturalised. In view of the suspicions attached to her husband, who is also on the Suspect List, it is thought that she is of doubtful loyalty and on account of the information concerning RAF and military locations of which she has possession, it is considered that she could and would assist the enemy on the event of an emergency.

Dunlop, Robert. (28) 147, Knella Road, Welwyn Garden City, Hertfordshire. This man is a specialist in Borosilicate High Vacuum Process and at present employed by Roche Products Ltd as a glass blower. Since 1935 he has played an important part in BUF activities. During that year he addressed twenty Fascist meetings and during 1936 and 1937 many more. On 3 May 1940 he addressed a meeting and introduced Sir Oswald Mosley.

In November 1940 his house at Croydon was searched and letters were found which showed that he had been connected with organising relief for members of the Fascist Party and had been detained under Defence Regulations. He is reported to have been in communication with G.F. Green who is well known for his Fascist opinions and who has been engaged in Fascist propaganda. He is also suspected of organising a National Socialist Society.

Durell, Miss Dorothea Vavasour, (57) Broad Green, Fort Road, Guildford removed to The Old Vicarage, West Wickham, Cambridgeshire. She then moved with her sister Phyllis to live in a caravan at Long Meadow, Riseley, Berkshire in September 1943. Fascist sympathiser with connections to the Guildford Branch BUF through her BUF activist sister Mrs Phyllis Vavasour Hook. Reported for her outspoken pro-Nazi views. When her house was searched in June 1940 she stated that she would be proud to be a martyr to the Fascist cause and at the same time made a violent attack on the present Government. Detained under DR 18B (1A) in July 1940. After her release in January 1941 it was reported she had been embittered by her internment, was of doubtful loyalty and could be dangerous in the event of invasion.

East, Frederick Robert, (33) The Bungalow, Avenue Road, Witham, Essex. East joined the BUF in 1934 and in the next four years was promoted three times. Thus, in 1934 he became Group Officer, in 1937, District Leader, first in Malden and later, when he had moved, at Chelmsford. In 1938 he was made County Propaganda Organiser, holding this post until he was detained in 1940.

Whilst in detention he made no secret of the continuance of his Fascist opinions. In October 1940 his case was heard by the Advisory Committee and although coming to the conclusion that he was a frank and intelligent young man, they recommended his continued detention. His case was reviewed by the Advisory Committee in August 1941. Camp reports had shown him to be quiet and well behaved and although still a Fascist he had moderated his views.

He was released subject to restrictions in October 1941. Since that time East lived quietly in Essex, his Fascist views however, are known to have increased in virulence. On 28 August 1943, he wrote: 'How foul a thing is democracy; the stinking miasma rising from the corpse of civilisation already moribund...'

In view of his past membership and prominent position in the BU and the apparent recent increase in the virulence of his Fascist views, it is thought East might be willing to assist the enemy in the event of an emergency.

Elliott, Charles and his wife Mrs Florence Elliott, 48, Poole Hill, Bournemouth. Both were active members of the BUF. Charles Elliott was District Leader of the Slough Branch BUF. They ran the branch together until Charles was interned in the summer of 1940. Released from detention in 1941, in 1942 it was discovered the Elliotts had been making regular visits to the home of William Webster at 3 Chalvey Court, Slough. Webster has been known for some time to retain strong Fascist principles, and since March 1942 he had been a member of a group of extreme Fascists who have started an underground Fascist organisation in London and the provinces. In April 1942 it became known that Mrs Elliott was attending meetings of this organisation in London.

Ellis, Charles, (58) Glaven Farm, Letheringsett, Norfolk. For several years this man was a prominent member of the Fascist Party and an associate of other leading members of the BUF. Up to May 1940 he was certainly very active in trying to obtain converts to Fascism. On 14 June 1940 a search of his house was made and large quantities of Fascist correspondence and literature were found. On 17 June he was suspected of sending up flares to guide aircraft but no evidence could be discovered to confirm this.

On 30 June he entered the White Horse Inn, Blakeney, and on seeing another Fascist named Charles Lambert gave him the Nazi salute. Conversation took place in which Ellis and Lambert were heard to state that this war was due to the Jews and that Chamberlain had double crossed Hitler.

On 19 July he tried to interest a farmer's traveller in the BUF and handed him a book entitled *Fascism* by Oswald Mosley to take away and read. He has complained bitterly because he has not been allowed to join the LDV and has at the same time protested his loyalty. He is also known to have had at least one visitor from Germany.

Essling, William George, (36), Fleece Hotel, Witney, Oxfordshire. Licensee of Fleece Hotel since August 1936. Frequently visited Austria before the war and even took parties there. Made regular Pro-Nazi statements. Further ground for suspicion rises out of information given by a taxi driver that Essling frequently hired to take him to Oxford where Essling meets a man with whom he converses in whispers in what the driver thought to be a foreign language.

Etheridge, Harry Eglinton, (47) Bibury, Packhorse Road, Gerrards Cross, Buckinghamshire. Reported for making Pro-Nazi statements. Claimed in a conversation reported to the police that he was a member of BUF Information and Policy department and a friend of John Beckett, Captain Ramsay and the Mitfords.

Finnie, Thomas Madeley, The Seven Stars, Cuddington, Aylesbury. Acting Deputy District Leader Chelsea BUF.

Firman, Kenneth Claud Richard, 68, Mount Pleasant, Maldon, Essex. Reported for making pro-Nazi statements.

Floring, Erich Artur, (40) 47 Commercial Road, East Dereham, Norfolk. This man was born at Barmen, Germany where he was educated. Between 1921 and 1931 he worked in Holland and Java in the Engineering trade in connection with the sugar beet industry. In 1932 he came to England and established a branch of the firm of Dreibholz Bros & Co Engineers at East Dereham to manufacture beet cutting knives. In 1937 while visiting Germany he married Lieselotte Schulte.

In 1938 he was granted a Certificate of Naturalisation. It appears that his naturalisation was not sincere because although he assured the police that he had no intention of retaining his German citizenship, the very same year he was writing to the German Embassy referring to himself as German-British and asking for a permanent visa for himself and his wife. In another letter to the German Embassy he refers to Germany as 'the homeland' and ends this and many of his letters with the words 'with German Greetings'.

On 24 April 1940 this man presented himself at Shoreham airport for embarkation to Amsterdam. He was stopped and has never given any satisfactory explanation of this attempt to leave this country for Holland shortly before the invasion of Holland. He is alleged to have many relations in Germany who are stated to be prominent in business and pro-Nazi. In addition he has a wide strategic knowledge valuable to the enemy of the Norfolk district.

Floring was detained on 9 July 1940 under DR 18B, however in September his case was reconsidered and he was released. In all the circumstances it is considered that this man would be disloyal to this country.

Floring, Mrs Lieselotte, née Schulte, (27) 47 Commercial Road, East Dereham, Norfolk. This woman was born at Velbert, Germany and first came to England in 1933 as a lady's help; she remained in this country for six months before returning to Germany. In 1937 she married Eric Artur Floring in Germany and came with him to this country. He is viewed with considerable suspicion and his name is also included on the Suspect List.

In 1938 she made a declaration of acquisition of British nationality when her husband acquired naturalisation. However, her husband, in spite of this declaration, in the same year wrote to the German Embassy asking for a permanent visa for this woman as well as for himself. In view of the suspicion surrounding her husband, and of her former German nationality, it is considered that this woman is of doubtful loyalty.

Floyd, Gilbert George, 51, Abercrombie Avenue, West Wycombe, Buckinghamshire. Blacksmith. Had a daughter in Germany married to a German officer. Reported for extolling the 'truth' of Lord Haw-Haw radio broadcasts and for making pro-Nazi statements such as 'The Nazi system is unique'; Germany is a better country than England; England is not worth fighting for; I would not hesitate to help the Germans if I had a chance.'

Flynn, Michael James, (40) (Irish) Licensee of the Red Lion Hotel, Bourne End, Buckinghamshire. Reported for making anti-British and pro-Nazi comments.

Foot, Edward Hammond Whalley (Born 1881) Wilton Corner, Beaconsfield, Buckinghamshire. Retired Army Officer. Member of the Anglo-German Fellowship and other pro-Nazi organisations. In 1937 Foot came to notice as a person who was in touch with Kitschmann, the assistant military attaché at the German Embassy.

Forge, Ernest George Frederick, c/o Gleesons Ltd, Cavenham near Bury St Edmunds, Suffolk. Member of Leytonstone Branch BUF and British Union London Defence Force.

Fortune, Miss Gladys, 69, Romney Court, Shepherd's Bush, London W2 removed to The Rustic, Sunnymeade, Wraysbury, Buckinghamshire. Secretary. Women's District Leader South Paddington Branch BUF. 'Rabidly pro-German.'

At the date of her detention this woman was living at 69, Romney Court, Shepherd's Bush, London, W2. She was employed as a secretary by Messrs Clare, Haynes & Co. Solicitors of Sicilian Ave, London, WC.

According to the official 'Gazette' of the British Union, which was published on 20 October 1937, Fortune had been appointed Women's District Leader of the South Paddington Branch of the British Union. There is no record of her having resigned.

According to information obtained from a reliable source, this woman is rabidly pro-German and claimed to be carrying on correspondence with people in Switzerland and Germany. She appeared to have a friend in Switzerland who has been assisting her to communicate with her friends in Germany. We know that after the outbreak of war she received a letter from an officer in the German Air Force which had been posted by someone in Holland. This letter was not dealt with by the Censor. At a meeting of the Nordic League she was heard to say that her great desire was to see Germany win the war. At one time she was on the Council of 'The Link', but her views were too extreme even for that organisation and consequently she was expelled.

She was also a prominent supporter of the British Union and a great friend of Mosley, who on several occasions had rebuked her for her revolutionary methods and statements at open-air meetings. She continually disregarded the orders of the BU and of 'The Link' Council.

On 18 September 1939 Gladys Fortune attended a meeting of the Nordic League at Lamb's Conduit Street. At this meeting she interrupted Gilbert and said that Mosley had good reason for not attacking freemasonry, but that she was prepared to do all she could to assist in stamping it out. She also boasted that she had obtained further converts to Fascism from the residents at Romney Court, including the porter and two young persons, who had previously been Communists. According to our information she appeared to be frightened at her own notoriety, and proposed to carry on her work of chalking seditious slogans on walls in another locality. This woman was also present at a meeting of the Nordic League held on 26 September 1939 at Lamb's Conduit Street. She said she has adopted new tactics; she used to visit restaurants where she started to discuss the international situation in a loud voice and, according to her, she was able to get everybody interested. She also said that although she had encountered some opposition, her efforts were meeting with quite a lot of success.

At a meeting of the Nordic League held on 2 October 1939, Gladys Fortune stated in conversation that she had been busy in Shepherds Bush and Kensington during the previous week, and had worked up till the early hours of the morning plaiting sticky-backs. Her favourite places for putting these were park seats, public lavatories and the telephone directories on call boxes. She also said that her flat was used as a 'Bureau' for the storage of propaganda and that although she had destroyed a number of documents, she has kept some German books and badges of all descriptions. She appeared surprised that she had not been arrested.

On 15 October 1939, Fortune attended a BU meeting at Stoll Picture House. At that time she was a kind of freelance private secretary to Pitt-Rivers. The latter has been detained and the Advisory Committee have recommended his continued detention.

In a letter dated 20 February 1940, W.A.T. Cross, the Acting District Leader of the South Paddington Branch, stated that he hoped Gladys Fortune had not given up her active work and he asked her to let him have 'an exact return of the results of contact work of the four teams for which you took responsibility last October'. In a letter dated 21 May 1940, the Senior District Leader of 10th London Area stated that she was the Women's District Leader of the South Paddington Branch and asked her to visit him.

In April 1940, Gladys Fortune received two pamphlets from the 'Home Defence Movement', one was 'News Commentary No. 15' and the other was entitled 'Easter Holiday Meditation, 1949'. The theme of both these pamphlets was 'stop the war'.

On 13 May 1940, Gladys Fortune appeared at Great Marlborough Street Police Court charged with 'using insulting words and behaviour whereby a breach of the peace was occasioned'. Police Constable Bell stated that on Sunday 12 May, he saw this woman surrounded by a hostile crowd at the Meeting Place, Hyde Park. She made various remarks which caused resentment, and amongst other things she said, 'to hell with the allies and their friends, to hell with the Jews', and 'in two months time Hitler will be here'. As a result of these remarks vicious fighting broke out, and attempts were made to strike this woman. After she had been arrested and was being taken to the station she remarked 'I am an active member of the Fascist Party, I still stick to my views.' When she was charged she said, 'The Jews are the enemy of my country. I say to hell with the Jews and all those who defend them.' This woman denied using insulting words and behaviour and said that she was indignant when she heard a speaker say, 'The time will come when you will bow the knee to the Jews, and they will crush you.' This magistrate said that if she had not been arrested, she would have probably been lynched. She was bound over in the sum of 40 shillings.

On 24 May 1940 the Hammersmith Police were informed by a resident at Romney Court that a fire had been found at the rear of those flats, and that Fascist literature was being burnt there. The police made investigations immediately, the informant who had helped the porter put out the fire, which had been lit in a dust bin, examined the contents and found the burnt remains of Fascist literature. The police officers made a further examination and found a partly burnt envelope on which were the words 'join the Link', Headquarters, 230 Strand WC2 which was addressed to Miss Gladys P.J. Fortune, 69 Romney Court, 45 Shepherds Bush Green, W12, and also a partly burnt postcard bearing a Berlin postmark dated 12 July 1937.

The police officer discovered that this woman had been seen by tenants hurrying along the ground floor passage which led from the rear of the flats, where the dust bins were. She had appeared somewhat agitated earlier that evening.

On 12 June 1940 this woman was staying with Pitt-Rivers at the Manor House, Hinton St. Mary. At a supper after a dance, which had been organised by the latter for troops at the Tithe Barn near this house, this woman spoke against the Czech refugees, and said that we should negotiate a peace with the Germans, and that if she had a son she would shoot him rather than that he should fight the Germans. She praised everything German and decried everything British.

This woman was a friend of Thomas Jabez Ashworth-Jones, who has been detained. The statement of case against him has been sent to the Advisory Committee. The following entries were found in the latter's diary:

11/6/40 I phoned Shepherds Bush – a happy thought, for Molver and Egan had arranged to meet me there. Anyway, Gladys Fortune suggested that I call and I did – arriving there at nearly midnight. I recognised her as a well known Blackshirt and we chatted and drank in her flat until 3am. She is a fine woman and most useful as a new contact. We are meeting again next week.

26/6/40 To Shepherds Bush this evening and to Gladys Fortune's place. Eddie there too and we chatted optimistically; listened to Bill Joyce from Bremen and toasted the day of liberation – 'Der Tag'.

3/7/40 Gladys Fortune round after eight and until midnight, for political conflab. The invasion is a long time coming! Do wish this war would end soon.

Statement: In May 1940, at a meeting of the Nordic League, I met Dr Leigh Henry and he invited me to his house. I went there once only, on Monday 27 May 1940. After a speech by Dr Leigh Henry to those present, four men and three women, the only one whom I knew was Professor Darwin-Fox, Dr Leigh Henry suggested that we each formed a small circle of Fascists. The intention was that we should accept his leadership and that the circle formed would keep in touch with each other. Nothing further than discussion was intended. I tried to form a circle with Eddie Molver, Denis Egan, Gladys Fortune and a man named Barnes. I understand from Eddie Molver that Egan has been detained by Police. I do not know Eddie Molver's address nor that of Barnes, who is a van driver. Gladys Fortune lives at Romney Court, Shepherds Bush Green.

Special Branch reported that this woman had been detained on 8 October 1940, and that her flat at Romney Court had been searched on 9 October. The following items were seized by the police officer:

1. Thin wire-bound red notebook containing (inter alia) particulars of men in the services.
2. Red address book containing various names including some in Germany.
3. BUF Diary for 1938 which contains many names and addresses including some German, and notes showing that Miss Fortune was at the time actively engaged in BUF matters, was interested in the 'Friends of National Spain' movement and in 'The Link'.
4. Various visiting cards (many German) and other pieces of paper bearing names and addresses.
5. Correspondence (mainly from Germany and written in English) from Curt Krieger, 45 Markgrafenstr, Berlin W. These letters express Nazi and Fascist sentiments. Photos of Miss Fortune and acquaintances some in Nazi uniform.

The police officer had been informed that two copies of the 'Uncensored British News Bulletin' had been pushed into a letter box of No. 69 Romney Court some weeks previously. When the flat was searched those pamphlets were not discovered; this woman admitted she had received them, but stated she had destroyed them.

British Union, Nazi, Fascist and Falangist flags, emblems, badges, photographs, periodicals and newspapers were also found but were not seized.

Fox, Seaton Henry Elliott, 16, St Peter's Hill, Caversham, Reading. Reported for making pro-Nazi statements.

Frowde, Henry Louis, (32) 59, Stanley Avenue, Gidea Park, Essex
On 15 May 1940 a report was received which showed this suspect to be of German extraction. His father is German and prior to the last war was a barber in London. He was interned in 1914 and was repatriated to Germany. He never returned to this country but remained in Germany where he had other children who are stepbrothers of the suspect. One stepbrother is now serving in the German Army. This person was formerly leader of the Hitler Youth Movement. The suspect is extremely pro-Nazi and once boasted of being a member of the Nazi Party and wore a Nazi badge in his coat.

He has often spoken in praise of German progress under Nazi rule and has belittled the fighting strength of this country. He once asked a soldier if they knew what they were fighting for. Frowde speaks fluent German and has made many visits to Germany, combining business with pleasure and visiting relatives. His stepbrother has also visited him in this country. In a letter of May 1940 a reliable source stated he had no doubt as to which direction the suspect's sympathies point and he suggests that in the event of an invasion Frowde would be an undoubted menace to the interests of this country.

Fuller, Major General John Frederick Charles, CB, CBE, DSO Oak Cottage, Compton, Berkshire.

Fuller came to our special notice in 1931, when an article in a periodical stated that even before Mosley resigned from the Cabinet he was friendly

Major-General John Frederick Charles Fuller CB CBE DSO.

with a 'brilliant General officer who mainly inspired the mechanisation of the British Army'.

By 1934 Fuller was closely associated with the BUF, and by 1935 his influence in the BU was being felt. Mosley was said to be under Fuller's thumb, and Fuller, who had been in Germany for about a fortnight, was reported to have been entrusted with carrying out a mission on behalf of Mosley.

During 1935 Fuller's influence increased and he became friendly with Lord Rothermere, who was a member of the Co-ordination Section of the BU, and was contributing to BUF periodicals. In an article in the *Daily Mirror* in 1935 he openly became a supporter of Mosley, and said, 'I would hand the government over to Sir Oswald Mosley on condition he made me Minister of Defence, ...We want a dictatorship, because we have three fighting services.' His journalistic activities extended and in the autumn of 1935 he went as correspondent of the Rothermere press to Abyssinia with the Italian Forces. On the way he had an interview with Mussolini, and Mussolini facilitated his travel arrangements. About the same time he became Vice-President of the University of London Fascist Club (described as a 'King and Country Club').

In January 1936 he was a director of *Action* Press Ltd., and by the end of the same year his name appeared on a list of BUF Candidates for the Parliamentary elections. He was to stand against Mr Duff Cooper at St. Georges, Westminster.

In November 1936 he delivered a lecture at the RA Institute, Woolwich, on the development of totalitarian warfare, as described as Nazi propaganda. He claimed to have met and talked with Hitler, Schacht, Goering, Hess and others and insisted on the desirability of an authoritarian system of government.

In February 1939, while on a visit to Germany, Fuller gave an interview to a German newspaper, in which he described the Governments of 'Certain countries' as 'pluto-canaille'. Any future war, he said, would mean for the democracies a struggle until their capacity to trade was exhausted; but the authoritarian states, on the other hand, 'could be wounded but not ruined'. On his return from Germany (where he had attended Hitler's birthday celebrations) he was noted as a speaker at meetings of the Nordic League on two occasions.

He wrote a letter to *The Times* on 27 April 1939 (after Bohemia and Moravia had been annexed) which consisted of an apologia for his visit to Germany, which had somewhat naturally come under criticism, and in it he claimed to be not 'anti-democratic, but a believer in the democracy of

Mazzini, who placed duty to the nation before individual rights'. This form of government, he said, did not exist in England, which was governed by a 'pluto-mob-ocracy, money at one end of our political system, and mass emotionalism at the other'. He said that he held that a new political idea, 'expressing itself as Fascism, National Socialism, etc., is also inevitable'.

In May 1939 he was noted as addressing a meeting of 'The Link' claiming that he had travelled over Europe regularly and was friendly with Ribbentrop. (That he was in close touch with German circles in London is known by the fact that he attended a dinner in honour of Ribbentrop in 1936. His menu card was signed by Pitt-Rivers (now interned), Major Yeats-Brown, with whom he is still friendly, Margaret von Trescow and others.)

Since the outbreak of war, his wife, who was born in Warsaw of Russian parents, has been reported to us as expressing pro-German sentiments.

Fuller himself was the recipient of a letter which Lord Tavistock sent out, inviting people to a strictly private meeting on 13 February 1940, for the consideration and discussion of his so-called peace proposals.

In the winter and spring of 1940, Fuller came to our notice in connection with meetings of pro-German individuals and of 'Information and Policy' supporters. He, together with Oswald Mosley, Maule Ramsay and others, was said to be trying to contact Sumner Welles in order to indicate a split on public opinion over the continuation of the war. His defeatist attitude is illustrated in the subtle phrase which he used in a letter in March 1940: 'I reckon that even should we win this war, we shall at once be faced by eight million unemployed.' His articles to the press contained similar subtle defeatist suggestions. He is known to have said that an alternative to negotiations for peace at once, taking the best terms offered by Hitler before it was too late, would be a coup d'etat by Mosley or some other leading Fascist.

Fuller was in close touch with John Beckett and his British People's Party down to the time of Beckett's detention. He is known to think that the country should be prepared for a new policy with a veiled dictatorship, since there is no really suitable person to fill the position of a Hitler or a Mussolini. His articles to the Press have raised concern to the DMI and to Sir Walter Monckton of the Ministry of Information. The American owners of *Time* agreed not to publish an article of an extremely gloomy character.

Fuller recently addressed a meeting of MPs and expressed very strong defeatist sentiments. His closing words were: 'I can see but to ends, (1) our defeat, which will surely carry with it the ruin of our empire, (2) our victory, which certainly must lead to anarchy throughout Europe in which we ourselves will inevitably be engulfed'.

In view of the fact that Fuller is a supporter of National Socialism and claims intimacy with Hitler and other leaders of the German Reich, believes in a dictatorship by Mosley or 'some other leader', and is himself an obvious alternative leader of the Fascist element in this country, MI5 are of the opinion that Fuller is likely to covet a position not dissimilar to that of Marshal Petain, and to assist the enemy if given a suitable opportunity.

Furre, Leif Arnor, The Thatched Cottage, Sindlesham, Berkshire
A young Norwegian who joined the Nasjonal Samling (Fascist Party led by Vidkun Quisling) in 1936. Furre would claim to have only joined the NS out of youthful curiosity, and to have resigned after a few months but he would also admit he was still attending NS meetings in June 1941. He had also been engaged to a Norwegian girl but she had left him because of his German associations and considered him pro-Nazi.

Furre was approached at least once by the Germans with a view to his spying on escape organisations in the Sundfjord area. Furre claims that he refused to do this.

In August or September 1941 Furre was called up by the Germans for service in the Merchant Navy. He tried to avoid this on the grounds of ill health, but without success. However, he managed to join an escape party which left Norway in the MV *Stolsgut*, which arrived in Scotland on 15 October 1941.

He was taken to the London Reception Centre, and when it became known to other Norwegians at the centre that Furre had been a member of the NS, they attempted to attack him. On interrogation Furre admitted that to some extent he agreed with the NS programme at the time. He had joined it in September 1940, but he also claimed that his motive in rejoining was to try to spy on the NS for the Allies.

Furre who has been described as of psychopathic type, is reported to be of unstable character.

Gardiner, Rolf, Fontmell Magna, Shaftesbury.
Farmer and owner of Flax Mills. He has founded an organisation known as the Springhead Ring. This society has the object of promoting or reviving interest in agriculture and rural pursuit and has a certain affinity with German work camps. He has frequently visited Germany, speaks German well and has many German friends. An informant states Gardiner has rooms at Slepe Mill near Bridport where he keeps Fascist literature and many books relating to Germany.

Gearing, Mrs Betty, 'Kuru' Flackwell Heath, High Wycombe, Buckinghamshire. Reported for expressing Pro-Nazi sympathies. Raised particular concerns in one conversation that was reported where she claimed to have been to Germany and to have German friends.

Gilbert, Oliver Conway, (born 1903) 3, Shouldham Street, Edgware Road W1 removed to 98, Spearing Road, Castlefield, High Wycombe.

Gilbert joined the BU in 1933 but appears to have resigned after paying three monthly subscriptions. He rejoined the BU in 1937 and took a prominent part in founding the virulent pro-German Nordic League, of which he became Chairman and treasurer.

Gilbert was at one time thought to have been in the pay of the German espionage service. In September 1938, at the time of the Munich crisis, he is known to have been visited by Kruse, a former U-boat commander, who was reliably believed to have come to London in order to obtain information for the German authorities about England's preparations for war. He visited the docks and places of military interest. Two days before his departure he paid a visit to 3 Shouldham Street, in order to see Gilbert, whose name and address was written on an envelope which he carried with him. Gilbert was out at the time and the two did not meet. The motive for this attempt is not definitely known, but it was thought at the time that Kruse was either hoping to recruit Gilbert as a German spy, or thought he might be able to give him information about Fascism in this country. In May 1939 Gilbert is known to have visited Cologne.

He appears to have held the position of BU propaganda officer for the district where he lived and was well known at BU Headquarters in Westminster. He appears, however, to have been distrusted by BU leaders on account of the extreme fanaticism of his pro-Nazi opinions. It was reliably reported that there was a feeling of satisfaction at the BU national HQ when they heard he had been arrested in September 1939. He was finally released in February 1944. Despite a professed change of heart MI5 were still of the opinion Gilbert's political record and his unreliability presented a danger to public safety in the event of an invasion.

Glasspool, Maurice, Station House, Romsey, Hampshire. An inspector for the Southampton Gas Light and Coke Company. Member of 'The Link'. Reported for making pro-Nazi statements.

Gloster, Alfred, (42) Park Street Lane, Park Street, near St Albans, Hertfordshire.
This man whose original name was Grunsberg was born in Germany in 1899, spent his early years in England but returned to Germany in 1914.

During the latter part of the Great War he served in the German Army in Macedonia and Albania.

In 1920 he went to Amsterdam as a representative of Orenstein and Koppel who have been strongly suspected of acting as a German Intelligence organisation. In 1925 he changed his name by deed poll from Grunsberg to Gloster. In the same year he came to England as Orenstein's representative and settled in London.

A colleague of Gloster's who worked in close touch with him between 1925 and 1932 states he idolised Germany and was contemptuous of England and the British race. The informant added that Gloster was considered untrustworthy by his business associates which is confirmed by reports from other sources. Particular concern is expressed about regular payments described as 4 per cent commission he received from Orenstein and Koppel (South Africa) Ltd and is strongly suspected of trading in goods of German origin.

Golder, Hugh Clifford, (Born 1906) 3, Church Cottages, Water Stratford, Buckinghamshire. Partner in a small engineering business employed by BSA Co. Golder first came to Dudley in March 1938 when it was alleged that he was taking an unusual interest in factories making aeroplanes and accessories. Reports of his pro-German comments led to police and MI5 enquiries which revealed Golder had spent several holidays in Germany, that he listened to German radio channels and the walls of his room were decorated with German calendars. In November 1938 Golder married Elsie Taylor, a woman noted in her workplace for her frequent comments of admiration for the German people and Hitler. After police received a tip off the Golders' flat was searched and a large quantity of books and printed material of Nazi interest were found along with a swatika and a cloth badge bearing the German eagle and swastika with the letters NSKK (*ie Nazionale Sozialistische Kameraden Klub*) along with gramophone records for learning Morse code.

Gollub, Werner Oswald Eric (40) Pond Hall Farm, Ipswich, Suffolk. Born in Germany and British by naturalisation in 1934. In 1936 he visited relations in Germany and remained there until 1937. From September 1937 when he arrived in England until May 1938 he was employed as a farm labourer by Mr Little of Levinstock Green, Hemel Hempstead, who states that he was an educated man with sympathies entirely with Hitler and the Nazi regime which would, he said, effect great improvement if the Nazis conquered England. In April 1938 he married an English girl of the domestic servant type.

Subsequently he obtained employment as a farm labourer with Mr Owen near St Albans, where he remained until 1940. This employer also reported

Gollub's strong sympathies with the Nazi regime. When HMS *Royal Oak* was sunk he said it was the great German Navy at its best and that it was the beginning of a new German Empire.

Goldsworthy, Mrs Jean, The Dower House, Truss Hill, Sunninghill, Ascot. Member of the BUF since August 1939. Reported for making pro-Nazi statements.

Golton, Cyril Robert, (Born 1903) 'Chantilly', Endfield Road, Christchurch, Hampshire. Employee at Aish & Company Electrical Engineers. When requested to join the Home Guard as part of his National Service duties his objections were expressed in such a violent and bitter way that it was considered desirable to interview him to ascertain his real political views. After refusing to fight 'for this bastard government' he stated he considered himself unfortunate to be a British subject.

The Chief Constable of Hampshire and MI5 are of the opinion that, in view of Golton's violent and irresponsible temperament, hatred of and disloyalty towards the Government of this country and the uncertainly of his attitude towards the Germans, it would be necessary in the interests of public safety and the defence of the realm to detain him in the event of an invasion.

Gore, Albert Edward (40) 16, Chase Avenue, King's Lynn, Norfolk.
This man is a person of some authority in the King's Lynn neighbourhood. For some time prior to his internment he had been a prominent and active member of the local Fascist organisation and had taken every opportunity to attempt to enrol recruits for the movement.

In April 1940, he is reported not only to have been indulging in pro-fascist expressions, but is stated by a reliable informant to have given tongue to pro-German and defeatist language, stressing the falseness of the BBC, the mastery of Germans in the air, that a great deal more shipping had been sunk than had actually been announced and that this country would be starved and was finished.

Later in the same month, a police officer who knew Gore and met him casually, reported Gore's defeatist sentiments and stated that Gore had boasted of his BU connection. In May 1940 a welfare worker who happened to be in King's Lynn, was so struck by the pro-Hitler views which Gore expressed, that she also reported him. His internment was ordered in June 1940.

In October 1940, his case was considered by the Advisory Committee and having heard it recommended Gore's release, although they described it as 'a difficult case which gave considerable anxiety' but they thought Gore's detention would ensure no such repetition of his former expressions. Despite the Advisory Committee's optimistic view, it is considered that this man cannot be regarded as above suspicion.

Gore, Frederick Charles, 89, Belmont Road, Reading, Berkshire. General Post Office employee reported for making pro-Nazi remarks. BUF Member and activist. Considered 'likely to help the enemy if given the opportunity.'

Gosling, Mrs Hertha Lina Hermine née Bilstein, (born 1902 in Germany) 59, Chessel Crescent, Southampton removed to 18a Spring Crescent, Portswood Road, Southampton.

Mrs Gosling is German by birth, she married a British subject 1933 and the pair lived together in Hamburg until they came to England. They lived at several addresses around the country and separated during the war years.

In June 1940, when filling in Form DR17, Mrs Gosling stated she had a brother in Germany, who had been in the habit of sending her money up to the outbreak of war. She told another neighbour that she had money in Germany which she had been unable to get out but she had received money from a stepbrother in Germany through someone who visited that country. Mrs Gosling has pro-Nazi sympathies.

Gosling, Stanley Frederick, 59, Chessel Crescent, Southampton. In 1930 Gosling went to Germany as a member of Harry Roy's dance band. When this tour came to an end Gosling stayed in Germany and played in various dance bands in Berlin, Munich, Hamburg etc. In April 1940 Gosling obtained a job at Southampton Docks with Messrs Risdon Beazley Ltd. He has been reported on several occasions for making Pro-Nazi comments. Gosling was also observed to be very inquisitive and tried to examine the inside of any vehicle, tank etc which was being handled at the docks. In May 1940 information reached the Home Office that Gosling was broadcasting information about the sailing and loading of military stores and equipment, particularly at the Sportsdrome, Southampton where he played in the band in the evenings. He was cautioned about this by a police officer in July 1940. Since he was given this warning Gosling appears to have been more discreet.

Gottlieb, Louis Karl aka Wust aka Charles West (born 1908) 28, Plummers Lane, Haynes, Bedford. District Leader Silvertown BUF.

This man was born in England of a German father and is a butcher by trade. He is at present employed as a lorry driver by a firm of contractors on an aerodrome site at Thurleigh. In April 1939 Wust joined the West

Ham (Upton) Branch of the BUF. On 1 March 1940 he transferred to the Silvertown Branch and on 6 March 1940 became District leader there.

Wust was detained under 18B on 1 June 1940. He duly appeared before the Advisory Committee who in view of the hardship Wust's wife had suffered through air raids and the loss of their home, they recommended Wust should be released.

Shorly after his release a report was received from his former internment camp which stated Wust was more pro-Nazi than genuinely British Union. On 28 October 1942 Wust registered as a Conscientious Objector and appeared before a tribunal where he gave his reason that he refused to take arms against his own flesh and blood.

Graves, George Woodley, 3, Coniston Drive, Tilehurst, Reading, Berkshire. Served in British Army during the First World War, subsequently married a German national. Employee at the Pulsometer Engineering Works. Reported for his pro-Nazi views and raised concerns when he made enquiries about where items made in his works were being sent.

Gray, John, 5 Altar Cottages, Crowhurst, East Sussex. Reported for making pro-Nazi statements.

Greene, Benjamin (48) Hall Cottage, Swingate Lane, Berkhamsted, Hertfordshire.
This man, whose mother was German prior to her marriage, is the eldest of five children. His sister is employed at the German Foreign Office in Berlin and is stated to be desirous of becoming a naturalised German.

In 1934 he was secretary of the Hemel Hempstead Labour Party and in 1935, when he was Deputy Chief Retaining Officer in connection with the Saar plebiscite, was prospective Labour candidate for Gravesend; he was not elected. It is thought that Greene's conversion to Nazism may have taken place during 1935. At the end of September 1938, at the time of the Munich Agreement, Greene appeared as a member of the Society of Friends and signed a joint peace manifesto issued by the Peace Pledge Union, Society of Friends, No More War Movements etc.

In January 1939 he was in touch with Herr Bohle of Berlin, a relation of the notorious head of the Nazi *Auslands-Organisation*; he informed Bohle that he was starting a Peace & Progress Information Bureau whose monthly bulletins were pure Nazi propaganda and offered to send him any information which he might require. By August 1939 there is evidence to show that Greene and Bohle were on friendly terms.

In September 1939 the business of which he is managing director, Messrs Kepson Ltd, was reported to be in a state of bankruptcy. It was at this time also that Greene became associated with John Beckett in the British Peoples Party in which he took the post of treasurer; this association continued in the British Council of Christian Settlement. Shortly after the outbreak of war Greene made a violently pro-Nazi speech.

In October 1939 the Hertford County Council took steps to have Greene's appointment as JP terminated on account of his pro-German sympathies; in November 1940 his name was removed by order of the Lord Chancellor.

From February until May 1940 Greene addressed meetings on behalf of the British People's Party and the British Council for Christian Settlement in Europe and actively worked on behalf of them. At one meeting he said that there was a state of peace in war which could continue only so long as Great Britain did not bomb civilians in Germany, as Hitler has given his word not to be the first to bomb civilians and there was no doubt that he would keep it.

On 24 May 1940 Greene was arrested and interned under DR 18B. He duly appealed before the Advisory Committee to whom he protested that if released he would do nothing to impede the war effort; he nevertheless refused to give any pledge that he would not devote himself to agitation against DR 18B.

It is not without interest in view of his membership of the Society of Friends and his signature on the above mentioned joint Peace Manifesto in September 1938 that when questioned by the Committee about the Peace Pledge Union, he described it as 'too negative'. On 8 January 1942, he was conditionally released. In view of this information, it is felt that he would undoubtedly assist the enemy in the event of an emergency; it is therefore recommended that he should be arrested if an emergency occurs.

Grosfils, Robert, (Belgian subject, born 20 January 1889) Rowanhurst, Hook, Hampshire. Formerly employed in the Belgian Consular Service, came to Britain in May 1940 as a refugee. Reported for being outspoken against Britain and sympathetic to Nazi ideology in conversation and correspondence.

Guest, Dr Harold Edward, (Austrian) 53, Lancaster Road, Basingstoke, Hampshire. In charge of the office of Messrs Cunningham and Gibaud, Surveyors and Assessors to Insurance Companies, 30, Portland Street, Southampton. Until shortly before the outbreak of war Guest lived in Vienna where he was employed as an assessor. Defeatist outlook and admirer of the

Nazi system, no matter what the conversation in his view things were always very much better in Germany.

One member of staff told police Guest had said to her: 'if the Germans get here, they will show you how to do things…The British have no chance of winning the war.' Another member of staff was told by Guest: 'The Germans have some awful gadgets prepared; one of them is to shower things like beans down, and if they hit a human being they will burn right into the flesh and nothing will get them out except a surgeon's knife.'

Habla, Mrs Berta, (Born 1896 in Blaschen, Sudetenland) 65, Park Street, Thame, Oxfordshire. Resident in England with her husband Rudolf since 1932 the Hablas were personal friends of Arthur Geyer. When Geyer went to Germany in March 1939 in order to take up an important post under the Reich Government as a ceramic expert the Hablas took over his house in Chippenham, Wiltshire. A number of aliens visited the Hablas at Chippenham and Rudolf Habla told the licensee of the Five Alls, Chippenham, that he had four German government officials to visit him on 18 April 1939.

In August 1939 it was known to MI5 that both Rudolf and Berta Habla were members of the NSDAP, and that Rudolf Habla was an active member. During this month Arthur Geyer flew over to England, stayed a fortnight with the Hablas and then returned to Germany. At the outbreak of war the Hablas' eldest son was in the German Army and the second son Rudolf Walter Werner Habla was about to go to Germany to enter a flying school. In the end he remained in this country with his parents. The Hablas were interned on 13 September 1939. Berta Habla was released in December 1939.

Hall, Olaf Lancelot Bjornson, Cressbed Cottage, Childrey, Wantage, Berkshire. British (mother Norwegian). BUF supporter who came to the notice of local police on a number of occasions as an active Fascist propagandist with pro-Nazi sympathies. Resided in Germany from August to November 1938 and from January to March 1939.

Hall, Richard Arthur (20) 7, Oxford Road, Bournemouth, Dorest. Team Leader, Herne Bay BUF, carried on clandestine meetings of his BUF group until his internment in 1940. On release in 1941 he obtained employment in a dance band.

Hallam, Frank, 9, Buckingham Road, Parkstone, Dorset. Engaged on Defence Works at Gosport. A convicted criminal with a number of convictions for larceny, shop and garage breaking. Described himself as 'anti-

British' and even 'what the newspapers term one of Hitler's Fifth Column'. The committee report concluded: 'Hallam is a lazy, unscrupulous individual whom, it is felt would be prepared to consort with the enemy in the event of an invasion.'

Hammond, Charles Hugh, Brimley Cottage, Stoke Abbot, Beaminster, Dorset. National Inspector BUF and BUF prospective Parliamentary candidate for Norwich.

Hammond, Yvonne Madeleine, Brimley Cottage, Stoke Abbot, Beaminster, Dorset. Reported for making pro-Nazi statements.

Hardingham, Harry, (born 1892) Gull Drove Crossing, Guyhirn, Cambridgeshire.

Hardingham has been employed by the LNER since 1913. Up to August 1940 he was a dock-gatesman at the Swing Bridge at Lowestoft. Shortly after the outbreak of war Hardingham came to the notice of the police through his pacifist and defeatist views which he was in the habit of expressing freely.

So far as it is known Hardingham was never a member of the BUF but he used to take *Action* the BUF newspaper up to May 1940, together with other literature circulated by the BUF. Although he did not indulge in active propaganda, he used to leave this literature lying about for his fellow workers to read.

He has always been anxious to dissociate himself as much as possible from the present war as shown by the fact that he at first refused to accept his gas mask. When the danger of incendiary bomb attacks were mentioned, Hardingham was heard to say that he would not lift a finger to extinguish a fire caused by enemy action. He also supported his son when he registered as a Conscientious Objector.

In February 1943 when completing Form ED.42 in respect of enrolment in the Home Guard, Hardingham said that he refused to serve and gave his reason as 'I am 100 per cent hostile to this war, I absolutely refuse to bear arms against the German Nation, especially my counterpart, that is transport workers.' As a result of this statement Hardingham was interviewed by the police. When asked whether he would resist the enemy if this country were invaded by Germany, he said that he definitely would not.

At interview Hardingham created the impression that he was sympathetic towards Germany as she had only done what she was entitled to do in the face of British aggression. It is feared that Hardingham may welcome a German invasion as an opportunity for overthrowing the British government.

Harper, Denis Malcolm George, (24) 'Venesia', Victoria Grove, East Cowes. Applied to join the BUF in 1934. In 1937 he spent a holiday in Germany, visiting Berlin and Leipzig. On 3 June 1940 when enemy aircraft were in the neighbourhood of Cowes, Harper was seen to flash a torch from an upper window at his home. Later that same night he was discovered inside the barbed wire fence surrounding the Kingston Electric Light Works, East Cowes. When challenged by soldiers guarding the place Harper ran away and dived into some bushes where he was caught. When asked what he was doing, he would only say that it was a mistake. Later, when Harper's room was searched at his home, a Nazi pennant bearing a swastika was found which he apparently brought back from Germany in 1937.

As a result of these events Harper was convicted at Ryde County Petty Sessions on 4 June 1940 of an offence against Defence Regulations and sentenced to three months imprisonment with hard labour. Since Harper's release from prison it has been reported to the police that he has been trying to obtain information as to the disposition of troops in the Isle of Wight. Although Harper appears to be mentally abnormal, the Chief Constable of the Isle of Wight is strongly of the opinion that Harper's anti-war opinions, lack of patriotism and complete irresponsibility is likely to lead him to assist the enemy if given the opportunity.

Harris, Sidney (alias Compton, Piers), Merlindale, Beaumont Rise, Marlow, Buckinghamshire removed to 'The Shieling', Milnthorpe Road, Kendal.

Born at Hammersmith 12 July 1901 Harris is an author, writing under the name of Piers Compton. His writings have been mainly in connection with religious history. He is now employed at the Standard Motor Works, Kendal.

This man first came to notice in December 1939 when he was interviewed at the War Office at his own request in order 'to clear his own character and offer his services to Military Intelligence'. He said he was a convinced anti-Communist and inclined to Italian Fascist ideals. He said that three years previously he had joined the South Bucks Conservative Society and started an anti-Communist propaganda centre. He attended a dinner of the Anglo-German Fellowship where he met von Ribbentrop and later von Dirksen [Herbert von Dirksen was a Nazi diplomat based at the German Embassy in London]. He saw a lot of Dirksen and was later passed on to Schacht's secretary, then to Dr Rosel and Fritz Randolf, the German Press attaché. Finally Harris was introduced to Captain George Pitt-Rivers who, he said, made it obvious that he was wanted for Nazi propaganda.

In November 1940 Special Branch reported that they had received information from Mrs Cathryn Young that Harris had Fascist views, never lost an opportunity of abusing Jews and Freemasons and was eloquent in his praise for Germany and Italy. Special Branch have also stated that during the Civil War in Spain Harris obtained a post for a catholic newspaper. His articles, however, were so violently pro-Fascist that they were unsuitable for publication in this country and it became necessary for the newspaper to terminate his contract.

[Author's note: Captain George Henry Lane-Fox Pitt-Rivers had been known to the Security Service since 1930 as a strong Fascist and associate of those who had similar views.[10]]

In September 1940 it was reported that Harris had claimed to have been a member of the Communist Party, of the British Union and of other organisations engaged in political propaganda before and since the outbreak of the war. Harris was heard to express satisfaction at the fall of France and held out threats of the fate in store for Great Britain should she fail to understand that she was ruled by a dictator and gangster in the pocket of international Freemasonry, Judaism and so forth. He said that no reliance could be placed upon the newspapers or official communiqués and that military damage greatly exceeded that admitted on our part. He was said to have previously stated the German-Italian case with conviction.

Hatten, Ernest John, 164, Kentwood Hill, Tilehurst, Reading. District Leader, Reading Branch BUF.

Heinertz-Gaate, Inga, (Born 1898) Bournemouth, Dorset (Swedish). Unreliable loyalty.

Henschker, Erhard, 'Tara', Compton Avenue, Parkstone, Dorset. Unreliable loyalty.

Henschker, Gertrud, 'Tara', Compton Avenue, Parkstone, Dorset. Unreliable loyalty.

Hetebrij, Gerard, (Born 1918 in Holland) Taplow Hill House, Taplow, Buckinghamshire.
    A Dutch subject serving in the Dutch Army. Arrived in Britain at the time of the German occupation of the Netherlands. In August 1940 Heterbrij was discharged from the army following a request by the Netherland Legation on the grounds of 'political unreliability', and was interned.

Shortly after his release in March 1941 a report was received from the Intelligence Officer at the camp at York where Hetebrij had been interned, stating that Hetebrij had consistently been a source of trouble in the camp where he actively associated with the Dutch National Socialist elements.

In July 1942 Hetebrij was convalescing from a throat operation at Little Wyreley Auxiliary Hospital, Pelsall, Staffordshire. During this time he came to notice on account of his pro-German statements and actions. On one occasion he gave the Nazi salute to one of the sisters in the hospital and said 'That is my salute'. When told he would get locked up for making such statements he replied 'I don't care, our gang will get me out when they come over.'

On 3 February 1943 Hetebrij obtained employment as a nursing orderly at the Dutch Sailors Home, Taplow Hill House, Taplow in Buckinghamshire

Hickman, Mrs Annie Josephine, (39) 23, Norfolk Road, Upminster, Essex (German born). Mrs Hickman, who was born in Cologne was reported for defeatist, anti-British talk in June 1940. Police investigation found her intensely pro-German; she had a framed photograph of Hitler who she holds in high esteem on display in her home and she took every opportunity to praise Hitler and his regime.

The expression of her views angered a number of women in the neighbourhood so much that information was received by the police that if Mrs Hickman was allowed to continue in her present strain they would take the law into their own hands. Mrs Hickman was interned in July 1940.

Hickman, Harold, (41) 23 Norfolk Road, Upminster, Essex

This man is of Welsh extraction, married to a Annie Josephine Hickman who is German by birth. He first aroused suspicion of the authorities when in August 1939 he was found to be a member of 'The Link' and had visited Germany shortly before the outbreak of war.

In May 1940 two independent reports were received from his place of employment, the Tithe Redemption Commission, where he was a temporary clerk, stating that Hickman appeared to be violently anti-British and to have strong pro-Nazi views; indeed so strong were some of his expressions that one informant added that they were causing dissension among the staff which would probably involve his dismissal.

At the end of 1940, yet another source reported that while holding a class at the Drury Falls School, Hornchurch, where he is employed as a language teacher, he refused to listen to the King's broadcast. The report added that Hickman is frequently trying to influence his pupils with his pro-German views, particularly those who are shortly due to be called up for service in HM Forces.

This report was further investigated and two pupils gave statements. One said: 'He stated that we (the Allies) were practically defeated in the war and that we could not hope for victory now. Our proper and most honourable course would not be to surrender as the Germans did in 1918. Our towns would be desolated if we did not surrender and he hoped that the war would be concluded in the Germans' favour by 1 July of this year as Hitler had promised. He said that Hitler is not too bad and their peace terms would not be so severe as those imposed by the Versailles Treaty at the end of the last war. The other added that Hickman had frequently attempted to persuade him to join 'The Link'. He was interned in June 1940 and was released subject to restrictions on 1 January 1941.

Hickman, Jack, 'Maywyn', West End Street, High Wycombe, Buckinghamshire. Language teacher at Drury Falls School, Hornchurch. Assistant District Leader BUF and member of 'The Link'.

Hignett, Cecil, (50) Three Gables, Letchworth, Hertfordshire.
Hignett became a member of the BUF in 1936 and was soon taking an active role. He also became a member of the British People's Party. He formed a friendship with Meyrick Boot, an ardent Fascist. He was also an associate of John Beckett and frequently attended Fascist meetings in London.

In 1937 he visited Germany combining business with pleasure and was greatly impressed by what he saw. Since June 1940 various reports from reliable sources have been received which allege that this man has given tongue to Fascist propaganda. Concern was also expressed over him engaged on various designs connected with aerodromes and Government factories in this region.

Hignett, Joan (22) Three Gables, Letchworth, Hertfordshire. BUF member. Miss Hignett lives with her father Cecil, she is also a member of the BUF but she claimed both she and her father resigned in June 1940. She has been and still is under the influence of her father, and so far as can be discovered, holds opinions identical with his. According to reliable informants, she was just as interested in Fascism as her father and almost surpassed him in knowledge of the movement; together they intensely hated the Jews and would prefer German methods introduced to this country.

Hill, Rudolph Heinrich, (Born 1904 in Germany) 'Ri-Ston', Appleton, Berkshire (born in Germany 1904). Representative of German nursery gardeners. His father, mother, brother and two sisters are still in Germany. He visited Germany in 1938 for ten days. Reported for his pro-Nazi views and concerns were expressed that he was living within four miles of Abingdon aerodrome, three miles from Harwell Aerodrome, three miles from Didcot Royal Army Ordnance Depot. In June 1940 the Metropolitan Police reported a reliable informant had stated that Hill was pro-Nazi in his views and would come out into the open as a member of Hitler's Fifth Column when the opportunity presented itself.

Hoare, Mrs Dorothy Lina, née Thurn, (Born German in 1891) Red Lion Inn, Lambourn, Berkshire. Reported for making Pro-Nazi and anti-Semitic statements.

Hoch, Matthias Julius Somerville, Little Hedges, Charmouth, Dorset. Unreliable loyalty.

Hogg, Dora, (40) Woodhouse Farm, Wormingford, Essex. This woman is the wife of Kenneth Hogg, whose name is also included in the suspect list. Prior to the outbreak of war she was in communication with Rolf Hoffmann of the Nazi Press Bureau in Hamburg and received bulletins from him. She has apparently always held pro-Nazi views similar to those of her husband and is reported still to do so. In all circumstances it is felt that she too should be arrested in the event of an emergency.

Hogg, Kenneth, Woodhouse Farm, Wormingford, Essex. Reported for making anti-British and pro-Nazi statements.

Hoggarth, George Fredrick, (30), Clint Farm, Eye, Suffolk. This man has been an active member of the BUF and was Treasurer for the Eye Division. At the end of August 1939 he was concerned with Ronald Creasy the District Leader in an incident when Creasy was roughly handled by the crowd as a result of distributing Fascist propaganda. Hoggarth was also suspected, although he was never caught, of accompanying Creasy on motor car expeditions for the purpose of chalking and painting Fascist signs and slogans on walls, roads and bridges.

As a result of these activities he was ordered to resign as a Special Constable. In May 1940 the Army authorities reported that there were indications that Hoggarth's activities were not confined to the normal working of the party such as selling *Action* and distributing political propaganda. He was released but subject to restrictions on 21 August 1940.

Hone, John Harold Mitford, (46) 27 Layton Avenue, Mansfield, Nottinghamshire. Former Assistant Director General of Organisation for the Northern Zone BUF. Hone first came to notice in 1934 when he was reported by the Dumfries police to be the BUF Organiser for Dumfries. At that time he was employed at Messrs Callenders Cable Construction Co at Dumfries. Other reports during that year showed that he was taking a very active part in BU activities, attending meetings addressed by Mosley and organising marches, meetings, social functions etc. In September 1934 Hone attended a Hyde Park Rally of Blackshirts. He left Callenders in 1935 for a paid administrative post at the British Union as National Inspector in charge of North-East England. By March 1936 he held the office of Assistant Director General of Organisation for the Northern Zone. Claiming to have had several differences of opinion with BU officials he left BUF HQ in 1937 and started work under the Ministry of Transport.

At the outbreak of war Hone was employed by the Ministry of Transport as a resident engineer at Hunsdon aerodrome in Hertfordshire. On 31 May 1940 Special Branch, New Scotland Yard, received reliable information that about two weeks previously Hone had been seen in Hundon wearing BU uniform.

The Rector of Hundon's sister reported that during his visits to the rectory Hone had expressed strong pro-Nazi views and had spoken so convincingly that he had almost converted the Rector to Fascism.

Hone was detained under DR 18B in June 1940. Evidence given before the Advisory Committee by the Rector of Hundon that Hone had been very incautious in his remarks. Other statements were made that Hone was highly spoken of by his employers and those who knew him. His release was recommended on the grounds that he would be of value to the war effort if he were sent to a different part of the country. On 14 January 1941 MI5 objected to Hone's release because there had been evidence which had not been produced before the committee. In the opinion of MI5, Hone was a calculating individual who would have no hesitation in going over to the enemy if he thought he would profit by such a move.

Hook, Mrs Phyllis Vavasour, (née Durell) (55) Broad Green, Fort Road, Guildford removed to The Old Vicarage, West Wickham, Cambridgeshire removed to Long Meadow, Riseley, Berkshire. Women's District Leader, Guildford Branch BUF.

Mrs Hook was in touch with Rolf Hoffmann of the Nazi Propaganda Bureau, who sent her the book *Hitler's Germany* and a photo of Hitler which she stated 'now has a place of honour on my mantelpiece'. She also stated that she was visiting Munich in May 1939. In November 1939 she was also in communication with George Hanson, a known Fascist sympathiser, then living in Copenhagen.

For a long time before the outbreak of war she had attracted adverse attention in Guildford. Fascist leaflets distributed in the town bore her name and address. She was also connected with the chalking up of Fascist symbols in the neighbourhood. Although she was never caught red handed she wrote in a letter to Hanson: 'The blackout has one advantage. The painters and decorators can get busy. Parts of London are a wonderful sight. The whole of Downing Street was done one night, I can't think how as it is very closely guarded.' As the graffiti only ceased to appear in Guildford after she had been detained, there is little doubt that she was responsible for organising this sort of propaganda. Witnesses also reported their concerns over the pro-Nazi views she expressed. A reliable informant describes her as a cunning woman who knows when to hold her tongue and is of the opinion that she might assist the enemy in the event of invasion.

Horsfield, James William, (55) Managing Director, The Ambassadors Theatre, West Street WC removed to The White House, High Street, Great Missenden, Buckinghamshire. Keen Member of BUF and 'The Link'. Nazi sympathiser. Horsfield did not speak on behalf of the BU on public platforms, but there is reason to think that his role was to spread BU propaganda among influential people whom he met in the course of his business, and to gain the support of powerful interests in the movement.

Howard, Mrs Anna née Koch, 48, Shaftesbury Road, Southsea. Born in Germany, British by marriage, believed to have five near male relations serving in the German army. Reported for Pro-Nazi and anti-British comments. Despite Mrs Howard being cautioned by the police, she continued to voice her Nazi sympathies and was detained under DR 18B in July 1940.

Howard, Wilfred Edmund, (34) originally 2, Great Eastern Avenue, Southend on Sea removed to 49, Horton View, Banbury, Oxfordshire.

Son of an English father and German mother. After his father left the family home his mother took Howard and his brother to Germany. Between 1922–1932 he was employed in Germany teaching and translating English. Between 1932 and 1935 he was a member of the German Austrian Alpine

Club which he states was non-political. In June 1940 the Chief Constable of Southend on Sea received three reports from different informants stating that this man and his family were pro-Nazi.

Police carried out a house search of the family home for evidence of pro-Nazi support but drew a blank, however, certain letters came to light that had been sent by Howard to his brother in Canada which reveal Howard to be pro German. At the beginning of March 1944 the Home Secretary made an order against Howard under DR 18B restricting him from being in an Aliens Protected Area. As a result Howard had to leave Southend and took up residence in Banbury in April 1944.

Hudson, Margarete aka Lutz, (28) Flat 1, Princes Avenue. Liverpool, removed to 1, Cherry Garden, Upper Bridge Lane, Chelmsford.

Born in Berlin in 1914 of German parents, after leaving school worked as a private secretary to Professor Hans Barthel, a tuberculosis specialist in Cologne. In the course of this employment she met Hitler on a number of

Aerial view of Liverpool one of Britain's great international ports and a recruiting ground for an ardent Nazi attaché to recruit agents c1939.

occasions. In 1935 while still in this employment, she first met her present husband who was in Cologne on holiday. In July 1936 she married Victor Ernest Dines Hudson in Manchester.

For some time prior to the outbreak of war she was a frequent visitor to the German consulate in Liverpool and associated with the notorious Nazi Consul Herr Walter Reinhardt who was withdrawn in 1939 at the request of the British Government after his consulate was implicated in the recruitment of agents for the Nazi intelligence service in Britain. Mrs Hudson often attended meetings at this consulate and was an apparently enthusiastic member of the *Arbeitsfront*. In view of these activities she was strongly suspected by Liverpool Police of being a German agent.

The 1939 Register shows Victor and Margarete Hudson were living at Flat 1, Princes Avenue, Victor as newspaper reporter, Margarete as a housewife. Neighbours at Flat 2 was Jack Benson a motor engineer and Captain in the RASC when on duty, and at Flat 6 was Agnes Reeve a postal censorship worker and her husband Wilfred who was working as a visiting officer for the Air Ministry.

On 27 August 1939 about a week prior to the war, without notifying the authorities or her friends, Margarete left this country for France. On her return she applied for employment in the Censor's office but was refused. In May 1940 she attracted the attention of the Essex police by frequenting public houses and associating with army officers. On her return to Liverpool in June 1940 she and her husband took rooms with an Italian who is regarded with suspicion on account of his anti-British views. While at this address she frequently associated with members of HM Forces at the most expensive hotels in Liverpool, although in the opinion of the police she could not afford to do so on her husband's income. During the course of these parties she is alleged to have been the worse for drink. On these occasions and when she was sober she vehemently upheld the policy of Hitler, exclaiming excitedly what would happen if the Germans were victorious as she believed they would be.

As a result of these associations she had frequent quarrels with her husband and just prior to her interment on 20 July 1940 they separated. Margarete was released from internment on 16 January 1941 and was rapidly added to the Suspect List.

Margarete Hudson died in Chelmsford in 1989 aged 74. Both the police and MI5 strongly suspected her to be working as a Nazi agent.

[Author's Note: The Home Office file on Margarete Hudson in The National Archives covering the years 1935 to 1943 exists but access is closed for 100 years. A request to access her file under freedom of information in 2017 was turned down and its contents remain closed to public eyes until 2044.]

Hunt, Hubert Aubrey Charles, (28)11, Elm Way, Rickmansworth, Hertfordshire. This man, a chauffeur-mechanic by trade, joined the BUF in 1934, having previously been a member of the ILP. At that time living at Dulwich and became the District Treasurer of the Dulwich branch. He left the BU in 1937 as a result of a dispute he had with Captain Hick of National HQ. Hunt was a great friend of William Joyce and a member of the National Socialist League and his quarrel with Hick was due to his championship of Joyce's cause against the main body of the BU.

In July 1939 he was fined £3 for possession of a firearm without a licence. In the course of enquiries his premises were searched and a black tunic, black shirt, pair of black high boots, black belt, three black German pattern uniform caps and four red armlets with flash or swastika designs were found. In July 1940 whilst living with Harry (aka Heinz) MacWilliams, with whom he had been closely associated for four or five years, he was detained. Both men are reported to have been imbued with Nazi doctrines and to have held Nazi views.

When Hunt made his first appearance before the Advisory Committee they came to the conclusion that he was still a keen National Socialist and recommended his continued detention. His case was reviewed in March 1942 and was reheard in June 1943. The Committee came to the conclusion that Hunt was a hedonist, desirous only of consulting his own comfort, pleasure and safety, who preferred the safe surroundings of the Isle of Man to doing his bit either in the Army or in outside work. Accordingly, they recommended his release. Hunt was released subject to regulation on 26 July 1942. He will not be accepted for service in any of the forces.

Huttl, Wilhelm Joseph, 37, Hillview Road, High Wycombe, British born of Sudeten German parents. Unreliable loyalty.

Jelfs, Charles John Chapman, (born 1890) and **Jelfs, Mrs. Harriet 'Peggy'** (born 1892). Lahana, Penyrheol Drive, Llanelly, Wales, later removed to 14, Spittal Street, Marlow, Buckinghamshire.

Mr Jelfs was a chemist and herbalist with a shop in Town Hall Square, Llanelly. His wife, Harriet is a member of the BUF. Prior to the war she always wore a swastika brooch. She has taken German lessons and about three years ago arranged a meeting with a few local women in an endeavour to start a Women's Branch of the BUF in Llanelly. Meeting was not a success. She and the speaker, a woman from London, were both dressed in Fascist uniform, and a swastika and photograph of Hitler were prominently displayed in the room. She expressed herself on numerous occasions as a very strong admirer of Hitler. She is stated to have been to Germany for a Nazi Party rally.

Jessop, Frank Piggott, (43) 51, Molewood Road, Hertford.
This man has a wife whose name is also included on this list and two children. At present he is employed as an electrician. In March 1934 he joined the BUF and in 1935 became a national organiser. This entailed him travelling about the country, inspecting various branches and opening up new ones etc. He resigned from this appointment in 1937 but continued to be a member of the BU. After a short period of unemployment he became a salesman for Hoover with whom he remained until the outbreak of war when he joined the army.

In July 1939 he wrote a letter to Rolf Hoffmann of the Nazi Press Bureau asking for a voucher copy of *News of Germany* and enquired where further copies could be obtained. He then asked if he would be allowed to go to Germany to live and take up German naturalisation because, he said 'England is becoming the home of the Jews.'

Jessop was detained on 19 June 1940, he had attained the rank of corporal and was at the time of his arrest about to go on a course leading to future promotion. Jessop appeared before the Advisory Committee in November 1941. When confronted with his letter to Hoffmann, he said he hated his job with Hoover and had become embittered by meeting German Jews who appeared much better off than he was, despite their stories of poverty. Jessop was released subject to regulations on 8 February 1942.

Jessop, Mrs. Margaret Emily, (35) 51, Molewood Road, Hertford.
This woman is the wife of Frank Piggott Jessop whose name is also on the Suspect List. During her husband's detention she wrote letters to him in which she expressed the view that she had lost all loyalty and respect for England and stated that she knew more about the BU, and she would do her best to soap box. In view of these expressions and of her bitter resentment of her husband's previous detention, it is felt that if an emergency occurs and he is again interned, she may prove herself of doubtful loyalty.

Johannesen, Maurice Richard, Leader of Cobham Branch BUF and his wife **Mrs Caroline Mary Johannesen** (born Caroline Mary Winchester in 1893) Surrey, removed to Coads Green, Launceston, Cornwall removed to Brimley Coombe Cottage, Stoke Abbot, Beaminster, Dorset.

Mr Johannesen was born in Aberdeen in 1887, his father being Norwegian and his mother Scottish. His wife was born to British parents in 1917. In 1934 Mr Johannesen and his wife both joined the BU and during the next five years they were very active on behalf of the movement. In one of the official BU lists Mrs Johannesen is described as District Leader. During this time the Johannesens, who were living at Cobham, Surrey, paid several visits to Germany and were treated deferentially by certain Germans with whom they came in contact. It is not known whether these visits were on behalf of the BU and whether this was the reason for the deference paid to them.

After the outbreak of war the Johannesens continued to take *Action* [the newspaper of the BUF] and attended both the big BU meetings at the Stoll Picture House, London, in November 1939 and also one of the Criterion lunches at which Mosley spoke in the spring of 1940. As a result the Johannesens were detained under DR 18B(1A) and when their premises were searched by Surrey police, photographs of Hitler and Mosley and two BU armbands were found.

The Johannesens appealed to the Advisory Committee and strongly protested their loyalty and support for the war effort: they attempted to minimise their connection with the BU after the outbreak of war. Mrs Johannesen, however, admitted to the Committee that she considered that Germany was too strong for us and we could never beat them. In due course the Johannesens were released from detention by order of the Home Secretary.

In April 1941 it was learnt that the Johannesens were living at Coads Green, Launceston, Cornwall and were associating with Dr Claude Gouldesbrough and his wife, who also lived there. Dr Gouldesbrough was formerly a BU District Leader in North London and was suspected of being in Mosley's confidence and of knowing where some of the BU funds had been hidden. He and his wife are bitterly anti-Semitic and he retains his Fascist beliefs.

At this time Mr Johannesen had obtained employment with the Ministry of Supply on forestry work. In May 1941 the Johannesens moved to Hawkchurch, near Axminster, Devon and moved again in November 1941 to Stoke Abbott, Beaminster.

In April 1942 Mrs Johannesen wrote a letter to the Gouldesbroughs which included an intriguing account of an enemy raid on the south coast:

> We were talking to a couple of soldiers in a pub one night and what they had to say was really dangerous. One was stationed in Dover and <u>swore</u> that the German commandos attacked Dover and captured the Barracks taking all prisoners – only four killed – he even gave the date 21 January. But of course one has to take everything with a grain of salt and we certainly

did not hear of it in the German broadcast. This man said he kept a pair of rubber shoes at his bedside ready to run like hell when things happened. When the manoeuvres were on the other weekend the looting was a despair. The marines were attacking round Hawkchurch and they broke into pubs and houses and drank and ate everything they could lay hands on.

Further letters show the Johannesens express deeply anti-Semitic views, were defeatist and remained pro-Nazi.

Johnson, Ms Selma, (29) 154, Waverley Road, Reading, Berkshire. Examiner, Royal Ordnance Factory, Theale, Buckinghamshire. Reported for her Pro-Nazi comments, Johnson was interrogated by an officer of MI5 in September 1941. She admitted that she hated Jews. She was sentenced to two months for spreading disaffection in October 1941

Jones, Mrs Karolin (née Voight), (Born 1910 in Germany) 60, Archery Grove, Woolston, Southampton. Housekeeper. Reported for her pro German sympathies that intensified after internment of her sister Gertrud Voight who was living with them.

Jones, Peter Richard Norman, (17) 60, Archery Grove, Woolston, Southampton. Mother German by birth. In 1925 Peter and his sister Sheila were taken from England to family in Germany where Peter became associated with the Hitler Youth. Returned to England 1935. Peter Jones visited Germany again in 1937. After the outbreak of war the Jones family continued to correspond with friends and relations in Germany via Holland. On 7 June 1940 a torch flash was spotted from a window in the Jones' house during an air raid at night. The police entered the house. In course of conversation Sheila Jones told police, 'Take no notice of my brother; he is a foolish boy.' It was also reported Peter's girlfriend had mentioned to the wife of a local policeman that Peter 'frequently declared that in the event of a German landing he would assist the enemy'.

Jones, Sheila Maria, (19) (German by birth) 60, Archery Grove, Woolston, Southampton. Housekeeper. Reported for making anti-British statements.

Jorgensen, Karl Viktor Emil, 3, Hostel Coppice, Mead, Stotfold, Hitchin, Hertfordshire. This alien was granted permission to land at Weymouth on 4 July 1940, on condition that he registered with the police and reported to the Danish Consul at Newcastle on Tyne and should not take any further employment at sea without permission from the Ministry of Labour – all of which he failed to do.

From 4 August to February 1942 Jorgensen followed various occupations without attracting attention to himself until February 1943 when the Clerk of Works to the Garrison Engineer at Drill Hall, Chepstow, gave a signed statement to a detective constable of the Monmouthshire Constabulary, which was corroborated by another man present at the time, regarding anti-British remarks made by Jorgensen, who is alleged to have said: 'If a fleet of planes came over and bombed your dirty little country and they left a little bit of it, leave it to me and I would see that there was nothing left of your dirty little country.'

On 13 August 1945, the foreman in charge of the timber cutters employed at the Ministry of Supply in Wickwar, Gloucestershire reported to the police that Jorgensen was causing trouble amongst the other employees making anti-British statements. Other similar reports would be made as he went from job to job. It is felt that Jorgensen would be likely to assist the enemy in an emergency.

Keller, Ernst Bampton, (born 1915) 24, Dewsbury Road, Dollis Hill, London NW10, later removed to Manor Farm House, Dummer, Hampshire. District Leader Willesden Branch BUF, a role he energetically continued until he was interned in 1940. Even after time in and release from internment his views did not change. In December 1943 he left London for Dummer, Hants, where he obtained employment with BUF officer Captain Charles Bentinck Budd.

Kemsley, Ronald Arthur, (born 21/11/10) The Cottage, Station Farm, South Leigh, Oxfordshire. In July 1940 Kemsley was employed by the NAAFI at Shrivenham, Wiltshire and was reported by the military authorities as having expressed pro-Nazi sentiments.

In March 1941 Kemsley was arrested on a charge of larceny (for which he was found guilty and sentenced to four months). In his suitcase was found a stolen passport, a copy of *Mein Kampf*, a swastika, sheets of paper with German and Dutch writing on them which showed that Kemsley had been studying these languages, and a piece of paper which showed that Kemsley had been interesting himself in an elementary code.

Kemsley was interrogated by the police and an officer of MI5 during which he admitted he had made short visits to Belgium, Holland and Germany on several occasions between 1930 and 1935. He has friends in Germany, one Litner and Rudolf Wendt, corresponding with the latter with a view to teaching him English. He was a member of the *Deutsche Fichte Bund*, an association for promoting better understanding between Germany and England, but had ceased this association before the outbreak of war. The swastika had been given to him by a party of Hitler Youth whom he had met at Southend. The code, he claimed, came out of a book called '*The Black Chamber*' by Captain H.O. Yardley.

Throughout the interrogation Kemsley made little effort to disguise the fact that his interest and affection lay far more with Nazi Germany than with this country.

Kemp, Jean Antoine William, (38) 204, Lyndhurst Drive, Hornchurch, Essex. He is a manager of a shop at Hornchurch and is in the habit of preaching the Hitler doctrine to customers, so much so local women have become distressed by his remarks. Among those reported were: 'It will be a bloody good job when Hitler does get here, we won't have to work any harder than we have to now.' 'It's no use, we shall have the Germans up the Thames in no time.' 'They have got anti-tank trenches in Southend as well as barbed wire entanglements inside the river, but that won't stop them.'

The suspect has relatives in Germany and has spent holidays there, the last occasion being 1938.

His father was interned during the last war and is now residing in the Peckham district, having become naturalised after the Great War. Local opinion is that the suspect would give every assistance to the enemy. He has not time for the present British Government and is in possession of a motor car.

Kier, Olaf, (41) (Danish) Keepers Corner, Wrentham, Norfolk.
This man who was born in Copenhagen on 4 September 1899 is a civil engineer and contractor by trade. On 1 June 1940 a reliable informant who has since confirmed his information, states that Kier had strong pro-German sympathies which he had expressed to him and added that in spite of them he was doing secret work for the Air Ministry in Lancashire.

On 28 June a further report was received that he was of pro-German sympathies. Enquiries revealed that he was much mistrusted by his fellow engineers and was alleged to have said when discussing Quisling: 'Hitler always looks after people who work for him,' and 'Denmark would be well off after the war as she did not oppose Germany' and that he intended to keep on the right side whichever way things went.

Kier was detained in June 1940. In view of representations made by various persons and not least his co-director who is serving in HM forces, on the grounds that Kier's firm were engaged on contracts of national importance, he was released in late August 1940. Enquiries were still continued, however, and information was received that he belonged to the circle in Denmark which was under the influence of Gunnar Larsen (the Danish Quisling).

In view of his association and his expressions of pro-German sympathies it is felt that he would, in the event of an emergency, be likely to assist the enemy not least through his knowledge of Secret Government contacts.

King, Charles Kenneth, (27) 66, Queens Road, Norwich, Norfolk. Assistant District Leader, Westminster (St George's) Branch BUF, he was detained under 18B on 20 July 1940. In June 1941 he was described in a detention camp report as very pro-German and pro-Axis and later as one likely to foment administrative trouble. After the September riot at Peel Camp, Isle of Man, King was transferred to Liverpool prison where he vigorously denied that he had played any part in the riot and complained that he had been victimised. As a result of a number of letters asking that his case should be reconsidered a further camp report was obtained which added that his associates were among the most violently anti-British and ended by saying: 'King has no sense of shame in expressing his miserably defeatist views. He may genuinely consider himself loyal, but he is that type of BU partisan whose narrow and bigoted views lead him to be a political conscious objector. Clearly "loyalty" of this description is of little use to this country.' In November 1943 it was eventually decided that King should be released subject to restrictions.

Kirkbright, Olga Agnes née Majewitz, born 1897 in Germany, married a British soldier in 1934. 11, Lewins Way, Chippenham, Slough. Since the outbreak of war she has come to the notice of police after she was reported for the pro-German tone of her conversation while employed at Weston's Biscuit Factory, Slough. She also failed to declare she had a brother serving in the Luftwaffe when she filled in Form DR 17.

Knight, Charles and Knight, Josephine, High View, Bury Road, Hemel Hempstead, Hertfordshire. Reported for making pro-Nazi statements.

Knowles, Dorothea Mary 'Dorie', (aka Knowles-Schulze) (17), St Leonards Avenue, Windsor, removed to 2, The Avenue, Datchet, Buckinghamshire.

Born in Berlin on 30 December 1921 the daughter of a British father and a German mother she was educated in Germany and had been living in

Britain in 1934 working as a secretary. Her family life had been marred by the arguments between her parents. Her mother, Dorothea would claim, 'hates England like poison' and instilled these feelings of hatred in her, a view her father and sibling did not share and she had become estranged from them.

During the autumn of 1939, Dorothea Knowles joined the Ealing Branch of the British Union of Fascists. She remained a member of the movement for a few weeks only, being asked to resign when it was discovered that she had German blood. At the Ealing branch of the BU she made the acquaintance of Frank Millbank, who gave information in October 1939 that Dorothea Knowles had asked him to help her in sending to Germany certain information concerning an explosive which she had gained while employed by a firm of chemical engineers. Although Millbank himself was not above suspicion (he was a member of 'The Link' as well as the BU), the information he supplied concerning Dorothea Knowles was confirmed by letters he had received form her which he was able to produce.

As a result of the information provided by Millbank, Dorothea Knowles' room was searched by Special Branch in December 1939. Among other things, the police found a collection of love letters written by Dorothea Knowles to a German, Kurt Schulze, in which she wrote of her love of Germany and her desire to serve the Fatherland. 'I am ready to sacrifice all for my country – my life in espionage, it doesn't matter at all, only I know that I serve the great sacred German country.' When questioned about these letters Dorothea Knowles explained that she was keeping a record of her daily thoughts and doings so that she could let Schulze read it when the war was over. She was detained under DR 18B on 19 December 1939.

While in detention Dorothea Knowles struck up a very warm friendship with Gladys Fortune, a British Fascist. She also became friendly with Mary Stanford, whose admiration for Germany and the Nazis is extreme. Dorothea Knowles' letters to these friends, and others, continued to be violently anti-British and pro-Nazi until the summer of 1942. During June of that year she wrote to the Home Office saying that her political views had undergone a radical change and asking for another hearing before the Advisory Committee. The Intelligence Officer at Camp W had an interview with Dorothea Knowles on the subject of her alleged change of heart. Knowles declared that she was sick to death of Germans now and completely disgusted by their behaviour and outlook. The childhood years she had spent in Germany had been very happy and the picture of Germany she had retained in her mind was that of a dream country and not the real one.

Since her detention she had come across many Nazis and her dream had been shattered. She was now anxious to do anything she could to help the British war effort. Knowles said that she had not heard from Kurt Schulze since the outbreak of war and did not care if she never heard from him again. The Intelligence Officer thought that her change of heart seemed genuine, although the District Superintendent of the part of the camp in which she lived said she was as unstable as a weather cock. It should be noted, however, that only a short while before her interview Knowles had written to her friend Mary Stanford saying that she was feeling better and that there was no possibility of her throwing in the sponge. She signed this letter '*mit deutschem Gruss*'. It should also be noted that in May 1942, she has been overheard to remark that it would be a good thing if England were invaded.

In September 1942 Knowles wrote to Kurt Schulze: 'If there are times when you feel as lonely as I do, do not forget even if the whole world stands between us that I think of you. Write to me if you can. It is a pity you did not write more often before. I have now five lines to tell you that which can be said in three words….if you do not hear from me for a long time do not worry. I can explain it all in due course later.'

Knowles' letters during 1943 did not refer to political matters. She continually stressed her unhappiness and her great desire to get away from the Isle of Man. On 13 June 1943 she wrote to Gladys Fortune telling her that she has made a petition for her release on the grounds that she annulled all claims to German nationality, that she promised not to take part in politics for the duration of the war, and that she could produce a guarantor for her personal conduct. Evidently she expected Gladys Fortune to blame her for having made such a petition, for she pleaded with Miss Fortune not to be cross, saying 'I know I shouldn't have, but it probably saved my reason.'

The Intelligence Officer at Camp W sent in a report on Dorothea Knowles early in July 1943, in which he described her as 'a most painful case of adolescence'. She had told him that she was sick to death of the war, fed up with the people she had to meet in the camp, and willing to do anything the Ministry of Labour might suggest in the event of her release.

In the middle of July 1943, Dorothea Knowles went on hunger strike, presumably in the hope of forcing the authorities to release her. She called the strike off after forty-eight hours, however.

Knowles sought an interview with the Intelligence Officer on 9 October 1943, in order to ask his advice as to whether it was any use her applying to join the WAAF. During this interview she mentioned that her friendship with Gladys Fortune has now been dissolved, largely because she could no longer share Gladys Fortune's Fascist views.

Knowles was interviewed again by the Camp Intelligence Officer in December 1943; she assured him very earnestly that she would never go to work for Claremont Haynes & Co and added that Windsor was the last place in the world where she would think of going. She said she would do any kind of work the Ministry of Labour might offer her if she were released and would be willing to join any of the services if the authorities permitted. She stressed the fact that she has changed her opinions over eighteen months before and had adhered to her conversion ever since.

Dorothea Knowles was released in March 1944 subject to an obligation to notify changes of address and to notify her movements monthly to the police. She is also subject to the usual restrictions on employment. On her release she went to stay with another ex-detainee named Erika Frey at 46 Leconfield Road, N.5. On 30 April she notified a change of address to Rushton, Sunnymeads, Wraysbury, which was the address of G.H.R. Tildesley of Claremont Haynes & Co. She told the Bucks police that she hoped to find employment in Windsor; the police formed the impression that Gladys Fortune was helping her in this matter. According to the Ministry of Labour Knowles is doing her best to evade a direction to work in a hospital in Huddersfield, urging her desire to work in a solicitor's office.

Knowles now calls herself Knowles-Schulze, although her father's name is Knowles. Her mother's maiden name was Schulze, as was her German ex-fiancé Kurt Schulze. This is proved by the fact that soon after being released she contacted Gladys Fortune an ex-detainee who is on the Regional Commissioner's Suspect List, and is now working with her in the firm of solicitors, Claremont Haynes & Co. of 51 High Street, Windsor. Knowles is doing her best to oppose the efforts of the Ministry of Labour to direct her to work in a hospital in Huddersfield.

In view of our knowledge of this young woman it is felt she would be a danger to the State in the event of invasion of this country by the enemy, and therefore it is the opinion of the Chief Constable of Windsor and MI5 that she should be arrested under DR 18B in the event of an invasion.

Knowles never appeared to have any genuine change of heart and Guy Liddell's description of Knowles, despite her youth, as *a sophisticated and confirmed liar*[11] in his diary in 1939 held just as true when the war ended.

Kookyer, Dr Leon, Guessens Court Hotel, Guessens Road, Welwyn Garden City, Herts. Unreliable loyalty.

Korkhaus, August Rudolf Herbert, 29, Hooke Road, East Horsley, Surrey, British by naturalisation, formerly German. Unreliable loyalty.

Korkhaus, Mrs Elizabeth Wilhelmina, British, formerly Russian, 29, Hooke Road, East Horsley, Surrey. Unreliable loyalty.

Kraaft, Mrs Matilda, (65), 'Nasova', Clifton Road, Parkstone, Dorset. (German) Mrs Kraaft is a naturalised British subject of German origin. Her activities have been investigated over a long period by MI5 and the police. The sources of information available are extremely delicate, but I have no hesitation in saying that this woman would be prepared to assist the enemy whenever the opportunity presented itself. She is known to have done so in the past and since the outbreak of war. Mrs Krafft is only at large at this time because it would be inadvisable to take any open action against her.

Mrs Diana Christine Madalene de Laessoe (née Stark), 1, Downside Crescent NW3 later Tasburgh House, Upper Tasburgh, Norfolk

She joined the BU only a short time before her arrest but was described by people who had attended BU meetings with her as being a fanatical Fascist. In the early part of 1940 she boasted that Hitler conveyed instructions to Mosley through a neutral country and that before long Hitler would be Dictator of England, with Mosley as Leader. Mrs de Lassoe was at first detained in Holloway Prison and a report from the Governor said that she had been difficult and antagonistic but she later became very co-operative but that she was disliked by most of her fellow detainees; her only friends being those whom she could dominate.

There seems no doubt that Mrs de Lassoe had a very strong sense of grievance and that her detention was in fact something of a hardship to a woman of her age…To show the unbalanced state of mind which she reached it is perhaps worth noting that when photographs of the detainees going to the Isle of Man were taken for passport purposes, she thought the photographs had been touched up to make all the detainees look like Jews, with thick lips.

As recently as June 1943 she told another visitor that the 1940 blitz was in the nature of reprisals and 'let it be understood that she considered Great Britain the aggressor in the present war.'

Mrs Laessoe made two appearances before the Home Office Advisory Committee and spent most of her hearing giving vent to her sense of grievance and injustice. She was released subject to restrictions.

Laessoe, Major Harold Henry Alexander de, (65) 1, Downside Crescent NW3 later Tasburgh House, Upper Tasburgh, Norfolk.

Born Danish but his father naturalised British in 1887. At the age of 17 Major de Laessoe volunteered and served in the Matabele Campaign of 1896 and 1897, afterwards he served in the Rhodesian Civil Service (1899–1909) at the same time filling the post of Native Commissioner and Magistrate and Manager of the Land Settlement Department. From 1909 to 1914 he was general manager of Rhodesian Estates of the Liebig Company which covered one and a quarter million acres. During the 1914 war he served in France and was awarded the DSO and MC. After the war he obtained employment with Messrs Bovril obtaining from them concessions in Angola amounting to a million acres. In 1923 he left their employment and settled in Angola.

He returned to UK in 1939 and quite by chance it seems joined the BU and should have risen to an important post in the organisation.

Prior to 1939 de Laessoe had not come to the notice of the authorities in a Fascist connection, no objection was raised to his accepting employment with Postal Censorship. This appointment caused him to move from London to Liverpool, where he immediately became prominent in the local BU Branch. On 11 December 1939 he spoke to a small private meeting and the speech which he made was described by one who was present as 'the most defeatist ever heard in the Branch'. He predicted, among other things, Britain and France would be left to fight a lone war, which they could not possibly win. He went on to say he believed the British Empire was disintegrating and if war proved to be a long drawn-out struggle a revolution would ensue and that this revolution would provide the opportunity for Mosley to come into power.

As a result of his Fascist activities de Laessoe was discharged from his employment. He returned to London and by April 1940 it was announced he was District Inspector for the Paddington, Westminster and Willesden districts. In addition to this appointment, he was placed temporarily in charge of Richmond and Kingston.

On 23 May 1940 de Laessoe and his German born wife who shared his opinion were arrested. Whilst in internment a report was compiled on him: 'de Laessoe is a man of a certain ability and education and has a great opinion of his own importance. He therefore considered that his arrest and the conditions of his detention were an appalling insult and injury to his dignity. He is not the type of person to have caused trouble in the detention camps or prisons, but he has been described as an exceptionally clever propagandist and an influential type.'

In April 1941 the report from Huyton Camp on de Laessoe noted he maintained his Fascist opinions: 'This man's views remain unchanged. He is a strong supporter of Mosley and all British Fascism stands for. He was against the war from the beginning and told me that there is not the slightest doubt of Germany's ultimate victory. Although he is quiet and unobtrusive in camp there is no doubt that he would disseminate his ideas amongst his fellows and being a man of some personality and position would strongly influence others of a weaker nature.'

In November of the same year a report on him stated he had 'the strongest and most unshakable BU convictions, in which he was perfectly sincere and outspoken'. In addition he was said to have proved himself to be a propagandist of the most insidious and forceful kind. In December 1942 he brought an action against the Home Secretary on the ground of wrongful imprisonment and breach of statutory duty. This action, in common with various other indications, shows he is extremely bitter over his internment.

On 18 November 1943 de Laessoe was released subject to restrictions which require him to report his address and any changes thereof to the police as well as making monthly reports. Since his release it has been confirmed from various sources that he still maintains his Fascist convictions and it is felt that his name should be added to the list of those persons to be arrested in the event of an emergency.

Lake, Mrs Annie, (57) 4, Barnard Road, Leigh-on-Sea, Essex removed to 'Holloways', Beaconsfield, Buckinghamshire.

She came to the notice of the Southend police in June 1940 on account of a number of reports alleging her to be a Fascist who was pro-Nazi and anti-British in sympathy; she was stated to be elated at British losses.

In July 1940 her house was searched and a number of letters were found; these ended TDT HM HH G and when interrogated about then she stated that the initials meant 'Till der Tag', 'Hail Mosley', 'Hail Hitler'. In writing to her son Gerald Mrs Lake addressed him as 'My dear Fifth Columnist', one was even headed 'From 5 Col: Eastern Counties HQ'. The tone of all her letters was extremely anti-British. When interrogated further she stated that she had joined the Fascist party in 1936 and had resigned in May 1940, but added that she spoke of Mosley as the leader, considered herself part of the movement and was in sympathy with it.

Detained under 18B in July 1940 she became very friendly with Frau Astor Wehran, one of the most enthusiastic Nazis in the Port Erin Camp. In November 1942 Mrs Lake was released from detention subject to restrictions. The camp authorities were surprised at this decision as they regarded

Mrs Lake as one of the chief trouble-makers owing to her continual jibing and criticism of all authority, including the Government, and her incitement of other detainees to insubordination in the camp.

Released but subject to restrictions, Mrs Lake could not return to Southend because it was an Aliens Protected Area so she took up work as a housekeeper in Beaconsfield.

Lake, Gerald McKenna, (21) 'Rangles', Shelburne Road, High Wycombe. Employee at Hydro Dividers Ltd, Aeronautical Engineers. Expressed strong anti-Semitic and pro-Nazi views in correspondence.

Langen, Mathias, (German) Spur Hill Avenue, Parkstone. Employee of the Loewy Engineering Company at Branksome, Dorset. Firm works on Government contracts but regarded with uneasiness by police and MI5 owing to the number of people with Nazi sympathies connected with it. He was also reported for making pro-Nazi remarks.

Laurie, Prof. Arthur Pillans, Bentwater, Churt, Surrey. Unreliable loyalty.

Larke, Donald Beverley, (52) Snipe Farm, Clopton, Woodbridge, East Suffolk. This man is a batchelor living alone in his farmhouse. He was formerly a chemist, is a deep reader of scientific books and has displayed pro-German tendencies. He was also a prominent and active member of the Suffolk Tithe Payers Association and is a headstrong and difficult man to approach.

In 1937 he is known to have been in correspondence with Roland Charles Lines the Birmingham Secretary of 'The Link' with a view to contacting a German prisoner of war who had worked on his farm in 1918.

Since the outbreak of war he has informed the local constable that the small countries which had been seized by Nazi Germany ought to be thankful for Germany's protection as they would be better off under Nazi Germany and he did not approve of British 'interference'. He was reported for making similar defeatist statements to his neighbours.

On 24 July 1940 his premises were searched under the Defence Regulations. A list of German wireless transmission times was noticed near the wireless set. A rifle was discovered in the house for which he had no licence and he was duly fined £2 at Woodbridge Petty Sessions.

Lees, Colonel Aubrey Trevor Oswald, (42) 48, St Andrews Road, Henley on Thames, Oxfordshire then Rosedean Cottage, Stowupland, Stowmarket, East Suffolk.

In the years before the outbreak of war Lees was a Colonial Civil Servant in Palestine but he was instructed to return to Britain early in 1939 as he had become so strongly anti-Semitic and Pro-Arab in his sympathies. Soon after his return to London he began to move in extreme right wing political circles and came into contact with Captain Ramsay MP, Davidson-Houston, Richard Findlay, Arnold Leese, Ben Greene, Miss Bothamley, the Nordic League and the BUF.

After the outbreak of war Lees tried unsuccessfully to get a job in military intelligence. On 22 January 1940 he wrote to Findlay:

I share your white hot indignation against men who are bent not only on wrecking world humanity but on assigning to Britain the dirtiest and filthiest role in the execution of that project…Disgust utter and complete, is my predominant feeling…One reason I find you so kindred a spirit is that you, like me, reserve your fiercest vituperation not for the Jews or other aliens but for our own apparently 100% English 'great men'…I think we might fill in the months of waiting by compiling our own Black Book – names of those who have betrayed their trust and every English tradition, such as…the festering Halifax and others…

On 10 February 1940 the Duke of Bedford wrote to Lees asking for 'a few spicy Palestine horrors to chasten a particularly patriotically self-righteous correspondent'.

In April 1940, Lees attended a meeting of the Pro-British Association and joined a committee of other members which included the Marquis of Graham, Lord Ronald Graham and Leigh Vaughan Henry, all well known for their Fascist and anti-Semitic views.

In May 1940 John Beckett wrote to the Duke of Bedford mentioning Lees' name as a junior minister in a 'Possible Coalition Government of National Security'. Lees was at this time reported to be attending meetings at 48, Ladbroke Grove, London at which Sir Oswald Mosley, Domvile and other extreme right wing leaders were present.

In June 1940 Lees was interned under 18B, his premises were searched on 20 June 1940 and literature of the British People's Party, BUF, Imperial Fascist League. Information and Policy and the Liberty Restoration League were found.

When Lees appeared before the Advisory Committee he was asked among other things whether he had ever said that he wished he had done as William Joyce had and stayed in Germany at the outbreak of war. Lees admitted he had often made remarks on these lines and contended he had not meant them seriously. His attitude before the committee was that he was not anti-British but considered that Britain had been betrayed by some so-called 'great men' who, though English, had led themselves follow Jewish practices.

In autumn 1940 Lees was released from detention and returned to London where he again got in touch with Major General J.F.C. Fuller and Mary Stanford and began attending meetings at the latter's house. Throughout 1941 and in the early part of 1942 he remained in touch with various well-known Fascist sympathisers and former members of the Right Club, as well as the Duke of Bedford; he co-operated with Captain Bernard Ackworth and Captain Rogers of the Liberty Restoration League.

Lee, Maria, 66 St George's Drive, Carpenden Park, Watford, Hertfordshire. Unreliable loyalty.

Liepmann, Leo, 38, Davenant Road, Oxford. Unreliable loyalty.

Lindl, Hans Albert, 2, Cardiff Crove, Luton. Unreliable loyalty.

Longdon, Oswald J, Morning Dawn Farm, Bures Hamlet, Essex. This man is the brother of Dora Hogg, whose name with those of her husband Kenneth Hogg and of the brother-in-law Robert Hogg are also included in the suspect list and whose neighbour he is, for the boundaries of Longdon's farm march with those of the Hoggs. Longdon is alleged to be a very close friend of his brother-in-law in whose company he is often to be seen, and to hold views similar to his.

A recent report states that he is a regular listener to the German news and said to be violently opposed to the present Government. In view of his close association with the Hoggs and his anti-British sympathies, it is felt that he is of doubtful loyalty and might assist the enemy in the evnt of an emergency.

Longhurst, Leslie, 61, Earlsbrook Road, Redhill. Reported for making pro-Nazi statements.

Lowe, Miss June Trixie Violet, (25) (German mother) The Willows, New Wokingham Road, Crowthorpe, Berkshire removed to Folkestone removed to Rippon Hall, Hevingham, Norwich.

This young women, who is a teacher by profession, is the daughter of a British father and a mother who was German by birth. Her father is employed as a servant in the Staff College, Camberley and her brother is serving in the British Army; she has a grandfather, an aunt, uncles and first cousins still living in Germany. Prior to the war she was employed in Paris and Belgium as a governess.

Between September 1939 and July 1940 she was the subject of a number of reports which alleged that both she and her mother, Mrs Maria Bertha Lowe, both of whom were living at Crowthorne, Berkshire, had strong German sympathies. When investigated in February 1940 Mrs Lowe was reported as saying her daughter was so pro-German she '... *would like to run Mr Chamberlain and Mr Churchill round Hyde Park with a pitchfork.*'

On 25 June 1940 police reported that complaints about Mrs Lowe and her daughter June continued to be received. June Lowe had been heard to say that we will soon be crawling on our haunches to Hitler. When British losses were known, both mother and daughter clap their hands and laugh.

On 29 June 1940 the police searched Mrs Lowe's premises in which June Lowe was also living. A quantity of literature referring to 'The Link', BUF and Imperial Fascist League was found, in addition to Nazi photographs, pro-German propaganda and a German edition of *Mein Kampf.* Most of the Nazi photographs were in June Lowe's possession and she told the police that she was responsible for the literature relating to 'The Link', BUF etc. Letters were also found from June Lowe to her parents expressing pro-German views, in one of which she says 'Hans Meyer or Heinz or somebody comes down in a parachute one day and in another she writes of having had 'a real German lunch'.

A number of love letters from a German named Heinz, who was in a Saxon unit of the German Army in Leipzig in 1938–1939, were also found in June Lowe's possession.

On 17 July 1940 June Lowe and her mother were detained by virtue of 18B. June Lowe appealed to the Advisory Committee and told them, among other things, that Hitler was a great man for his own people, that if in recent history England had been more willing to give and take some of the 'unpleasantness' might have been avoided and that she did not know what to think about the annexation of Czechoslovakia. These admissions by June Lowe are significant considering that they were made on an occasion when she must have been greatly concerned to try and vindicate her own loyalty to this country. The Advisory Committee, who were impressed with her attractive and agreeable personality, came to the conclusion that there was no sort of reason for thinking June Lowe had been, or would be likely to be, disloyal in act or word to this country. This view, however, was not accepted by the Home Secretary who on 14 February 1941 revoked her detention order but made a restriction order against her on 13 March 1941 requiring her in future to notify the police of her change of address.

On 5 August 1941 a report was received from the Isle of Man stating that when Mrs Lowe and her daughter were released from detention, they went round to each cell to say farewell and gave the Hitler salute saying 'Heil Hitler' as their parting greeting. Although this report should be treated with some reserve, it is not without interest to note that Mrs Lowe, prior to her detention was reported to have given the Hitler salute.

When she was released, June Lowe took employment as a teacher at the Convent School, Wokingham where she remained until 1942. Whilst she was there she expressed no views showing that she was favourably disposed to this country and is known on one occasion to have walked out of the room whilst other members of staff were listening to a broadcast made by the Prime Minister and not to have returned until the broadcast was finished. In 1942 Miss June Trixie Violet Lowe removed to Rippon Hall, Hevingham, Norwich.

Lowe, Mrs Maria Bertha, The Willows, New Wokingham Road, Crowthorne, Berkshire.

Mrs Lowe was German by birth, her maiden name being Finker. She acquired British nationality on her marriage in 1914. She has one son and is the mother of June Trixie Violet Lowe.

On 19 September 1939 Mrs Flora Kearney, High Street, Crowthorne stated to the police: 'About a fortnight ago a woman whom I know by the name of Mrs. Lowe, of New Wokingham Road, Crowthorne came into my shop and expressed sympathy with Germany and said to me, "I am prepared to die for my leader." She was very excited. She also said, "God help England, if they take my son and anything happens to him."

Amy Casserley of 'Locarno', Ellis Road, Crowthorne, stated to the police: 'On 3 September 1939 I was walking along New Wokingham Road, Crowthorne with my sister. When passing Mrs. Lowe's house, Mrs. Lowe's son came out of the house followed by his mother. The son was in khaki. Mrs Lowe shouted to us, 'I loathe to see my boy in that uniform. I wouldn't mind if he was the other side fighting for my big leader.'

Mrs Elizabeth Doherty of 'Cramon', New Wokingham Road, Crowthorne, informed the police that on 2 September 1939 she heard Mrs Lowe shout from her house 'Heil the Führer! Heil the Fatherland!' In February 1940 information reached the police that June Lowe was also pro-German; she was described as just as bad as her mother.

On 3 March 1940 a very reliable informant reported to the police as follows:

'On 28 February 1940 I spent about half an hour in Mrs Lowe's company at her residence at Crowthorne. During this time she was full of praise for Hitler, his activities and his officials. So ardent was her praise that she shouted in a loud voice, waved her arms about in an excited manner, and at times was almost breathless with exertion caused by her long high-pitched speeches in praise of the Nazi regime.

'She has a picture hung on the wall of Hitler and inserted in the frame are two German stamps showing this person. She also has a large picture of him which has been torn from a German magazine and also numerous picture postcards showing him at various functions. She told me that her daughter, June, has taken away her best pictures of him and has them with her in Folkestone; also that June is a keen supporter of the Nazi regime, and although British born is really a German at heart. It is her opinion that Hitler will soon win this war and when it is over she and her husband intend to reside permanently in Germany.

'She has an Ecko seven valve wireless which she says is her only link with her 'beloved Germany'. While I was there, she switched on the German news, which at intervals she interrupted with one of her speeches praising Hitler and denouncing the British people and their government. In April 1940 Mrs Lowe told the coalman, who refuses to deliver coal to her, that she admired Hitler, and when she finished speaking to him she said "Heil Hitler! Heil Hitler!"'

In June 1940 confirmation of Mrs Lowe's pro-Nazi sympathies was received by the Exeter police from a reliable informant, who had lodged at Mrs Lowe's house. On 25 June 1940 the police reported that complaints about Mrs Lowe and her daughter continued to be received. Mrs Lowe was stated to praise the Germans, hate the English and say that Hitler is her Messiah. June Lowe has been heard to say that we will soon be crawling on our haunches to Hitler.

The police searched Mrs Lowe's premises on 29 June 1940. Among the property found was a quantity of literature referring to 'The Link', the BUF and the Imperial Fascist League; a Nazi badge, which Mrs Lowe said was given to her by a relation in Germany who was a Black Guard; a large quantity of Nazi photographs and pictures; a quantity of pro-German cuttings; a copy of Hitler's speech at the Reichstag on 28 April 1939 in German and a German edition of 'Mein Kampf'.

On 17 July 1940 Mrs Lowe and her daughter were detained by virtue of an order of the Secretary of Sate made under DR 18B. Mrs Lowe appeared to the Advisory Committee and at the hearing of her appeal she told the Committee that she had a father, brothers, sisters, nephews and nieces living in Germany and had often visited them. She is of the opinion that conditions in Germany have improved since the Nazi regime came into power and that the German people never wanted this war. She also told the Committee that she did not care who won the war. On 14 March 1941 Mrs Lowe was released from detention, but is subject to restrictions on her movements.

Macdona, Major and Mrs Basil V de Landre, (Retired Royal Horse Artillery Officer) The Red Cottage, Great Kingshill, Bucks. Reported for his defeatist and pro German statements. Information was received by MI5 in August 1939 that Macdona, then living at 16, Roehampton Gate, London SW had advertised in *The Times* personal column for support for the Anglo-German Fellowship. It was also reported that 'The Link' held a number of meetings at the Macdonas' London home where Fascist literature was distributed. A letter received by Special Branch raised concerns about Mrs Macdona's very pro German sympathies and how she was 'confident of a German victory'. Both Macdonas were considered likely to assist the enemy if given the opportunity.

MacQueen, James Miller, Holme Park Farm, Sonning, Reading, Berkshire. MacQueen and his wife joined the Sonning Branch BUF in July 1939 and were connected with the Imperial Fascist League. Both came to the notice of the local police on account of their expression of anti-British views and their praise of Hitler, Lord Haw-Haw and the New British Broadcasting Station.

Marchfield, Gertrud, (Austrian) 24, Horsham Road, Dorking, Surrey. Reported for making pro-Nazi statements.

Mart, Linnell Bradley (born 1887) Grass Farm, Wallasea Island, Burnham on Crouch, Essex.

Mart has owned a number of farms in East Anglia and has visited the continent for holidays on a number of occasions. He first came to notice in 1936 when he wrote to the Home Office making application for a German named Alfred Hermann to visit him. Hermann was strongly suspected of espionage and twice in 1936 was refused leave to land. On his third attempt during July 1936, when he eventually landed he had in his possession an invitation from Mart. Enquiries made since reveal that Hermann contacted Mart through The World Union Club though Mart says he does not know how the union got hold of his name before he was asked to join it. Mart also denied any personal knowledge of Hermann prior to this visit and added that their friendship was based on an exchange of correspondence.

The circumstances of this visit therefore can only be regarded as curious and the suspicion concerning it has been considerably aggravated by the fact that a Miss Free stated that immediately prior to this visit Hermann wrote to her asking to be allowed to use her address for the Aliens Office.

It was not until late June 1939 that Mart came to notice again when he was reported to have been seen putting a small stake in the ground then running away from it and throwing himself on his face for a few seconds. When asked what he was doing he said that he imagined the stake was a stick of gelignite and was trying to see how far he could run in 30 seconds.

In view of his association with Hermann and of his eccentric habits, it is felt that he cannot be regarded as reliable and might assist the enemy in the event of an emergency, it is therefore considered that his name should be included on the list.

Martin, Harry Harold, 40, Granby Road, Southampton. Employed at Saunders Roe Ltd, Aircraft Manufacturers at Southampton. Member of the BUF. When his premises were searched in July 1940 a quantity of Fascist literature and two membership cards were discovered along with a number of letters that revealed that he and his brother Clarence were carrying on clandestine meetings of their BUF group.

Martin, Clarence Eric Alan, Willowdene, St Paul's Avenue, Shanklin, Isle of Wight. Civilian employee at the Mines Department, HMS *Vernon*, Portsmouth. Member of the Shanklin Branch BUF. Police were tipped off that Martin was a member of the BU which he denied. When his brother's premises were searched however in July 1940 a quantity of Fascist literature and two membership cards were discovered, along with a number of letters that revealed they were carrying on clandestine meetings of the BUF group.

McLean, Alan Stewart, The Cottage, Winterbourne, Newbury, Berkshire. Probationary Constable Brighton Police Force. In the summer of 1940 a family of enemy aliens named Handwerck, who were keen Nazi supporters, were interned and a search of their premises revealed that McLean was on close terms of friendship with members of the family. As a result McLean's rooms were searched and a number of books of a political nature were found including a copy of *Mein Kampf* and *Teach Yourself German*…A slip of paper was also found with the words '*Deutschland uber alles*' followed by an English translation. PC McLean also expressed defeatist and pro-German views to members of the public while on duty. He was dismissed from the force in June 1940.

Mellotte, Dr. James Henry, The Fort House, Hersham Road, Walton on Thames, Surrey. Unreliable loyalty.

Mendham, Frederick William, (34) Milkman 'Bank View' 138, Ware Road, Hoddesdon, Hertfordshire

This man, who is a milk roundsman by trade, joined the BUF in about 1937. In 1938 he became District Leader for South Hackney, a position which he was still actively holding in June 1940 when the Movement was proscribed. In June 1940 his premises were searched and Fascist literature including eight BU enrolment forms were found together with evidence of the enrolment of two members in May 1940.

When making his report on this case, the officer responsible described Mendham as 'one of the men most deeply steeped in Fascism in this country'. Mendham was ordered to be interned in 1940. When arrested he admitted that he was still active on behalf of the BU and stated that nothing would change his political outlook.

When he appeared before the Advisory Committee in January 1941 it was apparent his BUF beliefs were undiminished and his continued detention was recommended. In May 1942 he was the subject of a favourable report from the camp in which he was being detained. Apparently Mendham had expressed his willingness to serve the country in any capacity against any enemy. During November 1941 he was released subject to regulations. In view of his past activities and expressions he will not be called up for service in the Army, and on the same grounds it is felt that there is reason to consider him as a person of doubtful loyalty who is likely to assist the enemy at the time of an emergency.

Menuge, Auguste Eloi, Primrose Cottage, Worplesdon, Surrey. Unreliable loyalty.

Merriman, George Raymond, 32, St Michaels Road, Totton, later St Aubins, High Firs Road, Sholing, Southampton.

Merriman joined the Southampton branch of the BU in January 1940. He associated with prominent local Fascists, and in April 1940 attended a Fascist meeting in London. At the end of April 1940 he was dismissed from the Water Splash Hotel, Brockenhurst, where he was employed, as a result of the Fascist views he expressed.

Detained and released in 1940, in 1943 Special Branch reported that there coud be no doubt that Merriman remained an ardent Fascist and, although he was not known to be engaging in spreading Fascist propaganda at that time, he spent much of his spare time listening to German broadcasts.

Mills, Herbert Victor Townsend, (born 1898), 39a, Pelham Street, South Kensington SW7. Pro-Nazi. Chairman of 'The Link'.

Moir, Horace Ronald, 86, Eastney Road, Portsmouth. Employed in the City Engineer's Office. Reported for Anti-British and Pro-German comments.

Montgomerie, William Cumming, Brook Farm Dedham, Essex, then to Honey Hill Farm, Little Saxham, Bury St Edmunds and then 'Birchlands', Milland, West Sussex. BUF official who purchased the trawler *Crisia* and fitted up a powerful radio which he claimed he intended to use for propaganda broadcasts at sea on behalf of the BUF. This scheme was intercepted and prevented but Montgomerie continued to be reported for his defeatist, anti-Semitic and pro-Nazi comments.

Lady Diana Mosley (née Mitford), Shaven Crown Hotel, Shipton under Wychwood, Oxfordshire

Lady Mosley is the second wife of Sir Oswald Mosley, the Leader of the British Union of Fascists. She is the daughter of Lord Redesdale, and was previously married to the Hon. Brian Guinness. Her sister Unity Mitford, has been the subject of much publicity because of her association with Hitler and other Nazi leaders in Germany.

It is believed that Lady Mosley first made the acquaintance of Sir Oswald Mosley in 1933, and her interest in Fascism dates from then. When she appeared before the Home Office Advisory Committee on 2 October 1940, she made no secret of the fact that from 1933 up to the time of her detention she was a very strong supporter, not only of her husband, but of the BU of which he was head. An instance of this support occurred on 27 October 1935 when Lady Mosley attended a demonstration in Hyde Park against the Nazi regime and, after opposing a resolution advocating the boycott of Germany, gave the Fascist salute during the singing of the National Anthem.

Lady Mosley paid a number of visits to Germany during 1935 and 1936, and became on friendly terms with the Nazi leaders, including Hitler. This association led up to her being married to Sir Oswald Mosley on 6 October 1936 at the house of Frau Goebbels in Berlin, in the presence of Hitler. Lady Mosley told the advisory committee that this was arranged after a long discussion with Hitler, in which he had advised that it would be the only way in which the marriage could be kept secret. The secrecy was desired by

Sir Oswald Mosley because he feared that the announcement of his second marriage might do harm to the BU movement.

After her marriage, Lady Mosley continued to make frequent visits to Germany and – in addition to Hitler – Hess, Goebbels, Goering and Julius Streicher were among those with whom she became on friendly terms. This friendship was regarded as very valuable by Sir Oswald Mosley and it was a result of Lady Mosley's close friendship with Hitler that Sir Oswald Mosley was able in 1938 to enter into negotiations with the Nazi Government for the establishment of a broadcasting station in Germany, which seems to be used by an

Lady Diana Mosley. In 1940 she was considered by MI5 to be far cleverer and a greater public danger than her husband Sir Oswald Mosley.

English company, in which Sir Oswald Mosley and another member of the BU were the chief shareholders, for commercial broadcasting. The Advisory Committee came to the conclusion that Hitler's close acquaintance with Lady Mosley, and his friendly attitude towards her and her husband, was due to the support the Mosleys gave to the Nazi regime. Lady Mosley made no attempt to disguise from the Advisory Committee that she was a very great admirer of the Nazi regime.

There is reason to believe that Lady Mosley had herself told Hitler that Britain would never fight, and it is certain that it was a great disappointment to her when her conviction was proved wrong in September 1939. During the first nine months of the war she supported her husband's condemnation of it, and of his advocacy of making peace with Hitler at once. After the collapse of Belgium, she was reported to have said the British army was in a wedge, from which it could not possibly be extracted, and to have expressed her pleasure at this situation.

After the arrest of Sir Oswald Mosley and other BU leaders in May 1940, Lady Mosley kept in touch with members who were still at large and acted as go-between for Mosley and the remains of the BU organisation. She herself was detained under DR 18B at the end of June 1940.

The detention order against Lady Mosley was suspended by the Home Secretary on 19 November 1943, subject to a number of conditions, at the same time as the detention order against Sir Oswald Mosley was suspended on account of his state of health.

The Acting Chief Constable of Oxfordshire and MI5 are of the opinion that, in the interests of public safety and the defence of the realm, Lady Mosley should be re-detained under DR 18B (1B) in the event of invasion

Sir Oswald Mosley, Shaven Crown Hotel, Shipton under Wychwood, Oxfordshire

Sir Oswald Mosley was the leader of the British Union of Fascists, which he founded in 1932, and which was proscribed by the Home Secretary in July 1940.

He was detained under DR 18B by order of the Home Secretary made on 22 May 1940, on account of his belief in the desirability of the establishment of Fascism in this country, his association and that of British Union with Nazi and Fascist organisations and leaders in Germany and Italy for a number of years before 1939, his opposition and that of

Sir Oswald Mosley, Leader of the British Union of Fascists.

the British Union, which he controlled, to the British war effort during the first nine months of the war, and his advocacy of the Nazi and Italian Fascists' cause and doctrines. All of which made it necessary, in the interest of public safety and the defence of the realm, to deprive him of his liberty, and thereby prevent him from attempting to seek the support of Hitler and the Nazis in the establishment of a Fascist regime in this country, or to assist the enemy directly or indirectly in any way at a time when the military fortunes of this country were low, and the establishment of Nazi and Fascist regimes in most countries in Europe seemed possible.

On account of Sir Oswald Mosley's state of health, the detention order against him was suspended by the Home Secretary on 19 November 1943, subject to several conditions.

The Acting Chief Constable of Oxford and MI5 are of the opinion that, in the event of invasion, Sir Oswald Mosley should be re-detained under DR 18B(1b)

Above: the exterior and below: the lounge hall inside The Shaven Crown Inn, in the Cotswold village of Shipton under Wychwood, Oxfordshire where the Mosleys lodged after release from detention.

Mower, Mrs Marie, (22) (Austrian born) 3, Coopers Cottages, Great Wenham, Suffolk.

Born in Kreuzberg, Austria as Marie Eberhart, she arrived in Britain in 1937 and obtained a situation as a domestic servant. She visited Austria in April 1939 and returned in July 1939. On 2 September 1939 she married Stanley Mower a gardener and they lived at Great Wenham, Suffolk. She undoubtedly has a higher standard of education than her husband and generally her ways show that her affections still lie with Germany. At the present time various members of her family are serving in the German Air Force.

Last year this woman was reported for having urged a friend not to take a holiday on the continent and to have advised her that if she did so she was to be sure to retun to England by 1 September 1939.

Mrs Mower is forward in communicating to neighbours the German wireless news and her presence in Great Wenham has caused apprehension among local inhabitants. It is considered Mrs Mower would assist the enemy in the event of invasion.

Murphy, John Francis, (born 1893) No 2, Council Houses, Lower Road, Grimston, Norfolk.

This man came to notice at the time of the Munich Crisis in 1938 when his name was found in the possession of a German Naval Officer who came to this country to do espionage work. Enquiries at that time revealed Murphy had visited Germany in 1935, 1936 and 1937, and on the latter occasion had an interview with an official of the *Deutscher Fichte Bund*. As a result of that interview, Murphy agreed to distribute German propaganda leaflets to many of his friends and associates.

In 1938 he joined 'The Link' on the suggestion of Hoffmann of the Nazi Press Bureau and became an active and enthusiastic member. He was detained in June 1940. During his detention he created a somewhat confusing impression. He wavered from apparent loyalty to extreme pro-Germanism. He was also known to sign off his letters 'Auf Wiedersehn and may the protecting hand of providence guide Herr Hitler to the interests of the Fatherland. Heil Hitler.'

He was also believed to have been responsible for decorating his room with swastikas and photographs of Hitler. Although there was a suggestion that it was not he but his room mates who did this decoration, however, he made no attempt to remove it.

In March 1943 he was released from internment subject to restrictions. Between the time of his release and his arrival at King's Lynn, he regularly attended the unofficial Fascist meetings which are held from time to time in Hyde Park. Since he had been in King's Lynn his wife has continued to attend the Hyde Park meetings.

Murray, Mrs Maia, (45) 47, North Hill, Colchester, Essex. Born in Russia of Russian parents obtained British nationality on her marriage in 1922 to David Charles Graeme-Murray from whom she separated in 1936.

She is a great friend of Anna Wolkoff, who she has known since childhood. She has admitted to being an enthusiastic Fascist and she and Anna Wolkoff attended every possible meeting and rally. When her flat was searched on 1 July 1940 evidence was found of her interest and sympathy with the BU. She is reliably reported to be interested in obtaining information which might be of use to the enemy and that she claims to have two contacts at the German Hospital at Dalston who are Nazi agents.

Nash, George Edgar, (32) Meadow View, Stapehill, Wimborne, Dorset. Commercial traveller. Reported for making defeatist and pro-Nazi statements.

Newenham, Mrs Dorothy, 17, Roland Way, South Kensington, London SW7 and 14, Moreton Road, Oxford. Member of The Right Club and known associate of Anna Wolkoff. Another of her friends was Margaret Bothamley, a women who is at present in Germany, where she is thought to be working for the Nazis.

Mrs Newnham attended meetings of The Right Club. She was active in its interest by posting up sticky-backs which, besides being anti-Jewish, were directed against the war effort. We received information from two independent and reliable sources that Mrs Newenham used to advertise the NBBS in her conversation, and that she used to listen to these broadcasts.

She attended the British Union Earls Court Rally in 1938 and remarked afterwards that it was a wonderful meeting. We have heard recently from a delicate source that Mrs Newenham has stated that she is in sympathy with the British Union, although she is not a member. When her house was searched there was found a large quantity of anti-Jewish, anti-Communist and pro-Nazi literature.

Mrs Newenham was successful in deceiving the Advisory Committee as to her real views to such an extent that the Committee recommended her release. We objected strongly to this course and the Home Secretary maintained the Order for her detention. On 2 September 1941, however, the Detention Order against her was revoked, she was released but was subject to a restriction order requiring her to notify her address and any changes thereof and to report monthly to the police.

Shortly after she was released Mrs Newenham went to stay with a Colonel MacMillan at Ross on Wye. She remained there for nine weeks, during which time her general conversation and outlook indicated that she was quite incapable of keeping her views to herself. She repeatedly referred to Hitler as the Saviour of Europe and maintained Britain could not win the war.

In November 1941 Mrs Newenham returned to London, where she soon resumed her contacts with Mrs Ramsay, Ann van Lennepp and various other of her former associates. A Special Branch report dated 10 June 1942 states Mrs Collett, who does domestic work daily for Mrs Newenham, declares that Mrs Newenham is more pro-Nazi than ever, despite her period of internment. She states Hitler is the greatest leader the world has ever known and remarked 'in the event of an invasion we shall all be glad to run with open arms to Hitler to save our England'.

Observation kept by Special Branch on Mrs Newenham's flat showed that besides the people mentioned by Mrs Collett, Norman Hay and Captain Aubrey Lees have both visited Mrs Newenham.

One of the chief blessings of democracy is that it gives us liberty. Liberty to speak—to criticise if we think fit. Liberty to listen—to both sides of an argument. We shouldn't neglect this great advantage. In this country secret police don't enter our houses to destroy wireless sets that can 'get' foreign broadcasts. It is not a crime here, thank Heaven, to listen to the other man's point of view. Guard this freedom to listen—and *use* it.
E. J. POWER, *Managing Director*

MURPHY
RADIO

This advert for Murphy radios from November 1939 offers freedom to listen to any station, but by 1940, although it was not prohibited by law, listening to German propaganda stations broadcasting in English was strongly discouraged.

Nommenson, Dennis Max, 38, The Green, Richmond, Surrey later Tasburgh House, Tasburgh, Norfolk.

Born 26 December 1914 to a naturalised British father who was later de-naturalised and returned to Germany for refusing to do military service during the last war and is still in Germany. His mother, though British born, appears to have pro-German sympathies and is an associate of people with known pro-German sympathies.

In 1933 he joined the BUF and held various positions in the Richmond and Twickenham branches. He is also known to be one of the BU members who held secret meetings of that Party after it was banned, as late as July 1940 when arrangements were made for carrying on underground BU activities. In January 1941 he was detained and during the time that he was on the Isle of Man chose his associates largely from the pro-German type of detainee and is reported to have been one of those who remained seated during the playing of the National Anthem.

In March 1943 his detention camp report described him as a low type of person; who not only had no love for this country but is in himself a worthless man. It was noticed for example, that when the camp was divided into two factions, he kept in with the one faction only to be able to pass information about it to the leader of the other faction. He was released in September 1943.

O'Donohue, Brian, (born 1920) 11, Hamilton Road, Reading, Berkshire. Joined BUF in 1938 when living in Essex and became an activist distributing leaflets and selling *Action*. Subsequently moved to Worcestershire where he was fined £3 for painting Fascist slogans on walls. After release from internment he contacted several of his former BUF colleagues.

Panama, Ignatius Maurice, (born 1924, his father was a native of the State of Salvador) 'Holmfels', Devonshire Road, Amersham, Buckinghamshire. Occasional speaker at Fascist meetings 1939–40, drummer in the BUF Band and a fanatical supporter of Hitler.

Parsons, Harold James, 16, Hoe Road, Bishops Waltham, Hampshire. Shipping line cargo worker. Sub District Leader, Petersfield BUF. Parsons had joined the BU 1934 and by 1939 was a prominent member of the BU in Hampshire. From documents in the possession of MI5 it is known he used to communicate on BU matters with Mrs Muriel Whinfield of Shalden Lodge, Alton.

Pasold, Erich Walter, (born 1906 in Austria) The New Factory, Station Road, Langley, Berkshire. Partner with brothers in knitwear factory. Owned a plane which he used to fly to the continent and back before the war. Reported for making pro-Nazi statements.

Pasold, Rolf, (born 1914 in Austria) The New Factory, Station Road, Langley, Berkshire. Partner with brothers in knitwear factory. A keen glider pilot. Reported for making anti-Semitic and pro-Nazi statements.

Paulone, Anna, (born 1923 to Italian parents) 19, Queen's Road, Alton, Hampshire. The whole Paulone family were strong supporters of the Italian Fascist Party in Southampton before the outbreak and during the war.

Pawle, Mrs Nellie Abinger, Blomvyle Manor, Hatcheston, East Suffolk. Reported for making pro-Nazi statements.

Pearl, Charlotte Natalie (née Gunther) (45) 38 Princethorpe Road, Ipswich, Suffolk. Born in Berlin in 1897 of German parents, she has two sisters still living in Germany. She married her husband Bernard Leslie Pearl in 1924 and came to Britain in 1930. During 1940 when the question of evacuation of coastal areas was first raised Mrs Pearl said to her neighbour: 'Don't you go, if they (the Germans) come I will speak nicely to them and you will be all right.'

In August 1942 when in conversation with the same neighbour she said that she was a Jerry and proud of it and that she loved her country. Shortly afterwards when unable to obtain the name of the person that made a complaint concerning her Mrs Pearl said:

> *I demand it, my husband is in the British Army fighting for you swines. I will send him a telegram and tell him to finish with the army. I am a German and proud of it, you British never were any good, you schweinhunde. I shall get my husband to desert from the British Army and come home to protect me from the schwein police.*

It is felt that in view of her undoubtedly violent temper, she might easily prove unreliable in the event of an emergency and assist the enemy.

Pearl, Elfrede (née Ermert) (35) New House Cottages, Lorkins Lane, Twinstead, Essex, later 28 The Street, Assington, Suffolk.

This German woman was from Yelsen Kirtchen near Essen where she was educated until she reached the age of 17; she then worked in a hotel for four years and trained as a nurse for three years, then worked in hotels. She came to the UK in 1934 as a student to learn English. She was later granted permission to take domestic work which she followed until her marriage in December 1937 to a British subject who was ten years younger than herself, whom she had known only a few months. Her husband is of the farm labouring class, whilst she is said to be far superior. She has resided at her present address since marriage and in conversation has shown strong sympathies with Hitler and Germany.

In a statement given in May 1940 by an alien associate named Fuhry, it was claimed Pearl displayed the German and Fascist flags in her house and that her conversation was mainly in praise of Hitler. She also expressed her hatred of the English and stated if her husband was killed she would return to Germany with her pension.

Peters, Walter, (45) 270, Mawneys Road, Romford, Essex.
He was born in Liverpool to German parents who, with a sister, are now residing in Germany. His son, aged 17, worked for six months in a newspaper office in Hamburg which was under Nazi control. Peters has boasted that he had dined with Ribbentrop in Germany. He speaks German, Dutch, French and Hindustani fluently. He also visited India and is supposed to have met Gandhi. He listens to German broadcasts and says that the Jews in this country should be interned. German subjects, including Dr Carl Lowe who is alleged to be a cousin of Goebbels, have been known to visit his house. He owns a German made Hansa car, has frequented the Blackwater district and has referred to this spot when speaking of possible invasion by German forces. On each anniversary of the Armistice Peters visits the graves of the German airmen buried in Billericay in Essex. He is suspected of communicating with Germany through agencies in other countries. His premises were searched but nothing incriminating was found.

Pfingstmann, Canisuis (60) **Putheg, Chrysostomus** (61) **Staudacher, Carl Vincent** (63) **Weinmann, Reginald,** (50) The Priory, Hatfield Peverel, Essex.
A report of 4 August 1940 shows that these four named persons are German by birth and parentage, although they have since become naturalised British (South African) subjects. They are Lay Brothers of the Marianhill Mission, Natal, South Africa. Weinmann who is described as Superior General of the Mission, was in Germany from 1932 until 1938. When Austria was invaded, he went to Holland and eventually came to this country with four other German Lay Brothers who have since been interned under the Aliens Order.

On arrival at Harwich, Weinmann was found in possession of two, seven-chamber revolvers and 100 rounds of ammunition which were confiscated. He stated that he had bought them in Germany in 1933 and had carried them in South Africa for personal protection. This was clearly untrue as he had not been in South Africa at all after 1932. Three other persons named herein have since taken up residence. The premises have been searched but nothing of a subversive nature was found.

Local suspicion is high owing to the fact that they are German by birth. The monk Pfingstmann has been seen near an Air Ministry floodlight making notes in a book. On another occasion he was seen outside Langford Water Works with a large note book in his hand which he hurriedly pushed away under his jacket when he was seen by a witness who suspected that he was either taking notes or drawing. It is considered that these people would be likely to assist the enemy. There is a very large skylight in the roof of the premises which could be used for signalling.

Pfuller, Charles William Fritz, 131A, Banbury Road, Oxford.
Pfuller first came to notice when, in October 1934 he was in touch with Nazi Party headquarters in London. It is known that he was a member of the Nazi Party. He was then employed at the Savoy Hotel, London, as a receptionist.

Pfuller married a German National in December 1936. In May 1940 complaints were received by the Metropolitan Police respecting Pfuller, who was working at the Waldorf Hotel WC2. It was alleged that whilst employed at the Savoy Hotel he had praised Hitler's actions, attended Nazi meetings and openly boasted that he was in possession of a German and British passport. In addition, it was said that Pfuller had been so sarcastic in his remarks regarding the British people that employees of the Savoy Hotel with whom he came into contact were so resentful of his remarks that on one occasion blows had been exchanged.

Captain George Henry Lane-Fox Pitt-Rivers, (62) Manor House, Hinton St. Mary, Dorset. From late 1941 he resided at Ashurst Grange near Tunbridge Wells, Kent.

Pitt-Rivers has been known to the Security Service since 1930 as a strong Fascist and associate of those who had similar views. The following account is drawn from the MI5 file on Pitt Rivers.[12] It has been heavily weeded but the minutes give tantalising hints of the former contents.

In 1935 he founded the Wessex Agricultural Defence Association which brought him into close contact with Sir Oswald Mosley and the BUF, the main point of agreement being the agricultural policy put forward by Sir Oswald Mosley. The association with Mosley became so close in June 1934 we find him writing to Mosley that he was convinced that the Blackshirt movement offered the only sound prospect of ridding this country of party political shame and domination by international political financiers. He assured Mosley of his personal support but pointed out that because there were members of his WADA who were opposed to Fascism he could not openly declare himself a member. Mosley came to visit him at Hinton and meetings were held at an assembly hall on the estate.

Pitt-Rivers had also presided at a Fascist meeting at Poole, Admiral Domvile also visited and William Joyce had been a frequent visitor. When Pitt-Rivers was arrested they found a large quantity of correspondence, a plaque of Hitler and a number of photographs of the Nazi leader....The police officers found a copy of a letter from Pitt-Rivers to Hitler dated 22 June 1938, in which he expressed his thankfulness that the Anschluss with Austria had been accomplished under Hitler's leadership without bloodshed and with the rejoicing of all the German and Austrian people.

The local commandant of the Home Guard expressed marked uneasiness at having Pitt-Rivers at large in his district. The GOC-in-C, Southern Command and the Chief Constable considered Pitt Rivers a dangerous man to be at large. The Lord Lieutenant of Dorset said that in view of Pitt-Rivers' constant pro-German conversation he was not to be trusted and ought to be detained.

In June 1939 we were informed that Pitt-Rivers was intensely disliked and feared by his tenants and it appears that feeling against him is still extremely high. There were even stories of Pitt-Rivers being seen walking around his estate wearing a Nazi armband. The Chief Constable of Dorset thought that in the event of serious air raids on this country Pitt-Rivers might be lynched by his neighbours.

He spent the latter part of 1936 in Europe visiting Germany, Czechoslovakia, Belgium, France and Spain. He made a special investigation of the position in the Sudetenland and stated that facts relating to the extermination by starvation and persecution of the Bohemian-German population in Czechoslovakia were suppressed and distorted in England. On 8 September 1936 he was arrested in Karlsbad by the Czech Police on a charge of espionage. He has since stated that he was in Czechoslovakia working for Hitler.

Captain George Henry Lane-Fox Pitt-Rivers.

Later he went to Belgium where he met Leon Degrelle, the leader of the Rex Party and from there he proceeded to Spain as a guest of the Franco government. On 20 December 1936 he wrote to the War Office requesting removal of his name from the Regular Army Reserve of officers on the ground that he was 'not prepared to serve in any capacity…a Parliamentary despotism now styled as His Majesty's Government'. His letter was a long one in which he set out extreme political views about international Jewry and kindred topics.

We have been informed from a reliable source that in 1937 Pitt-Rivers had meetings in Munich with Baron von Redlitz, who was apparently employed by Ribbentrop to establish contact with such people as Mosley and Pitt-Rivers. In September of that year Pitt-Rivers was a member of the British Delegation at the Nuremberg Rally, where he expounded at great length rabid anti-British views to German audiences. He then wore, and has worn since, a gold swastika badge. He boasted that Hitler and Goering were his friends and we have been informed that he knew Ribbentrop, Biberstein and William Joyce.

Pitt-Rivers associated with some well-known Fascist characters in Europe, some of whom were in contact with Mosley. Among his contacts might be mentioned Domvile, [Léon] Degrelle and [Konrad] Henlein.

Pitt-Rivers expounded in no uncertain terms his admiration for the Nazi regime and his contempt for Great Britain. He was a firm supporter of the British Union and was a member of 'The Link' and the January Club. He was detained under DR 18B on 27 June 1940. Detective Inspector A. Knight of Dorset Constabulary submitted his account of the arrest and search of Pitt-Rivers' home:

On 27 June 1940 I went to the Manor House, Hinton St Mary, Dorset and there arrested Pitt-Rivers:

I served a copy of the order on Pitt-Rivers and explained to him that it would be open to him to make objections against the order to an advisory committee or he could make representations to the Secretary of State if he wished to do so.

Pitt-Rivers appeared to be taken aback but he nevertheless maintained a courteous attitude. He made some remarks about this being a reward for patriotism and referred to his service in the Great War, his literary work etc.

In the house as guests were Sir Barry Domvile, Lady Domvile, their son and daughter. Miss Winifred H.M. Farr of 3 Lorne Mansions, Gondar Gardens, London NW6 was also there and it is understood that she is employed by Pitt-Rivers as a hostess.

A search of the house was made including the rooms occupied by the Domviles. Nothing of significance was found except in Pitt-Rivers' study and office. From these rooms we took a large quantity of correspondence. We also found four pennants, apparently for use on a motor car. They were the Union Jack, the Swastika, the Spanish flag and the Italian flag. There was a plaque of Hitler and a number of photographs of Nazi leaders…

It is plain from the correspondence that Pitt-Rivers favours the Nazi regime. The case for the Nazis is always the right one as far as he is concerned and the Jews are the root of all evil. His contacts include Sir Oswald Mosley, Domvile, Sir Raymond Beazley, Degrelle, Henlein etc. There is one letter from America which congratulates Pitt-Rivers on being a candidate for Prime Minister and there is a copy of a letter from Pitt-Rivers to Hitler. An unsigned, unheeded letter refers to a meeting of persons 'who you met in London'.

Nothing openly seditious was found but it is obvious that Pitt-Rivers has a very strong bias in favour of the Nazis and it would seem that his idea of a suitable Government for this country would be one in which Mosley, himself and other persons of similar convictions took leading parts.

Interview

I saw this man at Brixton Prison on 2 July 1940…His pose was that of a gentle and patient literary man, detained for a reason he did not clearly understand but ready to assist the authorities with information as he had always done in the past. He seemed anxious to show that he was quite a different type of person from the other internees and referred to himself several times as a 'scientist' and a 'political diagnostician'.

It was almost impossible to keep him to the point. I said many times I was not interested in the stories he tried to tell of events twenty years old but would be interested in any recent information regarding subversive activities in this country. He appeared a little surprised that a literary man of retiring disposition should be expected to know about these things.

I asked him about the paper purporting to emanate from MI5…apparently the MI5 'Black List' and was given to him by Elwyn Wright or Professor Skeels, he claimed he did not recall which or when. He also referred to a meeting at which one of them spoke and to which he was taken by someone he could not remember. I told him I knew all about it and he had been taken there by his secretary Gladys Fortune.

The pose of the mild scholar was dropped for a moment when he assured me that David Vaughan (whom he assumed to be an informer) is a rat and Gladys Fortune a good, loyal girl with a tendency to hysteria…

We know that some fascists have announced their intention of pretending to be mentally unbalanced and Pitt-Rivers appears to be adopting these tactics. The interview was a complete waste of time.

J.G. Dickson 2 July 1940

He submitted several applications to the Home Secretary for release on the grounds of ill-health. He was released under a suspension of detention order. Considering the man's past activities it has been decided to place him on the Suspect List.

On 9 August 1945 R.G. Micklethwait minuted the application for a Home Office Warrant to intercept the post and communications of Pitt-Rivers:

Herewith HOW on Capt Pitt-Rivers, for signature, if approved.

Before the war Pitt-Rivers was a convinced National Socialist and had numerous Nazi and Fascist contacts in this country and abroad; details of these are set out in the statement of the case against him in volume 1 series 71a. In 1936 he was arrested in Czechoslovakia for espionage and he has since stated he was working for Hitler. He was detained under 18B from June 1940.

He did not appear to change his views. While at the Ascot Internment Camp he associated with Vaughan Henry and assisted the latter in his attempts to cause trouble to the officers in charge of the camp. When he was told he was going to be removed to Brixton Prison he sat on the ground and refused to move, he only got up when Vaughan Henry told him…There is no doubt Pitt-Rivers is a man of weak character and ready to become the tool of any fanatical Fascist whom he comes into contact with.

In his applications for release from prison Pitt-Rivers gave as sureties for his future conduct his wife, his eldest son and his solicitor. The problem was he no longer lived with his former wife and his eldest son was serving in the Welsh Guards…'

As regards his solicitor, we would not place any value at all on this undertaking, as it has been reported by the Chief Constable of Dorset that his solicitor George Henry Richard Tildsley is understood to be a Fascist himself and to be acting for a number of members of the BUF.

Pitt-Rivers was released from Brixton Prison at the end of 1941 on grounds of ill-health [acute arthritis which required Diathermic Treatment]. He also offered the Advisory Committee an understanding to refrain from all political activity for the duration of the war. It was also most undesirable that he should be in a position to give vent to his objectionable views in the

University as it appears he proposes to associate with the members of the senior Common Room of Worcester College.

A newspaper article in *The Star* on 6 February 1942 stated Pitt-Rivers had said:

> *I seek to have removed the stringent conditions imposed upon me at the time of my release which prevent me from returning to my old colleagues at Oxford to carry out important research work on agriculture.*

He also admitted his second cousin was Diana Mitford who married Mosley but Pitt-Rivers denied any link with the British Union.

> *I consider this relationship no more relevant than the fact that equally I am a cousin of Mrs Winston Churchill. I am not and never have been a member or supporter of the British Union I have never harboured or expressed anti-British views and am a loyal British citizen.*

Before his detention Captain Pitt-Rivers had a wide circle of all sorts of correspondents on all sorts of political and semi-political subjects and we are anxious to see how far he resumes his old associations.

After his release he resided 'in ill health' with his sister Mrs Astley-Corbett at Ashurst Grange near Tunbridge Wells 'and we have during that period been able to make arrangements for suitable observation to be kept on his movements.'[13] and was the subject of a HOW but this was cancelled in June 1943 since it showed Pitt Rivers was politically inactive.

Since then, it has become increasingly clear that he is as fanatical a National Socialist as ever and means to play a large part in any revival of Fascism in this country. He has discussed this on a number of occasions and is reported to favour a strong line. He associates with some of the most disloyal Fascist sympathisers in the country, such as Herbert 'Bertie' Mills, Captain Elwyn Wright, Leigh Vaughan Henry and Oliver Conway Gilbert. He had a number of Fascists living with him or in his employment. He has been reported to be compiling an index of National Socialist sympathisers in this country. When the German concentration camp atrocities were disclosed he said he did not believe them and when Hitler's death was reported he described it as 'one of the greatest tragedies of modern times'. He attends 18B functions and helped to compile and distribute their General Election Manifesto.

In August 1945 a note was added to the Pitt-Rivers file: '*I think it interesting to add, as a background to the case, that Pitt-Rivers is a man of depraved character.*'

Purser, William, Alban House, Watford Road, Hertfordshire. Reported for making pro-Nazi statements.

Ramm, Agatha, (27) 5, Merton Street, Newnham, Cambridge.
This woman, who is 27 years old, is the daughter of Reginald Ramm who is named on the Region 10 Suspect List on account of his pro-Nazi sympathies. Her mother is German born. At the time of the collapse of France a reliable informant said that Mrs Ramm 'would certainly commend herself to the Germans if they came; that she didn't mind at all what their Government did about Jews or anything else oppressive. What she did mind was her career; that 'if the Germans won, everybody would collaborate with them, and she herself certainly would'.

Recently (June 1942) when in conversation with the same informant and two other persons she expressed pleasure in the British reverses in Libya and prophesied the complete wiping out of the Allied forces in the Middle East. She also expressed the opinion that England had no right to interfere in affairs in Europe which ought to be left to settle its own problems…and anyway Germany had a perfect right to treat subject peoples as she liked. This woman, who is highly educated, has all the qualities of a Quisling and it is thought that in the event of an invasion she would not hesitate to assist the enemy.

Ramsay, Archibald Henry Maule.
Founder of the anti-Semitic Right Club in 1939. [Author's note: Ramsay was detained under DR 18B on 23 May 1940 and was not released until 26 September 1944. He has the ignominious distinction of being the only British Member of Parliament to be interned during the Second World War.]

Captain Archibald Henry Maule Ramsay, MP, founder of The Right Club and the only British MP to be interned under DR 18B.

Ratcliff, Mrs Dora Grace, (52) Little Vaggs, Hordle, Hampshire (German father) Pro German and Fascist sympathies. Dr Campbell, who had treated her for 'minor mental trouble', gave a statement recorded on her MI5 file in which he described her as 'a dangerous woman who would go to any length in carrying out anything she decided to do, regardless of the consequences'.

Raven-Thomson, Alexander, (Born 3 December 1899) 30 Overstrand Mansions, London SW11, later removed to 36, Acfold Road, Fulham SW6. Director of Policy British Union of Fascists.

This man is one of the most prominent members of the British Union of Fascists, and has been so for many years. There is reason to suppose that he is one of the most extreme members of the party and probably one of the more dangerous members. He was born in Edinburgh, the son of a solicitor. From 1921 to 1926 he was employed in an engineering business in Germany, and from 1926 to 1933 in an engineering business in England. He joined the British Union in 1933 and devoted his whole time to the Movement until his detention on 23 May 1940. His official position was that of Director of Policy, in which capacity he must have been largely responsible for the 'Mosley for Peace' campaigns which took place after the outbreak of war, and he was closely associated with the BU paper *Action* of which he was editor in 1939 and 1940.

Raven-Thomson is known to have been in contact with Nazi officials both in Britain and in Germany as far back as 1934. He has also visited Germany on behalf of the BU on several occasions, and in 1934 lectured on the British Union to students of Cologne University. In 1936, following a lecture at National Headquarters in reply to a question as to what would be the attitude of the BUF in the event of war between this country and Germany or Italy, Raven-Thomson said that he thought we should get at least two months warning before war broke out and if that was the case, the party could organise the country to the point of revolution during that time. Once German aeroplanes were actually dropping bombs on London, then there would be no option but to join up, but providing the movement got notice of impending hostilities, it could at its present stage of development bring the country to the brink of revolt. He also said that to the student of history, when contemporary events are analysed, it will be seen what a momentous decision was made when Oswald Mosley a little while ago said that the movement would not consider itself bound by treaties entered into by previous governments.

This man was to have been recipient of intercepted secret naval information and is known to have received secret information regarding British military orders for Ordnance Survey maps.

Raven-Thomson is married to Elizabeth Thomson, a German woman who runs A.G. Ltd (Anglo-German Employment Agency), known since the outbreak of war as Haymarket Equipment Company Ltd in London. The company has been in existence for several years. It was formerly engaged in providing employment, mostly of a domestic character, for young women of German and Austrian nationality. A few months before the outbreak of war Raven-Thomson set up New Era Tours, for the purpose of arranging tourist visits to Germany. Two tours took place led by Mrs Raven-Thomson and their daughter Helga.

Since the outbreak of war Mrs Raven-Thomson's Haymarket Equipment Company has devoted itself to the sale of ARP equipment of all kinds. She is known at one time to have been in communication with the *Landesgruppenleiter* of the Nazi Party in London.

Among the personal effects found at Thomson's house at the time of his detention were fourteen sheets of paper containing routes between large towns in Great Britain, thus:

A2 London to Dover
London–Dartford–Chatham–Sittingbourne–Faversham–Canterbury–Dover.

This may have sinister significance.[14]

Raven-Thomson was released from detention by an order dated 29 September 1944. During his detention Raven-Thomson made a very bad impression on the camp Intelligence Officer on the Isle of Man who described him as full of 'disgusting conceit and obstinacy'. He appears to have suffered something in the nature of a nervous breakdown, and has lost much of his following in BU circles. He is still, however, a Fascist of some standing and now that he is released may well resume his former contacts.

A note on Raven-Thomson's MI5 file dated 30 October 1944 confirms the fears voiced after his release. Immediately on release he proceeded to Leigh Vaughan Henry's address, but later spent a few days with Mrs Whinfield at Shalden Lodge, Alton, Hampshire.[15]

[Author's note: The MI5 files on Raven-Thomson at The National Archives that have been released to date only consist of photocopies of the annotated minute sheets that relate to over 750 letters, reports and enclosures in the file from September 1933 until November 1955 (Raven-Thomson died on 30 October 1955). Just over thirty photocopies of the letters, paper cuttings or documents they relate to are present. A rubber stamped note dated May 2002 states the original document has been 'retained in department under Section 3 (4) of the Public Records Act.']

Reale, Michael Anthony, 16, Amery Street, Alton, Hampshire. British but of Italian descent. Lodging house keeper and coal merchant. Joined the BU in 1936 and in the years before the outbreak of war was in contact with prominent BU supporter Mrs Muriel Whinfield of Shalden Lodge, Alton. On 10 November 1939 Reale informed the police that he had been approached by one Percival Vernon Christmas with a view to selling to Germany plans of aeroplane components and aerial bombs, which could be obtained from one Thomas Edminson who was employed at the Royal Aircraft Establishment, South Farnborough. Reale stated that the reason Christmas had approached him was because he was a member of the BU and might therefore be in a position to make contact with persons in Germany. It is very probable that Reale's motive for giving this information to the police was to curry favour with them since Reale was due to appear the following week at Farnham Petty Sessions on six charges of larceny of coke, of which he was in fact convicted and fined.

There is reason to think that there was some truth in Reale's story, and it is known that Edminson paid frequent visits to Christmas's house, that December. Edminson visited Reale on a number of occasions, and that Christmas made serious threats to his wife if she should divulge any of his secrets. Investigations which were made, however, failed to produce evidence on which action could be taken in this matter. Some light is thrown on Reale's lack of bona fides in this matter, however, by the fact that for several months after he had given information to the police about Christmas and Edminson, he continued to associate with them. This continued association was not at the request of the police, with whom Reale made no further contact.

In June 1940 Christmas was found in possession of two quartz crystal units used in wireless transmission and other property which had been stolen by Edminson from the RAF, South Farnborough. Christmas and Edminson were convicted on 17 June 1940 in respect of these offences and sentenced to imprisonment.

Curiously, a month earlier Reale built a pigeon loft on his premises for the purpose of keeping racing pigeons, but his application for a permit was refused. Reale had not previously kept pigeons.

Reb, Elizabetha, (27) 'Springfield', Goring-on-Thames, Oxfordshire.
Born in Austria. Reb arrived in England on 2 January 1939 and took up employment as a domestic servant in Kent and subsequently Surrey obtaining

her current position as a cook with Miss Ballasis of Springfield. She was reported for expressing defeatist and Nazi sympathies.

Redfern, Mrs Alida, (née Van der Vygh), Fairholme, Park Avenue, Ventnor, Isle of Wight British by marriage, formerly Dutch. Reported for defeatist and pro-Nazi statements.

Redfern, Cecil Augustine, Fairholme, Park Avenue, Ventnor, Isle of Wight. Reported for making defeatist and pro-Nazi statements.

Reichenbach, Fritz Ernst, (40) Saxon House, Wymondley Road, Hitchin, Hertfordshire. Weekday residence 13 Cameron Avenue, Leicester. Chemist.

Born in Limbach, Saxony, Reichenbach served in the German Army as a Corporal in 12th Section Heavy Artillery in 1918. He is alleged to have told a reliable informant that he was the seventh member of the Nazi Party although at a subsequent meeting he repudiated this and said that he was in fact the 1,007th member. This same informant claimed Reichenbach had told him that Hitler had warned him that it would not be safe for him to remain in Germany owing to the feeling of the Communist Party and he should leave as he was too valuable a person to lose.

In November 1928 he arrived in the UK giving his occupation as Glove Manufacturer. He was granted naturalisation in 1935. In 1938 he is alleged to have been very friendly with Hans Maier who was an active organiser of the Stutzpunkt and who left this country a few days before war broke out.

In the early months of 1939 Reichenbach left the Hitchin Glove Factory and joined Messrs Felt and Dampcourse Ltd of Welwyn Garden City. At their factory he was described as a very clever chemist who had discovered a process for manufacturing camouflage for RAF aerodromes which he frequently visited until the outbreak of the war in connection with this work.

After the outbreak of war his activities constantly gave rise to suspicion and many reports were received about the visitors who arrived at his house at all hours of the night. On 3 June 1940 his house was searched but nothing was found to show that he was engaged in any subversive activities, although his correspondence made it quite clear that he had communication with many members of HM forces.

On 10 June 1941 an employee at Messrs Felt reported that some time prior to the German invasion of Norway Reichenbach had said in the course of a discussion concerning the war, 'We don't have to fight for little countries, we just walk in and take them.'

On 23 June he was reported to have ordered half a gallon of Toluene and on 26 June he was interned before he received the order. [Toluene is a flammable liquid and products containing it can form an explosive mixture with air at room temperature.]

Reichenbach's name and address were found in the possession of Richard Adolf Carl Knop who had been interned in the First World War on suspicion of being a German agent and MI5 are of the opinion he is working as a German agent again.

Released from internment on 8 February 1941, an internee on the Isle of Man commented: 'The authorities were taking a grave risk when they released the anti-Semite Herr Doktor Ernst Reichenbach, ex German Army Officer, who it is thought is closely connected with Kapitän Reichenbach of the German Espionage Service in Berlin.'

Reya, Anthony de, 5, The Close, Fernbank Road, Ascot (Italian born). Unreliable loyalty.

Reynolds, Donald Edward, (born 13 Oct 1901) 33, Edgar Avenue, Stowmarket, Suffolk.

In May 1934, when Reynolds was employed at Birmingham, he was reported to be leader of the Stirchley Branch of the BUF. Towards the end of 1934 he was given employment by a subsidiary company of the BUF known as Abbey Supplies Ltd in London which is now defunct. On 19 November 1935 he was appointed National HQ organising officer and he held this position until 1937. In this capacity Reynolds worked on behalf of the BUF in various parts of the country. During this time he reorganised the Blackburn district and is known to have been active in Manchester during this period.

On 23 March 1937 Reynolds was appointed District Inspector of North Norfolk BUF but his appointment was cancelled the following month. From 1937 to 1940 he was variously employed by Electrolux, General Refractories and on his own as a commission agent.

Since the outbreak of war Reynolds has, on different occasions, boasted that he was political agent to Captain Ramsay and to Sir Oswald Mosley. Reynolds is at present employed as a clerk at the East Anglian Electricity Supply Company at Finborough Hall, Finborough, where it is alleged that he adopts the role of agitator amongst the employees whenever the opportunity presents itself and endeavours to fan small grievances into larger ones. He has openly boasted his former Fascist connections and claimed the acquaintance of William Joyce (Lord Haw-Haw).

In March 1943 Reynolds attended at the Labour Exchange asking to be registered as a Conscientious Objector. In completing the form Reynolds gave his occupation as 'Thinker, Writer, Fascist speaker and Organiser'. To the question 'What exactly did you do in this capacity?' he replied 'Worked for the liberation of Britain from the Jewish-Masonic oligarchy which now has her in its clutches.'

Reynolds, Ralph Kenneth, 16, Upper Redlands Road, Reading, Berkshire. Draughtsman at Thorneycrofts. Reading BUF member. Reported for boasting of his BUF membership and for expressing Nazi sympathies.

Rice, Edward Denis, (Born about 1900) Woolstone Lodge, Faringdon, Berkshire. Gentleman farmer and managing director of Direct Farm Meat Supply (Tilmanstone) Ltd, Rice owned several farms near the coast between Dover and Sandwich.

He was the Tilmanstone representative of the Eastry Rural District Council, Chairman of Tilmanstone Parish Council and Head Warden of the parish. He showed little interest in any of these roles. A relative of Archibald Ramsay and Mosley and a friend of Captain Robert Gordon Canning of Worth who were known to visit Rice on a number of occasions. Other visitors included a daughter of Herr Krupp the German Armaments manufacturer and Captain Alexander Proctor of Blairgowrie, Scotland, an agent for the sale of German machinery in England and the author John Scanlon, both of whom were known to be Nazi sympathisers. Rice was reported on several occasions for expressing pro-Nazi sympathies, evidence of which was confirmed as a result of meetings with Rice by an officer of MI5.

Rigby, Richard, (29) Muswell Hill removed to 'Minglee', Dedmere Rise, Marlow, Buckinghamshire. District Inspector, 11th London Area, BUF. When Rigby's flat at Muswell Hill was searched in May 1940 they found a complete Fascist uniform, a photograph of Winston Churchill with a jack knife inserted in the throat, and a quantity of Fascist literature and correspondence. There was also a rotary duplicating machine and a stack of sticky-back labels, some of which advertised the German broadcasting station NBBS. There was also an amount of paper ash in the grate of his flat to indicate a quantity of paperwork had already been destroyed.

Roberts, Lewis, (Born 1907) 42, Bradley Road, Slough. House painter and decorator. Reported for making pro-Nazi statements.

Rosa, Harry Aron, 64 Devonshire Road, Cambridge. Unreliable loyalty.

Rosa, Monica Deason, 64 Devonshire Road, Cambridge. Unreliable loyalty.

Rouse, Miss Katherine Helen, Vine House, Burton Bradstock, Dorset. Engaged to a German officer. Miss Rouse first came to the notice of the police as a result of her frequent expressions of pro-German views in the village. She is believed to have been on holiday in Germany during 1939 and has stated on a number of occasions that she is engaged to a German officer. From a letter in her possession dated 3 May 1940, it appears that she had been making enquiries as to the possibility of getting a message to her fiancé or his parents, in Germany. She also endeavoured to ascertain whether it was possible to travel to Germany by any route.

On one occasion she caused a scene in a shop at Bridport as a result of a statement to the effect that the Germans were better than the English, and were being blamed for a lot that the British had done. During this outburst a number of soldiers from a Scottish regiment passed by the shop and she said 'I would rather trust myself with a German any day than with the likes of those. German men are honourable, trustworthy, and of fine physique, and much more to be admired than that crowd.'

The mother of this women is believed to have died in a home for mental defectives and it may be that Miss Rouse has inherited some mental aberration. At the same time it appears that she might conceivably be an extremely dangerous person to be at large in the event of invasion.

Ryder, Miss Iris Katerine, (45) 47, Cadogan Street, London SW3, Sun House, Canford Cliffs Avenue, Poole, Dorset later Tasburgh House, Upper Tasburgh, Norfolk.

This woman was born in South Africa. Her mother Lady Isobel Ryder has been in a mental home since June 1939, her sister is mentally defective and she herself – though by no means insane – is inclined to be weak minded.

Before her detention Iris Ryder was living in Bournemouth on a small private income which she supplemented from time to time by taking employment. In 1934 she became interested in the British Union, absorbed the doctrines of the movement and thereafter devoted all her energies to propagating them. In 1938 she was fined £2 10s for using insulting words and behaviour and in 1939 £5 for painting Fascist slogans on ARP signs. In May 1940 during the Labour Party Conference at Bournemouth, she was selling *Action* in the street and so aroused anger of the public that she had to be removed by the police for her own safety.

In the early days of the war the leading male members of the Bournemouth branch of the BU left to join the forces or for other reasons, and from that time onwards Iris Ryder and three other women members – Florence Emily Hayes, Elizabeth Joan Griffin and Norah Constance Pearson carried on the activities of the Branch to the full. She was detained on 30 May 1940 and it is perhaps significant to note that after her detention and that of her three co-workers the painting of the Fascist slogans in Bournemouth ceased.

Whilst in internment Iris Ryder maintained her Fascist convictions. The Intelligence Officer at Port Erin compiled a Camp Report on Ryder in February 1943 which stated that she still had implicit faith in the sincerity of the BU's intentions for the betterment of Britain; our declaration of war on Germany was a 'tragic mistake', all that Germany was aiming for was the unification of the Balkans and the control of Europe.

Britain and Germany had much in common and should unite against the coloured races and menace of Bolshevism. Hitler had never wanted to make war on this country. Holding these opinions she could not bring herself to assist the war effort directly although she would be prepared to drive an ambulance, to do nursing, or horticultural work. The opinion of the officer interviewing her was that she was convinced that she was being truly patriotic in her support of the BU. She stated frankly that if she was released she would not refrain from expressing her views if she thought that by so doing she could help to bring about a negotiated peace.

In July 1943 she wrote in a letter to a friend:

I must own I am feeling embarrassed at my British nationality more than before, since our sickening bombing of the Ruhr dam happened an act of such barbarity that history can hardly equal...If you think differently I am sorry but you will not be surprised for why after all is it that I have been locked up...for more than three years in a land which is fighting for justice, Freedom, Humanity and Godliness.

On 5 November 1943 the Detention Order was suspended and Iris Ryder was released under the usual conditions and her name placed on the suspect list.

Sandwith, Mrs Maria E. née von Eckardt (60) Hinton House Cottage, Hinton Admiral, Hampshire, German born, known to MI5 having come under a certain amount of suspicion during the First World War. Reported for being violently pro-German and for spreading anti-British propaganda by listening to Lord Haw-Haw broadcasts and passes on what she has heard to friends and neighbours.

Saunders, Robert, (born 1910) Friar Mayne Farm, Broadmayne, Dorchester. District Leader, West Dorset BUF. Very keen and active worker on behalf of the BU before the outbreak of war and continued his activities afterwards.

Scanlon, John Templeton, Portsmouth Arms, Hurstbourne Priors, Whitchurch, Hampshire. Reported for making pro-Nazi statements.

Scott-Smith, Miss Joan (17) (Born 14 Nov 1921) 59, Southampton Street, Reading, Berkshire. Assistant shop-keeper and her mother **Scott-Smith, Mrs Mary** (Born 11 June 1891) (widow) Confectioner Tobacconist 59, Southampton Street, Reading.

Miss Joan Scott-Smith lives with her mother, who keeps a small general shop; she has a good education. She is in possession of a British passport issued in March 1939 which shows she visited Hamburg and Heidelberg in that year. From July to August 1939 Miss Scott-Smith was employed in the Royal Army Pay Corps Office but was dismissed for continually expressing pro-German views. Information reached Reading Police soon after the outbreak of war that Miss Scott-Smith and her mother held pro-Nazi views. In May 1940 a lodger who had been staying with the Scott-Smiths also reported to the police as a result of his experiences while staying with them he felt sure that they would offer their services to the Germans, and would offer shelter to any German parachutist.

It was also known to local police at this time that Miss Scott-Smith was corresponding with a German who was then in America.

Self, Frederick Wilsher 16, Friarage Road, Aylesbury, Buckinghamshire. Active member of Buckinghamshire BUF. The Advisory Committee formed the opinion: 'Self was not a normal type of man.' Inspector Rawlings of the Bucks Constabulary stated Self was 'generally speaking, a suspicious character who associates with persons of low repute.'

Severgini, Francis, (30) (British born to Italian parents) 11, Trent Road, Southampton. British born Italian father, renounced British nationality and took the Oath of Allegiance to Italy. MI5 received report from the internment camp where he was held with his brother that both displayed anti-British sentiments.

Severgini, Leslie, 24, Castle Crescent, Reading. British born Italian father, renounced British nationality and took the Oath of Allegiance to Italy. MI5 received report from the internment camp where he was held with his brother that both displayed anti-British sentiments.

Sherlock, John Edwin, (40) Hill Farm, Chediston, Suffolk.
Sherlock joined the Birkenhead Branch of the BUF in 1939 and was given notice by his employers so he bought a smallholding in Myddle, near Shrewsbury. He became the associate of two local Fascists, both of whom were detained in 1940 and therefore decided to have nothing further to do with the Party, although retaining his Fascist views as he 'had heard' that he was suspected of suspicious activities. A report of Sherlock by the Shropshire Constabulary dated 7 March 1941 summed him up as 'bitterly opposed to the Jews; undoubtedly a dangerous sort of person and absolutely anti-Government.'

At some point between 1941 and 1943 he left his smallholding at Myddle and came to Hoole near Chester. On 16 September 1943 he appeared at Chester Castle Sessions charged with failing to comply with a Ministry of Labour direction to attend an interview with a view to taking up Civil Defence work. The proceedings were somewhat strange. When asked to plead, Sherlock said: 'To hell with Britain and every Welshing Britisher.' When asked if he had anything to say he replied, 'No murderous King or his underlings is going to make a slave out of me.' On imposing a fine of £10 and a sentence of one month imprisonment the chairman said that this, the maximum penalty, seemed inadequate.

Sherston, William Edric, (31) Otley Hall, East Suffolk.
On leaving school this man travelled widely studying languages and in 1932 attended a foreigner's course in Munich. Two years later in 1934 he joined the British Union of Fascists. Sherston's progress in the BUF organisation was rapid and he became the close associate of a number of the highest officials. Sir Oswald Mosley stayed frequently at Otley Hall as his guest. He contested the Woodbridge Division in the BU interests. By June 1937 he had risen to be County Inspector Suffolk BUF and by July 1938 and had been promoted to Regional Inspector. In this year he visited Berlin and spoke in German on the radio. He was described by a British official in Munich as 'violently pro-Nazi and anti-Semitic'. Sometime during this period he attended the Nazi rally in Nuremberg.

From this time on Sherston's record has remained constantly Fascist. In August 1938 when his mother sent him a postcard of Goering he said 'Very good too. Have put it near Hitler in the business room.' When war broke out Sherston (who already held a Territorial Army commission in the Suffolk Regiment) was called up. He contacted various serving Fascists, notably Gunner P.T. Cook to whom he used to send notes on the progress of the Fascist movement, George Surtees, BU District Leader for the Lowestoft

Branch (whose name is already on the suspect list), Brian Smith, 'a very old BU member'; his Brigade Intelligence Officer ('we almost threw each others arms around one another on discovering we were both of the same thing, and old stagers at that…')

In March 1940 he was rejoicing that he had met several officers who were strongly anti-Semitic. In April he stated 'we should be able to keep on Otley Hall easily till the Leader comes to power…' The war he described as 'all a capitalistic ramp' to some soldiers.

In June 1940, for which year he paid his BU subscription, Sherston was interviewed. He would not admit until pressed that he had contacted Gunner Cook. Similarly, he denied having spread any BU propaganda in the army until faced with his remark that the war was a capitalistic ramp. He made it clear that his political views had not changed. The interviewing officer summed him up as bigoted, unbalanced and not altogether truthful. When his home was searched in July photographs of Hess, Goering, Himmler, Goebbels and Hitler were found.

Sherston was interned on 15 July 1940 and released on 26 October 1943. Whilst in internment his pro-German attitude appeared to have lessened.

Otley Hall, Suffolk, home of leading Suffolk British Union of Fascists officer William Edric Sherston. BUF Leader Sir Oswald Mosley frequently stayed here as a guest.

However, in April 1943 he was still reading *Vanguard*, a violently anti-Semitic publication. Despite the alleged change of views it was felt he could not be relied upon and he might assist the enemy in the event of an emergency.

Shipman, Mrs. Ellen Augusta Louise (née Stieg), (Born Germany 1898) 'Wadala', Manor Park Avenue, Princes Risborough, Buckinghamshire. Reported by several witnesses for her pro-Nazi views.

Simms, Gilbert Francis, (25) The Bungalow, School Lane, Lawford, Manningtree, Essex.

This suspect was first brought to the attention of the police as a Fascist in September 1938. A reported conversation in April 1940 shows when speaking to two persons on the subject of military service Simms said in the event of him being called up he 'would shoot as many officers in the back as he could and that he would do all the damage he could'. He stated that he would rather live in Germany than England and would do all he could to prevent England winning the war.

When Simms' premises were searched it appeared that he had expected this action by the police owing to the fact that he had taken the opportunity to destroy correspondence and Fascist literature which he undoubtedly possessed. He was found, however, wearing a BUF uniform belt in place of braces. A Fascist badge and armlet were found in his workshop. When entry was made he was listening to the German news broadcast in English.

He is described as being an ardent Fascist, very sly and plausible and possessed of strong pro-German sympathies. He is the owner of two motor cars. There is no doubt that he would lend assistance to the enemy in the event of an invasion.

Skinner, Alan Andrew, 80, Mullway, Letchworth, Hertfordshire. Reported for making pro-Nazi statements.

Smith, Mrs Alice, (formerly Stier née Fisch) 15, Gerrard Place, Cowley, Oxford.

Born in Vienna on 13 May 1905 of Austrian Jewish parents, she was brought up in Austria and married an Austrian Jew in Vienna. There was one child of this marriage, a daughter, Gerda, born two days after the wedding. The couple divorced in 1928. She then came to Britain as a housemaid in January 1939, in May 1939 she married William Thomas Smith, a lorry driver from Abingdon, Berkshire.

Mrs Smith had only known her husband a week before she married him, there was no child on the way, her haste suggests a marriage of convenience to obtain British nationality. Mrs Smith has protested that she is much hurt at this suggestion, but she is much given to dramatising herself and her misfortunes, and it is impossible to say now what her motives were. By September 1939 she had left Smith, whose former wife had returned home, which caused trouble in the household.

Mrs Smith has never been connected with any political party so far as is known. In a report of 6 July 1940 Special Branch noted: Mrs Smith has become violently anti-Jew in outlook and seems to blame every Jew for the fact that she has Jewish blood in her veins. This report further stated that she said to the police on 5 July 1940 'I am German: Germany is the land of my birth. I could not help it if I was born a Jew.' Since then the Jewish obsession has grown on this unbalanced woman.

Smith, Charles Horace, (born 1913) 13, The Drive, Earley Court Gardens, Earley, Berkshire. Ship's Engineer. Member of the BUF. Reported for his pro-Nazi statements subject of a detention order in October 1939. A search of his luggage revealed a large number of German books and periodicals, a Nazi flag and swastika, as well as a letter to Germany prefaced 'Heil Hitler' signed Karl Schmidt. There was also found a letter from Rolf Hoffmann of the Nazi Press Bureau in Hamburg referring to Smith's application to join the Nazi Party.

After numerous letters appealing for his release and a desire to assist Britain's war effort and long deliberation the Home Secretary suspended the detention order against Smith and he was released subject to keeping the police informed of his address and reporting weekly to the police. The camp authorities comment was that it seemed to be a very bad release as Smith had been regarded as one of the most pro-German and disloyal of the detainees.

In February 1943 the security services were informed that Smith was in contact with Edward Quentin Joyce, brother of William Joyce (Lord Haw-Haw).

Smith, Charles Cuthbert, 66 St James Road, Southampton. Governor of a Young Offenders Prison dismissed for BUF membership.

Smith, L. Vincent, Riviera Hotel, Bowleaze Cove, Weymouth, Dorset.
Former District Leader BUF. Smith came to this district from Lowestoft in 1939 where he had been prominently associated with the BUF. He made contact with local members of the BUF shortly after his arrival. Smith was a

member of the Lowestoft Hydroplane Club and visited Germany on many occasions before the war. He is said to claim acquaintance with Lord Haw-Haw (William Joyce) and a member of the Gestapo.

It is felt that Smith should be detained immediately in case of invasion, particularly as the Riviera Hotel is right on the edge of Weymouth Bay in a prominent position overlooking the sea.

Sohnemann, Jorgen Nissenius, (Born 1894) 1 Vaughan Road, Stotfold, Bedfordshire.

This man, though technically Danish, is German both by birth and upbringing. Sohnemann arrived in the UK on 12 May 1940 as Chief Officer aboard the Danish ship *Knut* by which time the ship had become SS *Knut* and was sailing under the British flag. Sohnemann was interviewed by the Danish consulate in Newcastle. His replies to questions and his general attitude were considered unsatisfactory and he was passed on to the immigration office for further interrogation. It was during this interview that he claimed he had served in the German forces during the last war and that his experiences there had made him a pacifist and he was unwilling to fight for either offensive or defensive purposes. In consequence of this he was refused leave to land and was detained in Durham Gaol until 15 October 1940, when his permit was granted and he was released.

Sohnemann then found work as an agricultural labourer and as a factory hand and was denounced on a number of occasions by those he worked with for making anti-British remarks.

In November 1943, the manager of the Coleman Foundry Equipment Factory reported that in his opinion some action should be taken against Sohnemann. Signed reports from fellow employees showed on one occasion Sohnemann had stated that his son was still in Norway and he hoped he was fighting for the Nazis against Britain. In view therefore of his German birth and upbringing, his German service in the last war and his probably anti-British bias, it is felt Sohnemann might assist the enemy in the event of an emergency.

Sperni, John Charles Gerald, 16, Amery Street, Alton, Hampshire.
Sperni was born in London in 1887, and is a self made man of Italian parentage who devoted his life to local politics in 1931 to the extent that he rose to the rank of councillor in the St Pancras borough as a 'Conservative' member, and was elected Mayor of St Pancras from 1935 to 1939.

He first came to notice from a subversive point of view at the time of the Italo-Abyssinian conflict, when as President of the Society of British born Italians, a message of loyalty (subsequently published in the Italian Fascist organ *L'Italia Nostra*) was forwarded to the King of Italy and Signor Mussolini.

Before organising the Society of British born Italians Sperni was actively concerned, in 1931, with the Mazzini Garibaldi Club which was taken over by the Fascist Party. During his term of office as Mayor of St Pancras, Sperni is reported to have become an open supporter of the BUF and in May 1938, when a BU meeting was addressed by Sir Oswald Mosley at St Pancras Town Hall, it was seen that Sperni was on intimate terms with him.

In November 1938 Sperni attended a dinner of the Italian Legation sponsored by the Partito Nazionale Fascista. On this occasion Sperni made a speech in which his strong pro-Italian sentiments were apparent, and which subsequently drew forth a letter of praise from a German NSDAP member to the London Nazi Party Leader.

When Italy declared war, four of Sperni's seven children left this country for Italy with the Ambassador's Party, and it has since been learnt that one of them (John) has broadcast in English from Radio Roma, thereby acquiring a label as the 'Italian Haw-Haw'.

Sperni was detained in August 1940 under DR 18B. The police reported him to be unscrupulous, anti-British at heart, an ardent follower of Mussolini and a potential source of danger. In May 1942 he was released subject to restrictions and after living at various locations he left London in July 1944 and took up residence with Michael Anthony Reale at 16 Amery Street, Alton, Hampshire. Reale is a former BU member, who has also been released from detention subject to restrictions and is included on the Suspect List.

Steegh, Hendrikus Stefanus Joannus, (Born 1910 in Germany) Taplow Hill House, Taplow, Buckinghamshire. Photographic instrument maker. A refugee, he arrived in Britain in June 1940 and was interned at the request of the Dutch military authorities on the grounds that he was 'politically unreliable'. Released late 1941, from May 1942 Steegh was employed at the Dutch Sailors Nursing Home at Taplow Hill House.

Self, Frederick Wilsher, 16, Friarage Road, Aylesbury, Buckinghamshire. Member of the Aylesbury Branch, BUF.

Stephens, George, 57, Hathaway Road, Grays, Essex. Reported for making pro-Nazi statements.

Stockdale, Mrs Valerie Frida (née Haberhauffe) (61) Hotel owner, Ventnor, Isle of Wight, later 5 Connaught Road, Hounslow, Middlesex.

Born in Germany of German parents she married a British man twenty years older then her. Together they ran a hotel in Ventnor, Isle of Wight. She joined the BUF in November 1938. Reports were received from several unconnected sources during the winter of 1939 and spring of 1940 that she expressed violently pro-German views. In May 1940 she was requested to complete form DR 17. She complied but refused to answer one of the questions because she had brothers in Germany whose whereabouts she was unwilling to disclose. In June 1940 she was sentenced to three months imprisonment for the failure to answer and was prosecuted for the offence against DR 80a, pleading guilty. On expiration of her sentence she was detained under DR 18B.

In November 1940 Mrs Stockdale appeared before the Advisory Committee, who came to the conclusion that she had considerable affection for Germany and some admiration for Hitler. The Committee did not consider her anti-British and recommended her release, the Home Secretary, however, maintained the Detention Order until January 1941 and then she was released subject to restrictions. MI5 was not consulted prior to her release. The camp report on Mrs Stockdale described her as difficult and disagreeable. There is no doubt that Mrs Stockdale holds thoroughly pro-German, pro-Nazi views and that she could not be relied upon in case of invasion.

Stokes, Frank Fernie, Fir Tree Cottage, Ashampstead Common, Newbury, Berkshire. Stokes is a thresher which entails travelling about the countryside. Before the outbreak of war he was known to the police as a distributor of Fascist literature and he continued this propaganda after the outbreak of war.

Stokes, Veronica Mary (formerly Taylor née Buettler) (32) 12, Cunningham Avenue, St Albans, Hertfordshire.

Veronica Mary Stokes was born on 28 Janury 1911 at Heswall, Cheshire, the daughter of the Captain Superintendent of Heswall Royal Navy School. She was privately educated and on leaving school attended the Albert Hall Dramatic School of Art. From 1930 to 1936 she was an actress. After she left the stage she worked at various stores in London as a shop assistant.

Little is known of Mrs Stokes' connection with the BUF before the war, but she was a member of the South Paddington Branch of the BU. She does not appear to have held any official position.

In March 1942 she wrote to the fascist E. Valeriani asking to be put in touch with 'our friends' (presumably BU sympathisers) signing the letter 'yours in union'. Shortly afterwards she wrote to the Chairman of the 18B Detainees (British) Aid Fund enclosing a long list of possible subscribers. It is thought Valeriani must have introduced her to members of the Fund's committee.

Mrs Stokes put in an appearance at the Fascist meeting place in Hyde Park in April 1942. Members of the Aid Fund's committee tried to stop her from getting involved with the more Fascist elements led by Moran and Watts, but Mrs Stokes decided she would like to do more active work for the 'cause' than that done by the Aid Fund and continued associating with the Hyde Park Fascists.

It was learned in June 1942 that she was living with a soldier who was an ex-BU member. The soldier heard he was to be sent overseas and considered deserting. Mrs Stokes did all she could to encourage him to desert, but the soldier joined his unit and proceeded overseas.

In July 1942 Mrs Stokes was stated to be extremely pro-Nazi. She spoke of German successes as victories, to her nothing British was good and everything German was right. On one occasion she commented on one of her BU acquaintances wearing a small tri-colour motif on his lapel. She stated she was surprised at his doing so since red, white and blue was the colour of everything evil, 'far better wear the swastika', she said, 'at least that is worth fighting for'.

Mrs Stokes has made every effort to avoid taking work which might help the war effort. She applied to join the women's branch of the Metropolitan Police as she thought she would avoid being directed to National Service. Her application was turned down.

In January 1942 she declared that she objected on political grounds to performing any form of National Service. She added she had been a member of the BU for seven years. The Tribunal ordered her name to be removed without qualification from the Register of Women Conscientious Objectors.

She left London in 1943 for St Albans where her mother lives. Throughout 1942 to 1943 when she left London Mrs Stokes continued to attend the Hyde Park Fascist meetings. Informants who met her there reported that she was utterly disloyal and wanted Germany to win the war.

On 25 September 1943 she married Major John Percival McLean Stokes and this is stated to have been Mrs Stokes' latest method of avoiding National Service. In view of Mrs Stokes' long Fascist history, and as she seems to be still active and enthusiastic, it is considered that this woman's name should be included on the list of suspects to be arrested in the event of an emergency.

Stuckey, Derek Richard, Broomfield Hatch Farm, Three Mile Cross, Berkshire. Joined the BU in February 1934 and rose up the ranks to become Reading BUF District Leader for Oxford and Combined English Universities. Stuckey was in charge of BU activities among school teachers. 'Extremely Pro-Nazi'.

Sturmann, Fritz Werner (German) Munslow, St Osmunds Road, Parkstone, Dorset. Employee of the Loewy Engineering Company at Branksome, Dorset. Firm works on Government contracts but regarded with uneasiness by police and MI5 owing to the number of people with Nazi sympathies connected with it.

Surtees, George Frederick, (50) The Old Rectory, Kirstead, Norfolk.
This man served through the Great War, first in the Army and later in the Royal Flying Corps. He married about 1919 and set up business as a garage proprietor in Lowestoft. He has a son and a daughter.

In 1929 and 1935 he visited Germany in connection with the Norfolk and Norwich Aero Club of which he was a member. In 1937 ad 1938 he was in Germany as a member of Oulton Broad Motor Boat Club which represented Great Britain in the International Outboard Racing. In August 1939 he spent about ten days at a Summer School in Berlin. It seems that his visits to Germany instilled in him an admiration for the National Socialist regime.

In 1936 he joined the British Union and became very active on its behalf. He arranged and addressed meetings both inside and outside Lowestoft and distributed propaganda. Shortly after the Munich crisis he arranged for Sir Oswald Mosley to address the Lowestoft Rotary Club. In December 1939 at the instigation of Surtees a Major Harris also talked at the Rotary Club and expressed Fascist views.

Shortly after the declaration of war, as a result of the many reports received concerning his pro-Nazi and Fascist sympathies, his house was searched and German propaganda leaflets were found. Various reports concerning Surtees' hostile sympathies continued arriving. As late as April 1940 he was stated to be attempting to persuade people to listen in to the NBBS. At the end of May 1940 one informant, amongst many who sent in reports, described Surtees as 'very anti-English and an ardent admirer of Hitler'.

On 4 June 1940 Surtees was detained and his premises were again searched. On this occasion a large amount of BUF literature was found together with one or two swastikas.

Since he has been interned he has appeared to be in sympathy with Germany and it has been noted that the detainees with whom he has been friendly are known to be pro-German. Given hearings by the Advisory Committee but his detention recommended on 31 March 1943; he was given a further hearing, but he still could not bring himself to express any concern for the people of Europe who had been downtrodden by the Nazis, nor to condemn the conduct of those who had directed German policy.

On 1 June 1943 he was released under restrictions. In view, however, of the above mentioned information it is felt that this man would assist the enemy in the event of an emergency.

Symonds, Alfred William Garland, 86, Hambledon Road, Waterlooville, Hampshire. Garage proprietor in Southsea. Member of Portsmouth Branch and County Propaganda Organiser BUF. Before the outbreak of war Symonds, who had retired from the Royal Navy, came to the notice of the Portsmouth police and MI5 owing to his membership of 'The Link' and his expressions of pro-German sympathies.

Tarry, Frank Gerald, Brightwell, Wallingford, Berkshire. Leader and Treasurer, Abingdon District BUF. Unreliable loyalty.

Taylor, James, 2, The Gables, Lent Rise, Burnham, Buckinghamshire.
Prior to 1940 Taylor was a close associate of active BU members in the Slough district. Although there is no conclusive evidence that Taylor was himself a member of the BU, he has been known to have Fascist sympathies, to have been closely concerned with the affairs of the local branch of the BU. He was also reported by numerous witnesses for his anti-Semitic and pro-Nazi comments.

Thompson, Ernest Samuel, Ship Inn, Oxford Road, High Wycombe, Buckinghamshire. Reported for making pro-Nazi statements.

Titcombe, Arthur 19, Albion Street, Aylesbury, Buckinghamshire. Assistant District Leader, Aylesbury Branch, BUF. Unreliable loyalty.

Tsakalakis, Anthony (Greek) 2, Ellington Gardens, Taplow, Buckinghamshire. Doctor of Law, Heidelberg University, came to Britain describing himself as an export merchant. At present (1942) Tsakalakis associates in the Taplow and Maidenhead districts with undesirable persons of the gambling and night-club type, he is known to be short of money. Special Branch described Tsakalakis as 'a crafty type of person, endeavouring to get rich quick, who would not shirk anything for money.' MI5 are of the opinion that Tsakalakis is an unscrupulous adventurer with no loyalty to the Allied cause and strong German sympathies.

Turton, Victor, Assistant District Leader Propaganda, Nottingham BUF. Unreliable loyalty.

Valls, Angeles, 'Ashfield', Reading Road, Yateley, Hampshire. Reported for making pro-Nazi statements.

Valls, Aurelio, 'Ashfield', Reading Road, Yateley, Hampshire. Reported for making pro-Nazi statements.

Vanneck, John Chalmers, Shearston House, Shearston, Bridgwater, Somerset, removed to Brook Street, Watlington, Oxfordshire. (South African)

Vanneck has a long association with the BUF. In October 1938, it is known that the notorious William Joyce (Lord Haw-Haw) wrote in a letter to a friend 'you can always communicate with Mr J. Vanneck…as to my doings'. In October 1939 a reliable informant reported Vanneck was doing important underground work on behalf of the British Union of Fascists and the Nordic League.

Vanneck's name has frequently appeared in letters between persons known to be engaged in Fascist activities, some of whom were detained in 1940. He is also known to have been continually in touch with many similar people. There were numerous reports made of his violently anti-Semitic and pro-Nazi comments.

Varicopulos, Else Wilhelmine Ina, 88, Dundonald Drive, Leigh on Sea, Essex. Unreliable loyalty.

Vas Benter, Louis H. 59, Southampton Street, Reading, Berkshire. 'A disgruntled and excitable person with strong Pro-Nazi and anti-British views and is completely unreliable. In view of this MI5 are of the opinion that he would assist the enemy, if given the opportunity.'

Velasco, Conrad Charles William Horatio, (36) 95, Victoria Road, Southend on Sea, Essex.

Velasco is a British born subject of a German father. A number of complaints have been received respecting this man's pro-German expressions. By reason of his occupation he has an excellent knowledge of the Thames Estuary. His father and brother reside in Germany. In the event of a German landing in this country his knowledge of the Estuary might be of invaluable assistance to the enemy.

Vock, Mrs Luise, 86 Inkerman Street, Luton, Bedfordshire. Unreliable loyalty.

Vogt, Marthe Louise, 59, Bateman Street, Cambridge. Unreliable loyalty.

Walker, Mrs Freda Maria Agnes (née Taube) (Born 1899 in Germany) 34, Woodlands Road, Cove, Hampshire. Reported for her pro-Nazi sympathies. Witness claimed she had candidly stated: 'If German parachutists or German troops came she would do anything in her power to help them.'

Wallace-Thomson, John J. 26, Richmond Way, Croxley Green, Hertfordshire. Reported for making pro-Nazi statements.

Wallis, Lewis Morden, 'Windrush', Eve's Corner, Danbury, Essex. District Leader Chelmsford BUF.

Watling, Robert Hammond (40) 155, Farnham Road, Guildford, Surrey removed to 449, Marston Road, New Marston, Oxford, removed to 11 London Road, Newbury. Factory time keeper at Messrs Dennis, Guildford. Assistant District Leader, Treasurer and Propaganda Secretary, West Lewisham Branch BUF.

Before the outbreak of war and between 1934 and 1938 Watling was a frequent speaker at BU meetings in Sydenham and Lewisham. Watling is known to have visited Germany on a number of occasions and to have corresponded with Nazi friends in Germany up to the outbreak of war. In February 1939 he was in communication with the Foreign Department of the Labour Office in Hamburg with a view to obtaining special privileges for a visit he proposed to make to Germany.

In March 1941 when Watling and his father the Rev. Gilbert Watling, were leaving London for Torcross, Devon, their luggage was examined and a Fascist uniform, membership and subscription cards for the BU and a large quantity of BU publications and Fascist and pro-Nazi books and pamphlets were found.

Visitors to the Watlings' home reported their concerns over the content of the family conversations which were defeatist, anti-Semitic and pro-Nazi.

Webster, William, 3, Chalvey Court, Slough, Buckinghamshire. During the first eight months of the war Webster was living in the Manchester district and was employed at the Fairey Aviation Works, Stockport. He was a sub-district leader of the BU and together with Thomas Hooker, used to frequent public houses in an effort to persuade customers to join the BU. He was also strongly suspected by the police of fixing Fascist labels on the windscreens of motor cars and of chalking Fascist emblems and slogans on walls. Webster was dismissed from Fairey in May 1940 and left the Manchester area. When the premises of an active Fascist were searched in 1940 letters from Webster were found that showed Webster's enthusiasm for the BU and in which he states 'given a free hand I could make Stockport into a little Fascist stronghold'.

Welsh, Joseph Henry, (born Josef Ferdinand Wellisch in 1883) Manager of the Duke of Cornwall Hotel, Mount Pleasant Terrace, Plymouth removed to 19, Jubilee Estate, Porton, Swindon, Wiltshire removed to 'Evergreen' Nortoft Road, Chalfont St Peter, Buckinghamshire.

Hungarian by birth, his correct name being Ferdinand Josef Wellisch, he became a naturalised British citizen in 1912.

Before becoming Manager of the Duke of Cornwall Hotel in Plymouth in 1937 he was manager of the Haymarket Hotel, London where he became a personal friend of Ribbentrop. He is also said to have received messages by courier from the German Embassy and to have entertained the couriers from Germany in private.

Welsh has been reported for making pro-Nazi statements, his son is said to be a member of the British Union and his brother-in-law, Emerich William Franzel, is known to have been a member in 1935 and to have been an active Jew-baiter. Welsh himself was composer of the Fascist March song.

The Duke of Cornwall Hotel is much frequented by officers of the fighting services. In 1940 Welsh's name was included on the Regional Commissioner's Suspect List, although he pretended to be a patriotic old gentleman, he was in fact known to harbour strong anti-British sentiments. MI5 are of the opinion that Welsh has strong pro-German sympathies and no sympathy for the allied cause.

Welsh, Mrs Louise née Hollisher, (born 1888) Duke of Cornwall Hotel, Mount Pleasant Terrace, Plymouth removed to 'Evergreen' Nortoft Road, Chalfont St Peter, Buckinghamshire. Born in Britain to German parents, educated in Germany. Wife of Joseph Ferdinand Welsh.

In December 1941 the Plymouth City Police reported that they had information in their possession that Mrs Welsh had spoken with intense bitterness against the Jews in Austria just before the outbreak of the war and had stated that she did not blame Hitler for punishing them. Her anti-Semitic and anti-British remarks were reported on several subsequent occasions.

Werba, Herbert, (34) c/o Herts War Agriculture Committee, Baldock. Czech (formerly Austrian).

Between 1937 and 1939 Werba divided his time between Sudeten German territory, Holland and the UK. In the Sudetenland he was regarded as exceedingly pro-German, his father was head of the German School and although there was no proof that the son was engaged in any subversive activity against the Czech state he was thought to be unreliable. What his activities in Holland were is not known for certain but it is perhaps sufficient indication that in December 1938 shortly after Werba's last pre-war arrival in England, a verbal message was received from the Dutch manager of Bata's that proof was held in Holland that Werba was a German agent.

Werba returned to England in April 1939 and worked for Bata's at Tilbury. Shortly before the outbreak of war he moved from there to a subsidiary company which Bata's had formed in Cambridge under the title of Abex (1939) Ltd. Here he was viewed with intense suspicion and dislike by his fellow Czechoslovakian employees, because of his pro-German attitude and his refusal to subscribe to funds in aid of the Czech troops in France. During this period Werba applied for an exit permit to enable him to join the Brazilian branch of Bata's. In consequence of the suspicion against him, this was refused much to the relief of his fellow national workers who had been terrified Werba would report to the Nazis in Brazil the names of those who had left Messrs Abex to join the Czech forces in France.

So far there was no definite proof against Werba but the cumulative effect of various suspicions was thought to be conclusive and he was detained in June 1940. This decision seemed to be justified by early camp reports which were 'uniformly unfavourable' and as recently as 23 February 1942 the Intelligence Officer at Camp X included Werba's name amongst the list of detainees to whose release he would be opposed in any conditions which could at this time be visualised.

Since that date, however, both the war situation and Werba's attitude have changed considerably. It is now thought Werba would support the war effort in all ways short of actual fighting and, although he feels himself to be a German and not a Czech, it is even thought that he would be willing to join the Czech forces had he no family in Czechoslovakia. However, a certain amount of doubt exists as to his sincerity and it is for this reason when Werba was released on 10 December 1943 he was released for agricultural purposes only and had a restriction order served on him and was added to the suspect list.

[Author's Note: The Home Office File for Werba, H aka Verba; Werba, S aka Werbova aka Diblik; WERBA, S; Werba, P R in The National Archives is closed for public access until 2048.]

Whinfield, Mrs Muriel Grace, Shalden Lodge, Shalden near Alton, Hampshire (where Admiral Sir Barry Domvile also came to reside).

Mrs Whinfield joined the BU in 1935 and in 1936 became a contact officer. From 1936 to 1939 she was a most active and enthusiastic Fascist, and was prospective BU candidate for the Petersfield Division of Hampshire.

Mrs Whinfield was in close touch with the principal BU officials in London, and during the winter of 1939–40 she was also invited to attend a series of meetings which were held in London at the house of a Mrs Huth-Jackson. These meetings were attended by Sir Oswald Mosley and other right wing extremists, such as Captain Archibald Ramsay MP and Admiral Domvile. Invitations were only sent to people who were considered to be of some importance. On a later occasion Mosley himself told the police that Mrs Whinfield was a valued member of the BU. In December 1939 Mrs Whinfield received a letter from Mosley thanking her for her 'work for the Cause'.

In December 1939 Mrs Whinfield received a letter from Francis Hawkins, an important official at BU HQ, suggesting that she should meet him in London to discuss a scheme regarding BU peace leaflets. She received personal Christmas cards from Mosley and she sent one of her friends a photograph of Mosley as a Christmas present. Mrs Whinfield also sent BU literature to several of her friends. This was not always appreciated and in January 1940 one of her friends wrote from Nyasaland asking a mutual friend to stop Mrs Whinfield sending him 'the most treasonable defeatist stuff I have ever read'.

In January 1940 Archibald Watts, District Leader Portsmouth BUF, wrote to Mrs Whinfield asking for help with a poster campaign which he was planning. A subsequent letter from Watts shows that Mrs Whinfield gave him financial assistance with this campaign.

Apart from her connection with the BU, Mrs Whinfield was friendly before the outbreak of war with Peter and Lisa Kruger, a German couple who ran the Anglo-German Academic Bureau in London. It is considered almost certain that the Bureau was used by the Germans for espionage as well as propaganda purposes, and that the Krugers were in fact German agents.

After the outbreak of war Mrs Whinfield's son, Edward P. Whinfield, was staying in Switzerland and was in touch with the Krugers who had by this time left England and were making arrangements for Edward Whinfield to enter Germany. But before he could do so, he was arrested by the Swiss police and deported from Switzerland. On arrival in this country he was re-arrested and is still in detention under DR18B.

In February or March 1940 Lisa Kruger gave a letter to a man [SNOW] who was travelling from Antwerp to England, with instructions that he should post it in England to one Eugen Horsfall-Ertz. The letter was as follows:

My dear Eugen, I quite forgot to give you the new address of Mrs M.G. Whinfield, Shaldon Lodge, near Alton, Hants. She is on the telephone in case you want to talk to her regarding the books, but you can always meet her personally if you like to, as she comes up to town frequently; bye bye and love to all. Yours, etc.

Three BUF women give the Fascist salute before going to a pre-war meeting to hear Mosley speak. Many members of the BUF arrogantly gave this same salute accompanied by 'Hail Mosley' when police came to take them into detention in 1940.

Horsfall-Ertz, who was subsequently detained under DR 18B is strongly suspected of having been a German agent, though this has not been conclusively proved. Nor has the true significance of this letter ever been established. When questioned about it subsequently, Mrs Whinfield denied all knowledge of Horsfall-Ertz, though she remembered that some strange men had written and telephoned her about some 'interesting books' which he thought she would like to see. She said that she had taken no notice of the matter and maintained that she never arranged any meeting with Horsfall-Ertz.

Confirmation of Mrs Whinfield's pro-German sympathies comes from Lieutenant Colonel Parkes, who has known the Whinfield family for several years and who reported that, before the war, he had on several occasions stayed at Shalden Lodge where he had met German Nazis and had heard very anti-British, pro-German and Nazi sentiments expressed.

On 23 May 1940 Mrs Whinfield was detained under DR 18B. When arrested she gave the Fascist salute and cried 'Hail Mosley!' During her detention Mrs Whinfield subscribed to the 18B Detainees (British) Aid Fund, which is organised and supported by former BU members. On 1 August 1942 the detention order against her was suspended by the Secretary of State, subject to the conditions that she should proceed to Shalden Lodge, Alton, should inform the police of her arrival, and should not travel more five miles from her place of residence without the permission of the Chief Constable of Hampshire.

White, Frederick Joseph, 64, Fair Cross Avenue, Collier Row, Romford, Essex. Unreliable loyalty.

White, Margarete (née Paukenheider), (26), 64, Fair Cross Avenue, Collier Row, Romford, Essex.

This woman was born in Bergreichsteen, Austria in 1915. She arrived in this country to take domestic employment in December 1937. In October 1938 she married Frederick Joseph White thus acquiring British nationality and took up residence at No 20 Loughton Grove, Sydenham. Her husband had taken a prominent part in the Lewisham Branch of the British Union since 1936.

In June 1940 information was received that White was a Fascist leader and that his wife expressed strong pro-Nazi views.

In September 1940 Kenneth Lyon, the son of Mrs Lyon, spent a great deal of time with the Whites in their house in Sydenham, whilst he was on 24 hours leave. Kenneth Lyon and his mother were members of the

Sydenham Branch of the BU. Mrs Lyon's name is also included on the Suspect List.

Later in 1940 both Margarete White and her husband joined Mrs Lyon in Hertfordshire and later they spent a fortnight in the same house as Mrs Lyon and the Watling family, one member of which is on the Suspect List in Region 7.

In view of Mrs White's hostile origin, of the fact that she is married to a prominent former member of the BU and her present close association with Mrs Lyon, it is felt that she might assist the enemy in the event of an emergency.

White, Roland Francis, Marsh Farm, Salcott, Essex. District Leader Wimbledon BUF. Unreliable loyalty.

White, William Cooper 56, Belfast Avenue, Slough, Berkshire. Member of Slough Branch BUF. White, who has been described as being of the 'thug type', is a restless, though illiterate, political agitator, with strong Fascist views and violent tendencies.

Wilkes, John Edward, Red Marley, Manton Drive, Luton, Bedfordshire. Reported for making pro-Nazi statements.

Wilton, Albert, Sunnydene, Boundstone, Farnham, Surrey. Reported for making pro-Nazi statements.

Wise, Leonard Francis, District Leader East Leyton Branch BUF. Unreliable loyalty.

Withers, Ronald William, 150, Gosbrook Road, Caversham, Berkshire. Manservant. Member of the Worthing Branch BUF. Visited Germany in 1939. An ardent Fascist, he listens to propaganda from German wireless stations. Known to have assisted with the painting of Fascist signs and slogans on railway property.

Wolf, Charles Frederick, (32) 113, Cambridge Avenue, Gidea Park, Essex. In reports and statements of July and August 1940 the suspect is referred to as a British subject of Germany ancestry. His father was German and his mother British. During the last war, his father was interned and eventually returned to Germany with his family and the suspect was educated there. In 1931 he married a German woman and returned to the UK in 1933 leaving his wife in Germany. She later divorced him. Father now deceased, suspect resides with his mother and his brother. He speaks fluent German.

From the several statements received he appears to support Nazism, which he has also preached among his fellow workers, constantly reminding them the German worker was much better off than the British. He argued that Hitler's action against the Jews was in order and that our statesmen were guilty of the war. He considered that we would be far better off under Hitler's rule.

Wolf, Gerald, (27) 113, Cambridge Avenue, Gidea Park, Romford, Essex

This man is the brother of Carl Frederick Vernon Wolf who is also on the Suspect List on account of his pro-German sympathies. Their father was interned during the last war and in 1919 when he was repatriated to Germany he arranged for his family to join him and both boys grew up there. Gerald Wolf returned to this country late in 1935 and obtained employment as an engineer with Messrs Briggs Motor Bodies Ltd of Dagenham, with whom he has been ever since.

In June 1943 he was interviewed by a police officer on the question of whether he should join the Home Guard. When asked if he would take up arms against the Germans if they invaded this country, he answered after a good deal of thinking, 'Well yes, I suppose so.' The police officer reported that he was not at all satisfied that Wolf would assist this country against the Germans.

Wrigley, Mrs Barbara née Wihl, (Born 1907, Germany) 14, Stafford Road, Sidcup, Kent removed to 65, Barnes Road, Bournemouth, Dorset.

Mrs Wrigley's father and sister are still living in Germany. She acquired British nationality in 1937 by her marriage to Sidney Wrigley a prominent member of the Imperial Fascist League and close associate of Arnold Leese, the organiser of the IFL. Before her marriage Mrs Wrigley's name appeared on a list of members of the NSDAP (Nazi party) in this country. She also joined the IFL. In May 1940 Special Branch reported that Mrs Wrigley was still an ardent admirer of the Nazi regime.

Wust, Karl Otto 'Charlie', Belgrave Road, Wanstead. Member of Wanstead Branch BUF. Unreliable loyalty.

Wutcher, Theodore, (Born Germany, 1905) 25, Neeld Crescent, Hendon. Rolling Mill Dealer (Engineer) Reported for making pro-Nazi statements.

Wutcher, Olga, (German). (Born 1909) 25, Neeld Crescent, Hendon. Reported for making pro-Nazi statements.

Yates, Anthony, Sub Post Office, Sterte, Poole, Dorset. Reported for making anti-British and pro-Nazi statements.

Zulueta, Alfonso del, Fyefield Road, Oxford. Born in London of Spanish parents. Unreliable loyalty.

Zuntz, Gunther (German) 37, Thorncliffe Road, Oxford. Unreliable loyalty.

Postscript

Many other MI5 case files exist relating to those believed to be agents embedded in our country and those who planned and indulged in covert acts of espionage against Britain. Some have already been released for public access, some still have release dates set for future years. Other cases are buried in files from various Home Office and Civil Service departments and drawing upon all these sources my next volume will reveal the stories of those who were literally 'The Enemy Within'.

On internments under Defence Regulations during the Second World War, The Earl Jowett who was Solicitor General from June 1940 until March 1942 concluded:

> *The suspension of Habeas Corpus, and the internment of suspected persons without trial – or even without an accusation – was a harsh and hard procedure and one which is opposed alike to our traditions and principles. But in view of our perilous situation, I for one do not question its necessity. No doubt, amongst those who were interned, there were some - and indeed perhaps many - who would never have contemplated taking any step, of passing information against the interests of this country. Yet, equally, I think it cannot be doubted that there were some who would have been willing, had the opportunity presented itself, to help the Germans.*[1]

Once the final victory had been achieved over Nazi Germany by the Allies in 1945 and the world saw the evil of Nazism exposed in every cinema on the films that showed liberated Nazi concentration camps, you may wonder what happened to those who had shown their loyalty to Hitler and the Nazi cause in Britain during the war years.

The Nazi agents that had landed in Britain and been tried and convicted under the Treachery Act had already been hanged. Most of those who remained were simply deported back to their country of origin where some of them would face trial and where they frequently avoided serious punishment by naming other agents and incriminating those further up the chain of command. Those who had become double-cross agents were usually given

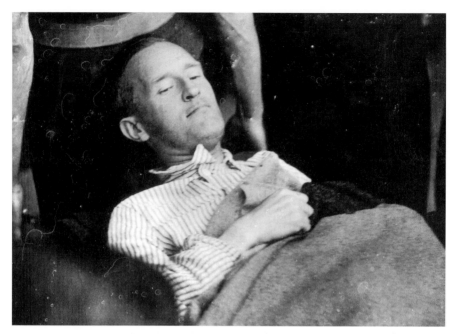

William Joyce, the main protagonist of German broadcasting in English who gave voice to 'Lord Haw-Haw' photographed shortly after his capture in Germany in 1945.

new identities, some of them choosing to live out the rest of their days in blissful obscurity 'somewhere' in the United Kingdom.

Sir Oswald Mosley made a number of unsuccessful attempts to return to politics over the years after the war, particularly with his new Union Movement. He died in 1980. Lady Diana Mosley, who obtained the sobriquet of 'The most hated woman in England' during the war, never lost her admiration for Hitler and the Nazis. She died in 2003 having remained unrepentant to the end. Oswald and Diana Mosley have recently featured as characters in the popular BBC drama series *Peaky Blinders*.

Leigh Vaughan Henry simply picked up his musical career again as if nothing had happened. He resumed his role as the musical director of the Shakespeare Festival Week in London in 1946 and enjoyed organising and conducting at British and Welsh festival concerts until his death in 1958. General John 'Boney' Fuller was never interned but was the only officer of his rank not to be invited to return to military service during the Second World War. He died in 1966 having spent his last years firmly believing Hitler had been the saviour of the west against the Soviet Union and that Churchill and Roosevelt had been foolish not to have recognised that 'fact'. Neither Vaughan Henry nor General Fuller, nor any of their collaborators were ever prosecuted in a court of law for their treasonous wartime plots.

The only former member of the British Union of Fascists to be prosecuted for High Treason was a certain William Joyce who had been the enthusiastic Area Administrative Officer for the West Sussex Division BUF. In 1937, after a few internal disagreements within the leadership team, Joyce found himself out of office as one of the BUF cutbacks, so he founded the National Socialist League. In August 1939 Joyce received a tip off that he was on the list of those to be detained on the outbreak of war so he and his wife fled to Germany. A mutual friend introduced him to her contacts at *Haus de Rundfunkhaus* (the German equivalent of BBC broadcasting house) in Berlin and he began broadcasting the propaganda-fuelled German news in English. Although there were several different presenters on the service it was the jeering, snobbish drawl Joyce adopted when reading the scripts that earned him the nick-name of Lord Haw-Haw.

Listening to the broadcasts was not illegal in Britain, thousands regularly tuned in because he gave information about British service personnel in German prisoner of war camps, and seemed to present news that was not covered on the BBC, but it was somewhat frowned upon and listeners could get into trouble if they began repeating the defeatist stories they heard during the broadcasts in conversations as facts.

Joyce was captured at Flensburg near the German border with Denmark by British soldiers on 28 May 1945. Handed over to British military police

The grave of BUF District Leader Ronald Creasy and his wife Rita in the churchyard at Monk Soham, Suffolk erected in 2004. Unrepentent believers in the Fascist case to the end, the centre stone of the kerb at the foot of their grave bears the Flash and Circle badge of the BUF.

he was transported to Britain where he was tried before Mr Justice Tucker at the Old Bailey for High Treason. Joyce was found guilty, his appeal was turned down and he was hanged by Albert Pierrepoint at Wandsworth on 3 January 1946. He was buried, as was customary at the time, within the walls of the prison where he was executed. After a campaign by his daughter Heather, Joyce's body was exhumed and re-interred in Galway, Ireland where he had lived with his family from 1909 to 1922.

Some of those who had been interned on account of their membership of the BUF and other far right political groups did return to the political forum after the war. Others simply washed their hands of political activism and never returned to politics save for debating their point on occasion with family members or friends. Some treated it all as a joke, some completely shut it away and their descendants had no idea that their dear old dad or grandad had been a member of the BUF before or during the war. That said, there were still those who 'carried the banner' of being a member of the BUF with quite some pride to the end and even beyond.

Ronald Creasy has the offices he held within the British Union of Fascists as Elected Councillor 1939, District Leader and Prospective Parliamentary Candidate carved upon his 2004 headstone in the churchyard at Monk Soham in Suffolk. He was joined by his wife Rita who died in 2008, who had been Women's District Leader and the subject of an MI5 investigation into her suspicious behaviour during wartime. The centre stone of the kerb at the foot of their grave bears the Flash and Circle badge of the BUF.

The British Union of Fascists was banned in 1940 but several far right political groups have been raised in Britain since the end of the Second World War. At the time of writing Italy has recently elected its first Fascist government since Mussolini and it is disturbing to see as the war years become more distant that the Far Right has an ever growing following across Europe.

We ignore the lessons of the past at our peril.

Notes

Chapter 1

1. Tyne & Wear Archives *Northern Civil Defence Region meetings of Police Security Officers PA.NC/2/2/46*
2. HO 45/25568
3. KV2/363
4. *Health and Beauty* No. 32 1937
5. *Daily Express* 1 April 1938
6. *Liddell Diary*, 23 January 1940 KV4/185
7. *Evening Standard* 17 September 1937
8. Nuremberg Trial Proceedings, 25 March 1946, morning session
9. FO371/21649
10. TS/27/533
11. Ibid
12. Tate, Tim *Hitler's British Traitors* (London 2018) pp209–14, 216–25
13. *Liddell Diary* 21 May 1940 KV4/186
14. *Liddell Diary* 21 May 1940 KV4/186
15. *Liddell Diary* 21 May 1940 KV4/186

Chapter 2

1. KV2/1700
2. KV2/12
3. KV2/12
4. Ibid
5. KV2/12
6. Ibid
7. KV2/1700
8. KV2/13
9. KV2/15
10. KV2/18
11. KV2/1701
12. KV2/1701
13. Ibid
14. KV2/1701
15. KV2/ 1701
16. Ibid
17. KV2/17
18. KV2/17
19. *Daily Herald* 2 October 1940
20. KV2/17

21. See *Dr Dearden's Report of an Interview with Vera on 9. 1.41* p.3 inKV2/15
22. Quoted by Petrie in his minute of 28.2.42KV2/15 encl 90a
23. Report by U.35 (Ustinov) KV2/15
24. Minute by D.G. White ADB126.2.42 KV2/15 encl 90a
25. *Liddell Diary* 4 October 1940
26. KV2/17
27. Butler, Memo 20.6.41 TNAKV2/15 encl 68b
28. KV2/15
29. Note of telephone call between Hinchley-Cooke and Stevens 25 February 1941 KV2/15
30. Milmo to Davies, Home Office 18.10.41 TNA KV2/15 encl 77a
31. KV2/15 encl 87k
32. Petrie to Maxwell KV2/15 encl 95a
33. Milmo to Davies, Home Office 12.2.42 KV2/15 encl 77a
34. *Liddell Diary* 8 October 1940
35. Cases of Edvardsen and Lund complied by Milmo, 31 October 1941 KV2/21
36. B.8 (L) Report 29 October 1940 KV2/21
37. Translation of statement by Edvardsen, 28 October 1940 KV2/21
38. Hinsley, F.H. and Simkins, C.A.G. *British Intelligence in the Second World War* vol. 4 p.325 (London 1990)
39. *B.8 (L)* Report 28 October 1940 KV2/21
40. Statement by Supt A.W. Stuart 27 October 1940 KV2/21
41. Letter from Scottish RSO to Dick White MI 527 October 1940 KV2/21
42. *B.8 (L)* Report by Robin Stephens dated 18 October 1940 KV2/21
43. KV2/1067
44. KV3/76

Chapter 3

1. Masterman, *The Double-Cross System* (London 2007) p50
2. *Northampton Mercury,* 18 May 1945
3. *Liddell Diary* 7 September 1940
4. *Liddell Diary* 8 September 1940 KV4/186
5. *Liddell Diary* 8 September 1940 KV4/186
6. *Liddell Diary* 22 September 1940 KV4/186
7. Memories and stories from residents in Willingham collected by the author when he researched the story in the 1990s, also see West, Nigel *Seven Spies Who Changed the World* (London 1991) pp.34–7
8. *Liddell Diary* 23 September 1940 KC4/186
9. *Liddell Diary* 11 October 1940
10. KV 2/60 - Caroli/SUMMER file
11. *Liddell Diary* 13 January 1941
12. *Liddell Diary* 16 January 1941
13. KV 2/2593 List of cases investigated by Camp 020
14. Masterman, J C *The Double-Cross System* (London 2007) p54
15. *Liddell Diary* 16 October 1940
16. *New York Times,* 23 October 1992
17. See article and statements by Smith, Keggin, Penn and Forth contributed by John Forth, WW2 People's War website.
18. *Liddell Diary* 5 October 1940

19. Ibid
20. Recollection of PC Forth contributed by his son John E. Forth, WW2 People's War website.
21. *Liddell Diary* 7 October 1940 KV4/187
22. Statement by Charles Baldock KV2/27
23. Statement by Captain William Henry Newton KV2/27
24. Translation of Statement by Josef Jakobs presented at his Court Martial KV2/27
25. Statement by Hinchley-Cooke KV2/27
26. See Ramsay, Winston G., *After the Battle, Number 11, German Spies in Britain* (London 1976) pp.24–25
27. Hoare, *Camp 020*
28. KV2/30
29. Ibid
30. KV2/30
31. Hoare, *Camp 020*
32. KV3/76
33. KV2/20
34. Pierrepoint, Albert *Executioner: Pierrepoint* (London 1974)
35. KV2/1936
36. KV4/192
37. Ibid

Chapter 4
1. Hayward, James *Double Agent Snow* (London 2013)
2. KV3/76
3. KV3/76
4. KV4/187 and KV2/1700 and KV3/76
5. *Liddell Diary*, 4 October 1940 KV4/187
6. KV4/122
7. KV4/122
8. KV4/122
9. KV2/25
10. KV2/26
11. Worcestershire Archives and Archaeology Service, Worcestershire Constabulary CID file Hagley Wood Investigation 4857/11
12. KV2/26
13. https://josefjakobs.info/story-of-clara-bauerle
14. *Liddell Diary* 5 November 1940 KV4/187
15. Bucks Constabulary Report KV2/114
16. Cambridge Borough Police report KV2/114 encl 4a
17. Cambridge Borough Police report re: Ter Braak KV2/114 encl 4a
18. Cambridge Borough Police report re: Ter Braak KV2/114 encl 4a
19. *Liddell Diary* 3 April 1941 KV4/187
20. Cambridge Borough Police report re: Ter Braak KV2/114 encl 4a
21. Report on W/T sets of Agents KV2/114 encl 5a
22. See Braak, Jan Willem Van den *Spion Tegen Churchill* (Zutphen, Netherlands 2017)
23. Masterman, J C *The Double-Cross System* (London 2007) p54
24. SIS report on Mörz dated 23 July 1939 KV2/1206

25. Statement by Heinrich Grunov translated and sent to Curry MI5 12.12.39 KV2/1206
26. SIS report on Mörz dated 23 July 1939 KV2/1206
27. Statement quoted in correspondence White to Vivian 30 December 1939 KV2/2106 encl 2a
28. KV2/2106 encl 7x
29. *Liddell Diary* 10 May KV4/186
30. KV2/2106 encl 11a
31. KV2/2106 encl 10a
32. KV2/2106 encl 10a
33. *Liddell Diary* 12 March 1940 KV4/186
34. See Metropolitan Police Special Branch report 4 September 1940 KV2/106 encl. 54a
35. KV2/2106 encl 21a
36. KV2/2106 encl 30a
37. KV2/2106 encl 43a
38. KV2/2106 encl 29q
39. Minute 53 KV2/2106
40. White to DAC Special Branch 7 August 1941 KV2/2106 encl 72a

Chapter 5
1. Letter from White MI5 to Stephenson SIS 28 July 1941 KV3/76 encl 74
2. *Liddell Diary* 20 June 1940 KV4/186
3. KV2/122
4. Tyne & Wear Archives*Northern Civil Defence Region meetings of Police Security Officers PA.NC/2/2/46*
5. MI5 *B Division Weekly Intelligence Summary No2,Part II Regional Summary* 16 October 1940 KV4/122
6. KV2/3874
7. KV2/680
8. Trythall, Anthony John *'Boney' Fuller : The Intellectual General* (London 1977)
9. McKinstry, Leo *Operation Sealion* (London 2014)
10. KV2/831
11. *Liddell Diary* 3 December 1939 KV4/185
12. KV2/831
13. Interim report May 1942 KV2/831
14. KV2/883
15. Ibid

Postscript
1. Jowett, The Earl, *Some Were Spies* (London 1954)

Select Bibliography & Further Reading

Addison, Paul & Crang, Jeremy A, *Listening to Britain: Home Intelligence Reports on Britain's Finest Hour – May to September 1940* (London 2011)

Andrew, Christopher, *The Defence of the Realm: The Authorized History of MI5* (London 2009)

Andrew, Christopher, *Secret Service: The Making of the British Intelligence Community* (London) 1985

Ansel, Walter, *Hitler Confronts England* (London 1960)

Atkin, Malcolm, *Fighting Nazi Occupation: British Resistance 1939–1945* (Barnsley 2015)

Barnes, James J. & Barnes, Patience P. *Nazis in Pre-War London 1930–1939: the fate and Role of German Party members and British Sympathizers* (Brighton 2005)

Braak, Jan Willem Van den *Hitler's Spy Against Churchill* (Barnsley 2022)

Brammer, Uwe *Spionageabwehr und Geheimer Mleldedienst. Die Abwehrstelle X im Wehrkreis Hamburg 1935–1945*, (Freiburg, Rombach, 1989)

Brinson, Charmian & Dove, Richard, *A Matter of Intelligence: MI5 and the Surveillance of Anti-Nazi Refugees 1933–50*, (Manchester 2014)

Brooks, Peter *Coastal Towns at War* (Cromer 1988)

Bushby, John R, *Air Defence of Great Britain* (London 1973)

Clarke, Comer, *England Under Hitler* (New York 1961)

Collier, Basil, *The Defence of the United Kingdom* (London1957)

Deacon, Richard, *A History of British Secret Service* (London 1980)

Dewar, Tom *Norfolk Front Line* (Brancaster Staithe 1998)

Engel, Major Gerhard, *At the Heart of the Reich* (Barnsley 2005)

Erickson, John, *Invasion 1940: The Nazi Invasion Plan for Britain by SS General Walter Schellenberg* (London 2000)

Farago, Ladislas, *The Game of Foxes: British and German intelligence operations and personalities which changed the course of the Second World War* (London 1971)

Fleming, Peter, *Invasion 1940* (London 1959)

Forczyk, Robert, *We March Against England* (London 2016)

Garnett, David, *The Secret History of PWE: The Political Warfare Executive 1939–1945* (London 2002)

Gilbert, Martin, *Finest Hour: Winston Churchill 1939–1941* (London 1983)

Glover, Michael, *Invasion Scare 1940* (London 1990)

Hayward, James, *Myths & Legends of the Second World War* (Stroud 2006)

Hayward, James, *Burn the Sea: Flame Warfare, Black Propaganda and the Nazi Plan to Invade England* (Stroud 2016)

Higgins, Jack, *The Eagle Has Landed* (London 1975)

Gillman, Peter & Gillman, Leni, *'Collar the Lot' How Britain Interned and Expelled its Wartime Refugees* (London 1980)

Hinsley, F.H. & Simkins, C.A.G., *British Intelligence in the Second World War Volume IV Security and Counter Intelligence* (London 1990)

Hutton, Robert, *Agent Jack: The Story of MI5's Secret Nazi Hunter* (London 2018)

Jakobs, Giselle, *The Spy in the Tower* (Stroud 2019)

Jeffery, Keith, *MI6 The History of the Secret Intelligence Service* 1909–1949 (London 2010)

Jowett, The Earl, *Some Were Spies* (London 1954)

Jonason, Tommy & Olsson, Simon, *Agent Tate: The Wartime Story of Harry Williamson*, Stroud 2011

Lampe, David, *The Last Ditch: Britain's Secret Resistance and the Nazi Invasion Plan* (London 2007)

Mackay, Robert, *The Test of War: Inside Britain 1939–45* (London 1999)

Macleod, Colonel R. & Kelly Denis, *The Unguarded: The Ironside Diaries 1937–1940* (New York 1963)

Masterman, J.C., *The Double-Cross System* (London 2007)

McKinstry, Leo, *Operation Sealion* (London 2015)

Morton, Andrew, *17 Carnations: the Windsors, The Nazis and the Cover-up* (London 2015)

Mosley, Leonard, *Backs to the Wall: London Under Fire 1939–1945* (London 1974)

Pawle, Gerald, *The Secret War 1939–1945* (London 1956)

Putlitz, Wolfgang zu, *The Putlitz Dossier* (London 1957)

Ramsay, Winston G., *After the Battle, Number 11, German Spies in Britain* (London 1976)

Ritter, Nikolas, *Deckname Dr. Rantzau*, (Hamburg, 1972)

Rowe, Mark, *Don't Panic: Britain Prepares for Invasion 1940 (*Stroud 2010)

Schellenberg, Walter, *Hitler's Secret Service* (New York 1971)

Schenk, Peter, *Invasion of England 1940:The Planning of Operation Sealion* (London 1990)

Scotland, Lt. Col. A.P., *The London Cage* (London 1957)

Simpson, A.W. Brian, *In the Highest Degree Odious: Detention Without Trial in Wartime Britain* (Oxford 1994)

Storey, Neil R., *Beating the Nazi Invader* (Barnsley 2020)

Storey, Neil R., *Britain's Coast at War* (Barnsley 2021)

Stourton, Edward, *Auntie's War: the BBC During the Second World War* (London 2017)

Strong, Major General Sir Kenneth, *Intelligence at the Top:The Recollections of an Intelligence Officer* (New York 1969)

Tate, Tim, *Hitler's British Traitors:The Secret History of Spies, Saboteurs and Fifth Columnists,*

Sweet, Matthew, *The West End Front: The Wartime Secrets of London's Grand Hotels* (London 2011)

Taylor, James, *Careless Talk Costs Lives* (London 2010)

Todd, Nigel, *In Excited Times: The People Against the Blackshirts* (Whitley Bay 1995)

Tremain, David, *The Beautiful Spy: The life and Crimes of Vera Eriksen* (Stroud 2019)

Trythall, Anthony John *'Boney' Fuller : The Intellectual General* (London 1977)

Verhoeyen, Etienne *Spionnen aan de achterdeur: de Duitse Abwehr in België, 1936–1945* (Antwerp 2011)

West, Nigel (ed.), *The Guy Liddell Diaries Vol I: 1939–1942* (London & New York 2005)

West, Nigel, *Historical Dictionary of International Intelligence* (Oxford 2006)

Wheatley, Ronald *Operation Sealion* (London 1958)

West, Nigel, *Seven Spies Who Changed the World* (London 1991)

White, John Baker, *The Big Lie* (London 1955)

Wighton, Charles & Peis, Günter, *They Spied on England* (London 1958)

The National Archives (TNA) (UK) (All KV, HO, ADM, FO, AIR and MEPO files cited in the text are held at The National Archives at Kew)

Newspapers and Magazines quoted are annotated in the relevant footnotes

Online:
BBC WW2 People's War website: www.bbc.co.uk/history/ww2peopleswar/
Coldspur, incisive analysis and research into spies and espionage: www.coldspur.com
Chain Home (CH) RDF System: ventnorradar.co.uk/CH.htm
Great Shelford Village: www.greatshelford.info/home
Josef Jakobs website: www.josefjakobs.info
Netherlands Intelligence Studies Association: Nisa-intelligence.nl
The Einsatzgruppen Trial: www.jewishvirtuallibrary.org/the-einsatzgruppen-2

Acknowledgements

The author would like to express his personal thanks to the following: The National Archives, Imperial War Museum, Aberdeen City and Aberdeenshire Archives, Manx National Heritage Library and Archives, Newcastle Local Studies Library, Gerry Jackson, BBC Look North, BBC Radio Norfolk, Norfolk Record Office, Lizzy Baker, Archives Lead, Tyne & Wear Archives, Worcestershire Archives and Archaeology Service, British Resistance Organisation Museum, Parham, The Coleshill Auxiliary Research Team, Milton Keynes Museum, Lieutenant Colonel Martin Valles, John Warwicker, Tim Tate, Matthew Hinchcliffe, Tim Bennett, Michelle Bullivant, David and Christine Parmenter, Ellengard Gertz, Oliver Rogge, Henry Wilson and all the team at Pen & Sword books, my old friends Stewart P. Evans, Bob Collis and James Hayward, my loving family and partner Fiona for all her love and support.

Index